The On-Line
Job Search
Companion

The On-Line Job Search Companion

**A Complete Guide to Hundreds
of Career Planning and
Job Hunting Resources
Available via Your Computer**

James C. Gonyea

McGraw-Hill, Inc.

New York San Francisco Washington, D.C. Auckland Bogotá
Caracas Lisbon London Madrid Mexico City Milan
Montreal New Delhi San Juan Singapore
Sydney Tokyo Toronto

Library of Congress Cataloging-in-Publication Data

Gonyea, James C.
    The on-line job search companion : a complete guide to hundreds of
career planning and job hunting resources available via your computer   /
James C. Gonyea.
        p.   cm.
  Includes index.
  ISBN 0-07-024068-X
    1. Job hunting—United States—Data processing.   I. Title.
HF5382.75.U6G66   1995
650.14'0285'46—dc20   94-23286
                                                      CIP

1 2 3 4 5 6 7 8 9 0 DOC/DOC 9 0 9 8 7 6 5 4

P/N 024102-3
Part of ISBN 0-07-024068
ISBN 0-07-024068-X

*The sponsoring editor for this book was Betsy N. Brown, the editing supervisor
was Fred Dahl, and the production supervisor was Suzanne W. Babeuf. It was set
in Palatino by Inkwell Publishing Services.*

Printed and bound by R. R. Donnelley & Sons Company.

 This book is printed on recycled, acid-free paper containing a
minimum of 50 percent recycled de-inked fiber.

*To Tom deBoor and America Online
for sharing my vision of the need for an electronic
on-line career and employment service,
and for giving me the opportunity
to make that vision a reality in the form of the Career Center.
And of course, to Pam
who has labored alongside me
to make the vision real,
and to Korie
who someday soon will carry on the dream.*

Contents

Foreword

Welcome to the future of personal career development and instantaneous electronic global job search.

In this fresh and informative orientation to a new era of personal mobility and employability, Jim Gonyea has laid out an important set of resources and techniques by which you can leverage your skills, interests, and personal career vision across thousands of opportunities resident in the fast-growing information superhighway. Plug in, beam up, and network into a world of job finding resources that may hold the key to your future.

Clearly, the information revolution is expanding in parallel with what may be called a worklife revolution: a revolution in how you construct your career and your way of marketing yourself to opportunities. In the past decade the already moribund employment contract has been revoked as regards all but a select cadre of high-priced executives with golden parachutes.

For the rest of us, the idea of job security is a fading memory. The only true security is your ability to know what's needed at any given moment, to package your customized set of skills, qualities, and competencies that meet these needs, and then communicate this to selected employers with impact and conviction. And to do this over and over and over as you fill in the details of your self-directed future.

The key change agent in all of this is, of course, IT—information technology. As companies expand their impact and productivity, their growth is based on greater linkages to outside providers; fewer core employees and more external contractors. Work that was once internal is now outsourced and subdivided. Individual workers are often independent contractors or telecommuters. The organization of the future will have relatively few people located in one place, and hundreds of linked resources in what is known as the virtual organization.

Which brings us to you. As the employee of the future, your way of connecting to future opportunities will be largely by way of data networks and computer software. In the emerging new economy, your job market may be a continent wide and include linkages to firms you have never even heard of. Your job search and the way you manage it are already changing, and changing rapidly as the information explosion meets the world of opportunity.

As a job seeker or career builder you can use information technology in several ways:

❏ To inventory and sort out your most relevant and marketable skills and competencies. *This will give you an instant advantage in being able to customize your "portfolios" (including your résumes and letters) and to communicate the most marketable aspects of your capability to the right situations.*

❏ To sort through current openings in databases and career development references and determine what skill sets you should target for personal development. In the near future, on-line services will give you access to courseware and reference to credentialed institutions for the study you need. *This will enable you to truly link your learning agenda with trends in job growth and to ensure relevance.*

❏ To place yourself on selected database services available to employers, search firms and consultant services. *This will allow you to be at all times available to be informed of skill matches that occur from thousands of employers—no need to post your entry only when you are in job search mode. A true electronic marketplace.*

❏ To search employer job listings worldwide from your armchair. *By "paging through" available job listings in different locations and in allied or even different fields, you are educating yourself, like a good marketing department, to the wealth of opportunity that is available, and to watch trends.*

❏ To post your qualifications, and communications to a selected employer by electronic mail. *By being able to make direct communication with employers you can skip time and distance requirements. As services become more sophisticated you will be able to add video clips, voice messages, and two-way screen-to-screen interviews.*

All this and more. This book by Jim Gonyea, a master in both traditional and electronic job search, is an intelligent and practical compilation of the technology job services available and the ways to make them pay off for you.

Tom Jackson
Woodstock, NY

Preface

Why, you might ask, would anyone consider writing another "how to conduct a job search" book considering the vast numbers of similar books on the market today?

The answer is simple. The way we communicate with each other—for all purposes including employment—is changing dramatically. The old methods took days to link one individual to another across town or from coast to coast, whereas today's electronic methods require only seconds to link one person with another regardless of their locations.

With few exceptions, the job-seeking how-to guides available today teach job seekers how to conduct a job search using traditional job-seeking methods and resources—methods and resources that have been in existence since the beginning of the twentieth century and are quickly becoming obsolete.

An examination of hundreds of job-seeking guides conducted by this author over the past two decades has revealed that the methods promulgated have changed little over time. Essentially, most guides instruct job seekers in how to prepare a written resume and cover letter, how to identify employers who may have a need for one's talent (both employers who have and have not advertised employment openings), how to "network" to increase one's chances of finding employment, how to prepare for the dreaded interview, and how to actually contact employers to inquire about employment and initiate the whole process of applying and being selected for employment. The "technologies" involved in these conventional methodologies have primarily centered around the use of the U.S. mail service, the telephone, and personal contacts and conversations.

While these methodologies still have some bearing for modern day job seekers, new electronic technologies have been created that have quickly empowered job seekers with the ability to outdistance, outpace, and—simply stated—beat out conventional job seekers for the available jobs. Computers, faxes, on-line information services, software, and CD-ROM programs, and the like now can be used to more quickly find and secure employment.

As of the time of this writing, only *one* book on the market instructed job seekers in how to use *electronic* resources in search of employment—and that book failed to provide readers with the actual software necessary to use today's ultra-modern electronic resources.

Bob Dylan once told us in a song that the "times they are a-changing" and Allan Toffler confirmed, in his best-selling book, *Future Shock,* that those individuals unable to adapt and adjust to change are doomed to the past. The old methods of job hunting are quickly becoming extinct.

There's a new breed of job seekers in our society armed with a vast arsenal of electronic resources—all designed for one purpose, to beat out the competition. While the new electronic technology can empower us all to higher levels of success and productivity, its use is not automatic, nor is it instinctive. It must be learned and there must be guides to teach the way.

The *On-Line Job Search Companion* was written to guide you in using today's high tech electronic resources to increase your job seeking capability. It is the way most employers and job seekers will find each other in the years to come!

For those readers who wish to contact me to share their experiences or recommendations for future editions, please feel free to contact me using any of the various options listed below.

Email addresses:
America Online = CareerDoc
CompuServe = 70233,177
Prodigy = CVTD03A
Internet = CareerDoc@AOL.com
Phone: 813-725-9600
Fax: 813-799-4668
Mail: Gonyea and Associates, Inc.
    3543 Enterprise Road East
    Safety Harbor, Florida 34695

Acknowledgments

Without the help of the following individuals, this book would not have been possible.

I would first like to thank Kelly Richmond and Marshall Rens at America Online for providing our readers with free software to access the Career Center on America Online.

To Tom Jackson, I am most honored by your comments in the Foreword of the book. Your leadership over the years has and will continue to be an inspiration—you set a high standard for the rest of us to follow. Your friendship is treasured and deeply appreciated.

I wish also to extend a very special thank-you to Rich Watson and his colleagues, and to Wayne Gonyea and Theopholis Benderschwitz for their persistence and resourcefulness in gathering the volume of information available in the Power Tools chapter of the book. It was a tough assignment and you guys were terrific! Get some rest.

Special acknowledgment must be given to Bill Warren at Online Career Center for his contribution in writing the chapter on the Internet, and to Dr. Steve Eskow of the California Institute of Integral Studies and Sarah Haviland Blackmun of the Electronic University Network for their work in preparing the chapter on on-line education. I am equally indebted to Dr. Jamie Huntington-Meath for his writing of the chapter on commercial computer network services and for his continual support of the Career Center over the years. Many thanks to Ward Christman of Online Opportunities for jumping in at the last minute and preparing the chapter on Bulletin Board Systems.

A large debt is owed to Pam Gonyea, Keeley Wood, Korie Gonyea, and Kevin Machos for their help in editing and preparing the final copy of the hundreds of profiles on electronic resources found in the Power Tools chapter. Let's break for lunch!

I cannot stress strongly enough my deep appreciation to all the current and past members of the Help Wanted-USA Employment Consulting team. Without your commitment and hard work, we'd still be matching employers and job seekers the old-fashioned way. Keep the faith!

And finally, to Betsy Brown at McGraw-Hill for her belief in and support of this book and for her assistance in bringing the manuscript to life.

James C. Gonyea

Introduction

Computers, computers, computers—they're everywhere! Whether you love them or hate them, three facts are undeniably true: They have invaded and automated just about every aspect of our lives, they are here to stay, and their use will only increase.

While only a few decades old, they now have taken control of most of our daily activities. Look around and you can find them controlling our automobile engines, operating the medical life support systems in our hospitals, adjusting the temperature of our homes, answering our phone calls when we're away, piloting the planes we fly on, monitoring and forecasting the weather minute by minute, as well as helping us to write letters, to balance our checkbooks, and to communicate with each other across the miles of electronic hyperspace.

Some computers work silently beside us and are hardly noticed, while others demand a great deal of interaction and input from us to function properly. Feared by some, accepted by most, and lovingly embraced by a growing number of people, computers can, given the opportunity, improve our lives in many ways. Few people who have accepted their role in our modern society, and who have mastered the basics of their use, will disagree that they can dramatically increase our productivity. Who among us would really want to return to the days when all work was done by hand?

From accountants to zoologists, more and more professionals have come to the realization that their future success hinges greatly on their ability to use and incorporate computer technology and skills into their workplace.

While there are many benefits that can be derived from their use, one major payoff from the embrace of computer technology is the fact that they can empower us with skills and capabilities impossible without their intervention. For example, within seconds of your command, your personal computer can reconcile your checkbook. By hand this task could take hours or days to complete. One person today, armed with a personal computer and the proper software programs, can accomplish far more work in a given amount of time than dozens of individuals working at the same task by hand.

What then does this mean for career planners and job seekers? Simply this ...

If you are attempting to determine a career direction, or seek employment and are not using the power of a personal computer to aid you in your search, then you will be less productive and less successful than those individuals who do!

There is little question that the competition for most jobs over the last few decades has been fierce. All indications point to the fact that this trend will continue in the foreseeable future. As evidence of this, consider the fact that some experts predict that the number of employees laid off by American employers in 1994 will be greater than those laid off in 1993—and 1993 set an all-time record for corporate dismissals!

If there ever was a time when job seekers needed a competitive edge, it is now. Beyond the normal factors of education, skill, experience, and personality style that separate one job seeker from another, there is one factor accessible to every job seeker that can help you beat out the competition—your personal computer!

The purpose of *The On-Line Job Search Companion* is to show you how to use the power of your personal computer for selecting a career direction and for finding employment. You will be introduced to hundreds of electronic resources that will enable you to compete on a higher level, such as:

❏ Audiocassettes

❏ CD-ROM programs

❏ Commercial computer network services

❏ Databases of help wanted ads

❏ Fax services

❏ Government, state, and private bulletin board services

❏ Online databases

❏ Phone services

❏ Resume banks

❏ Software programs

❏ Video cassettes

The On-Line Job Search Companion combines the best traditional strategies for selecting a career direction and for conducting a job search with the latest leading-edge electronic career development resources. This book is both a guide for determining a career direction and for conducting a job search, as well as a directory of electronic resources that can help you accomplish both goals using the advantages of ultra-modern technology.

Most of the resources listed in *The On-Line Job Search Companion* can either be loaded into your computer or accessed with a modem connection through your telephone line. All of the resources listed can empower your career planning to a higher level of productivity and success.

Traditional career guidance and job seeking resources—those normally found in print format—are not listed in this book. Plenty of books exist on the market today containing print-based resources; there is no need to duplicate them here. Also, many of these print-based resources can be found in the Career Center on America Online (see Chap. 10 for details). *The On-Line Job Search Companion* is, however, your gateway to today's and tomorrow's leading-edge *electronic career development technologies*—the means by which most employers and job seekers will find each other in the last half of this decade and from that point forward!

Turn on, log on, get a job!

By using a computer and various computer on-line network services, you can gain immediate access to an incredible library of information, people, and services. As pointed out recently by Richard Hart, host of *The Next Step*, a popular high-tech television program, you can now access more information electronically then you can in print!

These two factors—immediacy and access to vast amounts of information and numbers of people—can enable you to operate on a far more productive plane than possible if you were to follow the traditional methods of career planning and job hunting. To illustrate this point, consider the following career crisis scenario.

The traditional way...

Day 1: Your boss has just informed you that your services will no longer be needed. You've just been fired! You clean out your desk and head for the safety of your home.

You spend the rest of the day in denial and soliciting support from your family—your dismissal was not your fault!

Day 2: You awaken in a panic. You've got to get another job or the bank will repossess the house, your spouse will leave you, and the world will come crashing down around you.

You determine that you've got to rewrite your resume and immediately start looking for work.

Day 3: You've spent six hours writing and rewriting your resume on your old manual typewriter, and while it's not quite right you've got to get it out the door. But to whom do you send a copy?

Day 4: You've just spent the better part of the day calling all your friends and business colleagues and visiting the local library to produce a list of employers to contact. At least you're on the right track. Or are you?

Day 5: You've typed up your cover letter, made copies of your resume at the local copy center and dropped off 25 letters with resumes at the post office. Your "m" key on your manual typewriter is bad and your letters and resume reflect this, but it's the best you can do for now. You think you can relax a bit as you're bound to get a few requests for interviews next week. After all, you've got 30 years of experience and you're damn good at what you do.

Tomorrow will be a better day!

Day 6: Nothing arrives in the mail, no one calls you by phone! Not to worry, it's only the first day.

Day 7: Same thing happens. You're getting a little nervous.

Day 8: Same thing happens. You take the kids to the beach to forget your problems.

Day 9: You panic! There's still nothing in your mail box, the phone is gathering dust, and just about any job opening would look good at this time.

You need help!

Day 10: You call several employment placement agencies and beg for assistance. They offer to meet with you, but not until next week.

Day 11: Thinking it's a numbers game, you send out a total of 100 resumes and letters. That should do the trick!

Day 30: In spite of all your work, including the several interviews you've had with employment head hunters, the best you've accomplished so far is six letters saying, "We're sorry, but we have no openings at this time."

The world is now crashing in around you in a big way! Now you begin to understand why so many job seekers remain unemployed for months, if not years. There must be a better way?

Enter your personal computer!

Here's how the same scenario can be played out today utilizing electronic resources:

Day 1: Less than one hour ago, your boss gave you the pink slip. After soaking your head in the rest room sink to calm yourself down, you returned to your desk to clean it out. But before you leave, you decide to get your job search started using the power of your personal computer and several on-line network services.

You boot up your computer and log on to the America Online network service. In less than 10 minutes you have accomplished the following tasks:

(a) You've downloaded dozens of sample resumes of people working in your career field (that you will use later tonight to assist in editing your own resume with your home computer).

(b) You've identified 60 employment agencies in your region to contact for help who specialize in placing individuals with your career expertise.

(c) You've scheduled a counseling session on-line with a professional job counselor to talk about your job search.

(d) You've downloaded 20 profiles on companies that you've heard about in the industry that you want to consider as employment targets.

With your office possessions in hand, you leave for home determined to overcome the setback handed to you today by your boss.

Day 2: You've used the sample resumes you downloaded yesterday and your word processing program to write your new resume. Total time—less than 2 hours. Before lunch, you upload it using America Online to several resume banks used by tens of thousands of employers nationwide.

You still have half the day in front of you. After lunch, you log back onto America Online and check out the help wanted ads in the Help Wanted-USA database. With over 5000, updated weekly, to choose from, you download 87 position announcements that seem appropriate. Your local paper this morning had only 2 jobs that matched your interests and needs!

After dinner you log back on-line and chat with a job counselor for an hour about how to best use electronic services to conduct a job search. Without leaving home and from the comfort of your easy chair, the counselor is able to introduce you to several on-line employment listing services where appropriate positions may be found. Now, using various computer bulletin board services, you have immediate on-line access each and every day to over 100,000 help wanted ads nationwide! A quick search of several databases adds another 37 job options to your previous list of 87—now you have 124 positions ideally suited to your qualifications to consider. Your local paper is looking less and less useful each day!

You go to bed blessing the day you bought your new computer!

Day 3: While you sleep, your computer has , following your directions, mail merged your employment inquiry letter with your list of 124 positions. Using your computer and its built-in modem, your fax and laser printer, you send out all 124 letters and resumes in less than 2 hours! Before the end of the day, you received email and fax messages from 5 companies interested in talking with you about various positions. Three companies actually offer to talk with you on-line to discuss your qualifications!

You begin to think all's well with the world!

Day 4: Your day begins early as you jump back on-line using America Online and chat keyboard to keyboard with the three Human Resource Directors scheduled the day before. The interviews go well. You like two of the positions and are asked by one director to forward more information about your background.

In less than two hours you've met with three potential employers located at different ends of the country—all possible with your computer and on-line conferencing.

By noon you have drafted the necessary information using your word processing program and have emailed it back to the company.

Knowing there is no such thing as having too many job offers, you go back on-line and dial up Access-FEO and check out several hundred federal employment openings in your region of the country. Several seem appealing and you add them to your growing list of targets.

Your best friend, who is also unemployed at the time, not using electronic resources, and totally stressed out, drops over for coffee and actually asks why you seem so happy? You only smile!

Day 5: You turn on your computer, log on to CompuServe and find an email message waiting for you from one of the companies you interviewed with on-line. They are impressed with your background and ask if you would like to interview in person at their Tampa headquarters. You've always dreamed of moving to the sunbelt, so you send a return email message to indicate your willingness to participate in the interview. The actual interview goes well, you're offered the job, and you start packing up the house and family

In less than one week you've gone from being fired to your next job—all electronically!

You've stopped the sky from falling and you decide to take the whole family to the beach to celebrate your new job. Job hunting is not as bad as some claim!

Now, let's be real. Will the second scenario always happen as illustrated? No. Is the second scenario becoming the norm? In today's and tomorrow's society, most definitely yes!

As Tom Jackson points out in his best-selling book *Guerrilla Tactics in the Job Market,* "It's not the most qualified persons who get the best jobs, it's those who are most skilled in job finding." In the business of job finding today, being able to get immediate access to more information and more people, faster and easier than other job seekers gives you the competitive edge. And to do this requires the use of a personal computer. With the proper tools you are able to follow the age-old philosophy of "work smarter, not harder!" Many people work very hard and seem to get nowhere in life, while others who work less hard are successful. It's not always how hard you work, but how smart you work.

How important is having a competitive edge today? Consider one comment made by Walter Cronkite in a recent television program entitled *Help Unwanted*, "America is producing a permanent class of citizens who, while wishing to work, may not find employment."

Also consider a comment made by this author in an article entitled *The Absolutely Last Job Hunting Guide You'll Ever Need,*

> The fact of the matter is this . . . American employers do not have enough jobs to employ all those who wish to work! While there are several factors that have brought about this condition, the one common factor is economics. American employers facing increased world competition are adopting policies designed to save money, while improving productivity. Some common cost cutting measures include downsizing and merging facilities, moving plants overseas, discharging senior-level executives, hiring part-time workers or subcontractors rather than full-time employees, and increasing the work load of those employees who are retained.

In the ever evolving cycle of business, one fact remains constant: New technology continues to replace old technology. First a phone was necessary to conduct business, now a fax is standard, and automated voice mail created by a personal computer is the next leading-edge technology. Companies that incorporate new technology are able to succeed where those who remain tied to the past fail. Accordingly, career planners and job seekers who use electronic resources will succeed more often, whereas those who rely solely on traditional methods will fail more often.

The On-Line Job Search Companion will help you find those electronic resources that will give you a competitive edge in your career planning and job hunting.

As a result of using this book, you can expect to learn:

❑ About hundreds of electronic resources that can help you select a career direction that matches your personality style.

❑ How you can complete a vocational/technical or college program of study at home or from your office through your personal computer.

❑ About hundreds of electronic resources that can help you conduct an effective job search.

❑ How you can gain access to over 135,000 actual help wanted ads updated weekly and available nationwide to help you find your next job.

❑ How to upload your resume to several resume talent banks accessible to over 27 million viewers across the United States and in 140 countries worldwide to increase your exposure to employers and employment opportunities.

❏ How you can gain immediate access through your personal computer to the Career Center on America Online for the purpose of using any of the career planning and job hunting resources available from America's leading electronic career guidance service.

❏ How to access commercial computer network services, bulletin board services, and the Internet—America's information superhighways used by millions of career planners and job seekers to reach their career goals.

The On-Line Job Search Companion is the last job hunting guide you'll ever need!

Such a bold statement requires an explanation! If you are like most career planners and job seekers, you have purchased this book because you want to learn how to use electronic resources to advance your career development. If you are a professional employment recruiter, counselor, or similar professional, you probably have purchased this book to identify electronic resources that can be of value to your clients.

While *The On-Line Job Search Companion* contains information on hundreds of electronic resources, it does not list all the resources that exist—no book can do that since new resources are being created daily. However, any book that fails to provide some method of updating data quickly becomes obsolete.

Unlike most career planning books that are available only in print, this book will never become out of date or obsolete due to the fact that it is connected electronically to the Career Center on America Online. See Chap. 10 for more information about this service.

By becoming a member of America Online, and by using the services of the Career Center, you will have continual access to new electronic resources and services for as long as you wish—all accessible from your personal computer. As new resources and services become known to us, we'll post them in the Resource Library area within the Career Center. Any time you want to learn what's new in the industry, just check the Resource Library.

Travel the information superhighway with us!

Consider *The On-Line Job Search Companion* to be your personal guide to electronic career planning and job hunting resources available on the information superhighway. Get ready to travel as the ride is fast and furious! Sitting at your home or office computer in California, you can within minutes be in Chicago accessing information on health care employers from a university database, and in less than a few minutes later jet electronically to Washington, D.C. to pull information on industry trends out of a federal database. Time and distance are no longer barriers to your success. You are free to travel as far and as wide as you wish armed only with your personal computer.

Like Aladdin on his magic carpet, your computer can take you anywhere you want to go any time you wish to travel!

1

How to Use *The On-Line Job Search Companion*

This chapter presents information regarding who the book was written for, and how it may be best used by readers to satisfy their career development needs.

Who Can Benefit from Reading This Book?

This book has been written for individuals who are interested in (1) selecting a career direction or in finding employment through the use of electronic resources, or (2) guiding other individuals in learning how to use electronic resources to accomplish these tasks. *The On-Line Job Search Companion* is especially appropriate for the following groups of individuals:

❏ Adult workers who wish to explore a mid-life career change

❏ Adult workers who have been dismissed and must find new employment

❏ Military personnel who wish, or who are being forced, to seek civilian employment

❏ High school and college students about to select their first career direction, or seek their first professional job

❏ Career and employment professionals who wish to guide others in electronic career planning or job hunting

❏ Information brokers and researchers who wish to provide clients with information regarding electronic career planning and job hunting resources

❏ Librarians wishing to provide library patrons with a gateway to electronic career planning and job hunting resources

How Can This Book Best Be Used to Help You with Your Career Development Needs?

Option 1. As a guide to electronic career planning and job hunting resources.

If you wish to follow a prescribed guidance program designed by professional career counselors to help you determine a career direction or secure new employment through the use of electronic resources, then you should complete Chaps. 2 and 4, respectively.

Chapter 2 outlines several steps that are recommended if you are experiencing difficulty in determining a career direction. If you are unsure about which direction is best for you to pursue, it is suggested that you carefully review the career planning steps outlined in this chapter.

Chapter 4 outlines several steps that are recommended for conducting an effective job search. If you know the career direction you want to pursue, have the necessary qualifications and are ready to search for employment, it is suggested that you carefully review the job hunting steps outlined in this chapter.

Next to each step in Chaps. 2 and 4, you will find reference to an item called the Cross Reference Table (see page 245). This table will help you identify electronic resources that can aid you in completing each career planning or job hunting step.

Whenever you determine that you want or need to complete a particular step in either chapter, refer to the Cross Reference Table to identify electronic resources that can help. For more information about any resource listed on the Cross Reference Table, refer to Chap. 9.

Chapters 2 and 4 have been designed to provide you with a step-by-step program of career guidance—a program that can help you identify a career direction in line with your individual personality style, and then to guide you in securing the kind of job you want in the field you prefer. *The On-Line Job Search Companion* combines the best of two worlds—traditional, tested methods of career guidance with today's leading-edge, high-tech electronic guidance resources.

If you wish to explore the possibility of completing a vocational or technical program of study, or a college education, on-line through the use of your personal computer, please refer to Chap. 3.

If your schedule or lifestyle is such that you cannot attend school or college in the traditional manner, you should carefully consider "on-line education" or sometimes referred to as "long-distance education." It is now possible to complete fully accredited programs of study or college degrees (both undergraduate and graduate) through special network services with schools and colleges nationwide—all on-line and from your personal computer.

Option 2. As a reference source when you need to learn about specific electronic resources appropriate for career planning or job hunting.

If you wish to quickly identify resources that can satisfy specific career planning and/or job hunting needs, and if you know what those needs are, you should refer to Chaps. 2 and 4. Here you will find a list of suggested resources that are appropriate for various steps associated with career planning and job hunting respectively.

If you know the name of a specific resource and simply want more information about it, such as a description of the resource or how and where to obtain the resource, refer to Chap. 9 for an alphabetical listing of all resources contained in this book.

If you do not know which career planning or job hunting step is normally associated with the resource you wish to find, or the actual name of the resource, then you may wish to review the resources arranged alphabetically in the Index of Resources. Here you will find all of the resources contained within *The On-Line Job Search Companion*.

Option 3. *As a gateway to a leading commercial on-line network service, which, in turn, will provide you with access to the Internet, and hundreds of bulletin board services that offer electronic resources for career planners and job seekers.*

Refer to Chap. 10 to learn how to install the enclosed software program to become a member of America Online—the nation's fasting growing, private commercial computer network service. By doing so, you'll have immediate and direct access to the Career Center—America's premiere electronic career and employment guidance service.

The Career Center offers many services to career planners and job seekers, where you can:

❏ Receive on-line advice from professional career and employment counselors.

❏ Access thousands of help wanted ads—updated weekly.

❏ Upload your resume and reach thousands of potential employers.

❏ View complete profiles on hundreds of occupations.

❏ Identify employment agencies that can help you find your next job.

❏ Download sample resumes to help you write your own resume.

❏ Leave and view bulletin board messages as a means of communicating with other career planners and job seekers.

❏ Read articles on various career planning and job hunting issues.

❏ View profiles on major corporations nationwide.

❏ Meet thousands of individuals nationwide who share your interests—expand your network of contacts.

❏ Meet and interview with employers on-line—from all locations nationwide and around the world.

Refer to Chap. 5 to learn how you can gain access to the Internet—the information superhighway of the twenty-first century! The Internet currently links more than 27 million people worldwide, with over 1 million new members joining monthly.

Learn how you can travel the Internet to gain access to databases, information services, government/state/private bulletin board services, news groups and people anywhere in the world—all from the convenience of your personal computer and accessible in only minutes.

Refer to Chap. 6 to identify electronic services that are available from America's most popular commercial computer network services. Here you will find listings of electronic services available from America Online, CompuServe, GEnie, and Prodigy. These services are available to anyone with a personal computer and modem for a reasonable monthly membership fee.

Refer to Chap. 7 to identify bulletin board services (BBS) across the country that offer career and employment information and services.

2

Career Planning
the Electronic Way

This chapter outlines a number of activities (in the form of sequential steps) that can help you identify a suitable career direction or goal. Next to each step, you will find suggested electronic resources that, with the assistance of your personal computer, can help you accomplish each step.

If you are unsure of a career direction, or are confused about which occupation you should pursue from several you are considering, then this chapter is for you!

This chapter is *not* appropriate if you have already determined a career direction and are now ready to train for that direction or start searching for an actual job. If you have selected a career direction that you want to pursue, you should refer to Chap. 3 to learn about on-line educational programs that may help you prepare for your career goal, or Chap. 4 to learn how to identify electronic resources that can help you actually land a job in your chosen career field.

Guidance That Works!

The career guidance steps outlined in this chapter have been developed by the author over a 22-year period, and have been used by tens of thousands of individuals to chart a career direction. These steps have formed the basis for several books dealing with career planning, workshops, and courses on career decision making, software programs that have helped users identify occupations related to their interests and abilities, as well as the approach the author has used when counseling individuals about career decision making and planning. These steps have been thoroughly tested, are constantly updated and refined, and can help you chart your own career direction.

Following Your Own Self-Directed Search

The steps outlined in this chapter form what is often referred to as a *self-directed* program of career guidance. While the information presented has been developed by an experienced career guidance professional, you are free to decide which steps you want to complete and how long you want to work at any one step. It is recommended, however, that you start with the first step and continue forward completing each step in sequence.

In reality, you are setting off on a search for the perfect career. The strategy you will follow begins with a close examination of yourself to identify personality factors that define who you are as an individual. Factors such as interests, skills, values/needs, and behavioral traits will be defined. These factors will be used later in the program to help you evaluate the merits of various occupational options. The search will also require you to review information on occupations in general, identify those that seem to match your personality style, and research the most promising occupations to fully understand their nature. Finally, you will be guided in selecting a specific career direction and in developing a road map for realizing your new career goal.

How Long Will It Take?

One question often asked by individuals who are about to begin the following process is, "How long will it take me to complete all the steps?" Unfortunately, there is no one single answer for this question. Some steps can be completed in a matter of hours, whereas some steps may take several days or weeks to complete. Also, some individuals can complete a particular step in only a few hours or days, whereas other individuals require longer periods of time to complete the same task.

How fast you can progress through the guidance program depends upon certain factors, such as (1) how quickly you understand how to complete a task, (2) how much time you can devote daily to the requirements of the program, and (3) how quickly you can obtain the necessary resources listed for use with any step in the program.

Do not expect to complete the program in a day or two—this is just not realistic! Career planning is important to your life. If done properly it can result in increased job satisfaction and success—two very important factors in creating a more rewarding lifestyle! It is true that career planning as a task can sometimes be difficult to complete. Therefore, you should not attempt to rush through the program. To do so only invites the possibility of disappointment. If you can work full-time at the program on a daily basis, you can expect to complete the entire program in approximately one or two weeks, depending upon how quickly you can gain access to the necessary resources. If your schedule is such that you can work only part-time at the program, then give yourself several weeks to complete all the required steps.

The important factor to remember is not how quickly or long it takes you to complete the program, but whether you actually do complete the program.

Help Is Available If You Need It!

If you run into any difficulties attempting to complete any step in the program, or have any questions, you are encouraged to email your questions to the author using the America Online service.

The steps outlined in this chapter include:

❏ *Personality Assessment*—identifying your interests, skills/aptitudes, values/-needs, and behavioral traits

❏ *Occupational Exploration*—identifying occupations that seem to match your personality style

❏ *Occupational Profiling*—researching your career options to learn of their true nature and promise as career goals

❏ *Decision Making*—selecting a specific career direction

❏ *Planning*—developing a plan of action to reach your new career goal

For each step listed, you will find the following information:

❏ Objective

❏ Expected results

❏ How to complete

❏ Suggested electronic resources

Step 1—Personality Assessment

Objective. The goal when conducting an assessment of your personality style is to identify the underlying elements that define who you are as an individual. By recognizing the true nature of your personality, it is possible to obtain clues concerning which occupations might be appropriate as career goals. Plus, knowing the elements of your personality style provides you with information necessary for evaluating the merits of one occupation versus another.

The underlying philosophy of this approach is simple: When selecting a career direction it is wise to select one that best matches your overall personality style. By doing so, you increase the likelihood that you will enjoy your work, that you will have the skills necessary to succeed at your work, that your work requirements will not conflict with your personal values, that your work can satisfy many of your human needs, and that your work environment is one in which you can behave naturally and feel comfortable about your behavior.

Of all the steps outlined in this chapter, this step is by far the most important. Without a clear understanding of your personality style, it is not likely that you will make wise career choices. This is one of the main reasons why some people jump from job to job—they simply do not know which occupations can best meet their needs. This is also one reason why so many people dislike their work and feel trapped. While they may hate their work and want to leave, they do not know which occupation they should pursue. Do not attempt to shortcut this step, or partially complete its requirements—to do so could, and probably will, subject you to continued confusion and dissatisfaction about your career direction.

Expected Results. By conducting an assessment of your personality style, you should be able to define your:

Interests—the activities that you most enjoy doing.

Skills/aptitudes—the activities that you can do best (skills), or have the potential (aptitudes) for doing well.

Values/needs—the factors in life that define your beliefs and attitudes (values), as well as those factors that you feel you need in order to maintain a sense of well-being needs.

Behavioral traits—the mannerisms that describe how you normally function or behave, especially in work settings, or how you normally react to any given work-related situation.

How to Complete. Three common methods of gathering the previous information exist including self-assessment, peer-assessment, and professional assessment. Review the following three options and then decide which option or options you would prefer to use. Try to use at least two options to ensure that you will gather comprehensive and accurate information about yourself.

Self-assessment is a process whereby you conduct a review of your past life history, reflecting upon all that you have done and accomplished in life, and then prepare a list of what you believe are your most dominant and descriptive interests, skills/aptitudes, values/needs, and behavioral traits.

Upon first encounter, you might conclude that self-assessment is a difficult task to accomplish, especially if you have experienced a long life and/or are uncomfortable examining your personality style. However, it is actually very easy and emotionally safe to complete. The key to this process is to remember that the clues to who you are lie in your past history and are especially visible when recalling the major activities of your life. Consider this task to be similar to writing an autobiography about yourself, but only in outline form.

If you could play a videotape of your entire life (naturally, sped up to save time), you could fairly easily identify times and places when your interests, skills/aptitudes, values/needs, and behavioral traits were obvious. However, since no videotape exists, we have to rely on your memory of the past.

The human mind is a marvelous machine that, if asked to recall the past, can do so with a great deal of clarity. To conduct your own self-assessment, you should schedule several sessions of quiet time. Armed only with a notepad and a comfortable chair, close your eyes and let your mind wander back in time to recall all the major activities you have been involved in over your life. Starting with the present day and working backward in time, attempt to recall each of the following:

❏ The various jobs you have held

❏ The educational/vocational training programs you have enrolled in or completed

❏ The personal hobbies that have brought you the most enjoyment

❏ The volunteer activities in which you have been involved

❏ Your military experience

❏ The recreational activities you enjoy most

❏ The spiritual activities that you have enjoyed

Start with one category and work your way back in time from the present day back to your mid to late adolescent years. Do not rush the process, let your mind recall activities at its own pace. Try to visualize each activity in its fullest. As you recall a particular activity, examine it for clues about your interests, skills/aptitudes, values/needs, and behavioral traits. Write down what you recall. Continue this procedure for all categories. This will take you several hours to complete. Feel free to return to this task on separate occasions rather than trying to complete it all at one sitting.

Of all the assessment options possible, self-assessment may be the most difficult to complete but offers the greatest potential for revealing the most comprehensive and accurate amount of information about who you are as an individual. After all, who knows more about you then you?

Advantage/Disadvantage: Self-assessment can usually reveal a great deal of information about yourself. It is relatively easy to complete and always inexpensive do to. However, for some individuals, it sometimes can be difficult or uncomfortable to undertake.

Suggested Electronic Resources

To obtain a list of suggesed electronic resources useful in completing this step, refer to the Cross-Reference Table on page 245.

Peer-assessment is a process whereby you use the opinions of other people concerning your personality style to help draw a picture of your personality style. While other people seldom know as much about you as you do, they are privy to much of your inner workings and can, therefore, shed light on who you are.

To conduct a peer-assessment, it is recommended that you prepare copies of the Peer-Assessment Survey Form found on page 18, and provide each peer with a copy. Enter your name as the Career Planner and the name of the person conducting the review as the Peer Reviewer. Also indicate the date you would like the survey form to be returned.

Distribute copies of this survey form to as many peers as you can. The following individuals make excellent peers:

❏ Friends

❏ Coworkers

❏ Cousins

❏ Family, religious, or spiritual leader

❏ Grandparents

❏ Job seekers, support, or club members

Peer-Assessment Survey Form

Career Planner: _____

Peer Reviewer: _____

Return By: _____

Directions: please review the questions below and provide an answer to each based upon what you personally know to be true of the Career Planner. Use additional paper if necessary.

1. What are the Career Planner's main interests in life?

2. What are the Career Planner's best skills (things that he or she can actually do well)?

3. What aptitudes does the Career Planner possess (things that he or she has not yet done but could probably do well)?

4. What values are most important to the Career Planner (or what does the Career Planner seem to need most to maintain a satisfying and fulfilling life)?

5. What are the Career Planner's most common or normal work-related behavioral traits?

❏ Neighbors

❏ Older brothers and sisters

❏ Older children

❏ Parents

❏ Psychologists or counselors you have seen

❏ Spouse

❏ Teachers and professors

❏ Work supervisors

In short, just about anyone who knows you can be used to gather information. Encourage each peer to supply honest information and to return the survey form to you by a specified date. Some individuals may be hesitant to reveal such information for fear of offending or hurting your feelings. Encourage all peers to be complete and honest. Assure them that you will accept all information and not challenge any comment that is made, either positive or negative. Such a disclaimer is necessary if you hope to gain the largest amount of information that exists about you. Even with such conditions, it is not likely that everyone will share everything they believe they know about you, especially if what they believe may be taken as negative criticism of your personality. Some individuals may wish to return their survey form to you anonymously through the mail. This practice should be encouraged.

When you have received all completed survey forms, review all information and attempt, if possible, to identify the descriptive factors that were mentioned by more than one individual. The more a particular factor is seen and recognized by other individuals, the more likely it is to be a true element of your personality style.

Using a clean copy of the Peer-Assessment Survey Form, prepare a summary report listing what your peers believe are your main interests, skills/aptitudes, values/needs, and behavioral traits.

Advantage/Disadvantage.   Peer-assessment can usually reveal a good deal of information about yourself, but not as much as the other two options outlined in this step. It is relatively easy and quick to complete and always inexpensive to do. However, for some individuals, it sometimes can be uncomfortable or difficult to complete.

Suggested Electronic Resources.

To obtain a list of suggested electronic references useful in completing this step, refer to the Cross-Reference Table on page 245.

In the professional assessment process, you work with a professionally trained career counselor to identify your personality style. Depending on the training, philosophy, and past experiences of the counselor, he or she may use any number of strategies to help you learn more about yourself. For example, a counselor may use a question and answer strategy in an attempt to help draw conclusions about your personality style. The use of standardized test materials may also be used to help you identify your interests, skills/aptitudes, values/needs, and behavioral traits. Whatever strategy and resources are used, the outcome should always be the same—a list of factors that the counselor believes defines the elements of your personality style.

Professional assessment may be conducted on an individual basis when you work privately with a counselor. Or it may be offered in a group setting, often in the form of a course, workshop, seminar, or group counseling session on career planning.

Advantage/Disadvantage. Professional assessment can usually reveal a great deal of information about yourself. It usually takes longer to complete than the other two options and may be moderately expensive. However, it is possible to sometimes receive professional career counseling at little or no cost. Such low-cost counseling is often offered by colleges, universities, social service agencies, and church organizations. Check with these institutions in your community to learn what free or low-cost services are available for your use.

Suggested Electronic Resources

To obtain a list of suggested electronic references useful in completing this step, refer to the Cross-Reference Table on page 245.

Now, decide which assessment options and electronic resources you want to use. Follow the previous directions for completing the options you wish to use.

Review all the information you have gathered regarding your personality style from all assessment options used. Decide which factors best describe the elements of your personality style. Go with your best judgment. Do not include information that you do not believe is true, and do not exclude information that you know to be true but dislike about yourself. Using the Personality Profile Final Summary Chart on page 21, list what you believe are your most important, or most descriptive, interests, skills/aptitudes, values/needs, and behavioral traits.

After completing the Personality Profile Final Summary Chart, move on to Step 2—Occupational Exploration.

Step 2—Occupational Exploration

Objective. The goal of this step is to translate what you have learned about your personality style into *possible* career goals. Specifically, to identify occupations that *seem to* best match your interests, skills/aptitudes, values/needs, and behavioral traits.

It is important to note that you are not making final decisions regarding a career direction at this point in the program. What you are doing here is establishing a starting or focal point for your career search. Therefore, do not feel bound to any occupation at this time. However, do include any occupation that you think might ultimately be appropriate.

Personality Profile Final Summary Chart

My main interests are ...

1. _____

2. _____

3. _____

4. _____

5. _____

6. _____

My strongest skills/aptitudes are ...

1. _____

2. _____

3. _____

4. _____

5. _____

6. _____

(Continued on next page)

My most important values/needs are ...

1. _____

2. _____

3. _____

4. _____

5. _____

6. _____

My most descriptive behavioral traits are ...

1. _____

2. _____

3. _____

4. _____

5. _____

6. _____

This task, without guidance, can often be difficult to complete for several reasons. First, not everyone has a clear concept of their personality style. You no doubt learned new things about yourself from completing step one that you did not know beforehand.

Second, the world of work offers many occupational choices. According to the U.S. Department of Labor, there exist over 13,000 different occupations in the United States today—and this number is constantly changing and growing. With so many options to choose from, it is not surprising that we all may be "occupationally illiterate" about the world of work.

Finally, the ability to actually identify occupations from among the many that exist that best fit your personality style is a skill in itself—one that is not usually taught or learned from the course of normal everyday living. It is a skill, however, that can be learned.

If you feel confused, overwhelmed, and frustrated when you attempt to select a career direction, you are not alone. With time and proper guidance, your confusion will give way to a clear sense of direction.

Expected Results. By completing this step, you will develop a deeper understanding of various occupations that form our world of work, plus you will create a list of occupations—by job title—that you believe match your personality style, and are worthy of serious consideration as possible career goals.

How to Complete. Three common strategies exist that can help you identify occupations that may match your personality style. These strategies include (1) using a cross-walk classification system, (2) completing a series of career assessment inventories and tests, and (3) talking with a professional career counselor. Review the three options and then decide which option or options you would prefer to use. Try to use at least two options to ensure that you can generate a workable list of possible career options.

Cross-walk classification systems are long lists of occupational titles, prepared by experienced career counselors or occupational analysts, arranged according to some criteria, such as interests, skills/aptitudes, values/needs, or behavioral traits. The term *cross-walk* simply means that information has been prepared that can help you identify occupations related to a particular criterion. Therefore, if you know the criterion (e.g., interests), the system will walk you to related occupations. Think of a pedestrian cross-walk—it can take you from one side of the street to another. Similarly, an occupational cross-walk can take you from knowledge about yourself to knowledge about related occupations.

For example, if you want to identify occupations that match your interest in music, you should use an interest cross-walk classification list. Such a list would contain occupations that are normally pursued and found to be enjoyable by individuals with an interest in music.

If you want to identify occupations that match your ability in math, you should use a skill or aptitude cross-walk classification list. This list would contain occupations that are normally pursued and found to be enjoyable by individuals with math ability.

A great deal of research work has been conducted over the past few decades on the subject of cross-walk systems. Their use can help you quickly identify possible career options.

Advantage/Disadvantage. The advantages of using cross-walk systems are that they are easy to use and cost little, and do not require the intervention of a trained professional to use. The disadvantage is that cross-walks do not yet exist for all known personality factors, especially for values/needs and behavioral traits.

Suggested Electronic Resources

To obtain a list of suggested electronic references useful in completing this step, refer to the Cross-Reference Table on page 245.

Career-assessment inventories and tests can provide you with solid and accurate information regarding occupations related to your personality style. These devices have been carefully developed (in most cases) from years of research by experienced assessment specialists and can usually offer you a higher level of understanding concerning possible career options. Technically, some of these devices are referred to as "inventories" and contain long lists of questions or statements that you are asked to respond to. Such questions or statements usually center around which activities you prefer or value, or how you behave. Some devices are actually considered to be tests and are most commonly used to measure your ability to complete certain tasks.

Assessment inventories and tests usually require the intervention of a trained professional if they are to be administered, scored, and interpreted properly. Such devices are not considered by professional career counselors as self-directed instruments.

Advantages/Disadvantages. The main advantage of these materials is that they can reveal a good deal of information about yourself and related occupations. Also, there exist inventories and tests for all known personality categories mentioned. The disadvantages include the fact that a trained professional is usually required to use these materials. Finding such professionals is not always possible in every community, and, due to the need for a trained administrator, the use of these devices usually involves a fee.

Suggested Electronic Resources.

To obtain a list of suggested electronic references useful in completing this step, refer to the Cross-Reference Table on page 245.

Working face-to-face with a professional career counselor, one trained in cross-walking systems, is yet another excellent way to identify occupations related to your personality style. While it is unfair to expect that any career counselor, regardless of training and experience, can identify occupations related to each of your known personality traits, it is fair to expect that counselors can help you identify many options, as well as point you toward resources that can also help you identify additional options.

Advantages/Disadvantages. The advantage of working with a professional counselor is that he or she, from training and experience, can usually identify occupations that you may not know exist. The disadvantage is that you usually have to pay for this advice.

Suggested Electronic Resources

> *To obtain a list of suggested electronic references useful in completing this step, refer to the Cross-Reference Table on page 245.*

Go ahead now and decide which exploration options and electronic resources you want to use. Follow the preceding directions for completing the options you wish to use.

Review all the information you have gathered regarding occupations that seem to be related to your personality style. Decide which occupations you believe best match your personality style and are most worthy of further consideration. Using the Occupational Possibilities List on the next page, list the job titles of the occupations you wish to seriously consider as possible career goals. List all occupations that you feel are appropriate. At this time, do not attempt to make final decisions about which career direction you will ultimately pursue. Keep in mind that you may later drop some of these occupations from your list, and that others, not yet listed, may appear as appropriate career goals and should be added to your list.

After completing the Occupational Possibilities List, move on to Step 3—Occupational Profiling.

Step 3—Occupational Profiling

Objective. The goal of this step is to develop a profile (i.e., brief report) on each of the occupations listed on your Occupational Possibilities List. As you recall, the purpose of Step 2—Occupational Exploration was to identify occupations that *seem* to be appropriate. In this step, you will determine if your selections are appropriate for serious consideration. The purpose in profiling is to gather information that can help you determine if each occupation is appropriate.

Effective decision making requires accurate knowledge. The old adage, "Don't judge a book by its cover" is very appropriate here. Many occupations may seem on the surface to be ideal. However, many career planners, thinking that a particular occupation may be well suited to their personality style, change their mind after researching the occupation and discovering what it's really all about.

Consider also that most occupations require some period of training, often in the form of a formal vocational, technical, or college program of study. How disappointing it is to discover, when one finally enters a chosen career field after spending years in training and thousands of dollars, that the job is not at all as it was expected to be!

Expected Results. As a result of completing this step, you will have a report pre-

Occupational Possibilities List

The following occupations are those that I believe best match my personality style *at this point in the program*, and, therefore, are worthy of serious and continued exploration:

Job Titles:

1. _____

2. _____

3. _____

4. _____

5. _____

6. _____

7. _____

8. _____

9. _____

10. _____

11. _____

12. _____

13. _____

14. _____

15. _____

pared for each occupation on your Occupational Possibilities List containing the following information about each occupation:

❑ Main goals and objectives

❑ Main duties and responsibilities

❑ Required or recommended areas of knowledge and skills

❑ Preferred entrance qualifications

❑ Preferred training options

❑ Typical entrance and experienced salary levels

❑ Benefit options

❑ Positive and negative working conditions

❑ Problems and obstacles commonly encountered

❑ Common advancement opportunities

❑ Future employment outlook

❑ Type of employers

❑ Typical coworkers, customers, and clients

❑ Related occupations (job titles)

❑ Sources of additional information

❑ Professional and trade associations

How to Complete. Three methods of profiling occupations are recommended. These methods include (1) using occupational briefs and biographies, (2) talking with people who work in the occupation, and (3) trying the occupation out yourself.

Reviewing occupational briefs and biographies that have been written about your selected occupations is very easy to accomplish. Occupational researchers working for several private commercial companies, as well as for the federal government, have compiled extensive and detailed reports on thousands of occupations.

Information contained in these occupational briefs and biographies is collected from a variety of sources, including individuals who actually work in the occupation, state and federal government reports, information collected from professional and trade association reports, information from educational institutions, and information supplied by private research groups. Such information is the equivalent of what you might obtain if you had the opportunity to interview dozens of people about your chosen career options.

Advantages/Disadvantages. The advantage of using occupational briefs and biographies is they are easy to obtain, often detailed in the content, and cost little to nothing to use. The disadvantages include the fact that not all occupations that exist in the United Staes have been profiled, sometimes the information is out of date, and even after using several different sources you still may not have all the information you desire.

Suggested Electronic Resources

> *To obtain a list of suggested electronic references useful in completing this step, refer to the Cross-Reference Table on page 245.*

Talking with people who actually work or who have worked in the occupations on your list is another ideal way of obtaining solid, accurate, and timely information. No one can speak more authoritatively about an occupation than someone who has done it, and done it well, for years. Also, individuals such as teachers and college professors, who train others for a particular occupation, and personnel directors and/or human resource managers who hire people for particular positions are excellent people to talk to about your chosen occupational options.

Advantages/Disadvantages. The advantages include the fact that you often get the true picture of what it's really like to work in a particular occupation. Also, by talking to someone working in the field, you can usually get answers to all your questions. The disadvantages include the time usually required to find someone willing to talk with you, and the fact that some people are biased in favor or against their occupation and, therefore, do not present the true nature of the occupation. Another disadvantage is that it's not always possible to find someone within your community to talk about a particular occupation. *Note:* One advantage of using electronic resources, especially on-line conferencing, is that you can meet and chat with people from all over the country and around the world.

Suggested Electronic Resources

> *To obtain a list of suggested electronic references useful in completing this step, refer to the Cross-Reference Table on page 245.*

Trying out an occupation for a brief period of time to get a true feel for what it's really like, is often referred to as "volunteering for work" or "shadowing an occupation."

For several hours or days you actually get to do some of the work, or at least follow (shadow) someone who is doing the work. This firsthand exposure can often reveal information about the job unavailable through any other means of investigation.

Advantages/Disadvantages. The advantage of this option is that you can see for yourself what the job is all about. The disadvantages include the fact that this option is less practical then the first two—it will be more difficult to find employers willing to let you volunteer your time or shadow workers than it is to read literature or find someone willing to talk to you about their job. Many occupations simply do not allow volunteers or shadowing due to the unique training and preparation requirements of the position. Imagine volunteering as a brain surgeon—just not practical or wise!

Suggested Electronic Resources

> *To obtain a list of suggested electronic references useful in completing this step, refer to the Cross-Reference Table on page 245.*

Occupational Profile Guide

Directions: Make a copy of this form for each occupation on your Occupational Possibilities List. Using the occupational research options you have selected, seek answers to the following questions for each occupation. Record the information you obtain from your research below each question.

Occupational Title of This Profile:

_____

1. What are the main goals and objectives of this occupation?

2. What are the main duties and responsibilities of this occupation?

3. What areas of knowledge and skills are required or recommended for this occupation?

4. What are the preferred entrance qualifications?

5. What are the preferred training options to prepare for this occupation?

6. What are the typical entrance and experienced salary levels?

7. What benefit options are typically offered by employers?

8. What are the positive and negative working conditions of this occupation?

9. What problems and obstacles are commonly encountered in reaching the goals of this occupation?

10. What common advancement opportunities exist?

11. What is the future employment outlook or need for this occupation?

12. What type of employers typically have a need for this occupation?

13. Who would be my typical coworkers, customers, or clients for this occupation?

14. What related occupations (i.e., job titles) exist for this occupation?

15. Where can I obtain additional information about this occupation?

16. What professional or trade associations exist for this occupation?

Now decide which profiling options and electronic resources you want to use. Follow the preceding directions for completing the options you wish to use.

Using the profiling option or options you prefer, prepare a profile on each of the occupations listed on your Occupational Possibilities List. Use a copy of the Occupation Profile Guide (page 29) to record your findings.

As cautioned in the previous step, it is not recommended at this point in the program that you make any decisions regarding which occupation you want to pursue as a career goal. Decision making will be dealt with in Step 4. It is possible, however, that you may, through your research, discover that an occupation is grossly unsuitable or undesirable for you. In such cases, you may delete those occupations from your list. Conversely, you may discover new occupations from your research that were not on your list when you started your research, but feel are appropriate for consideration. Add these job titles to your list and complete a profile of each.

When you have completed a profile on each occupation on your list, move on to Step 4—Decision Making.

Step 4—Decision Making

Objective. The objective of this step is to provide you with a decision making system that will enable you to determine which of your occupational options is best for you to pursue as a career goal. Specifically, your task is to determine which occupation *best* matches your overall personality style.

Caution! Considering the number and kind of personality traits that you have, it is not likely that you will find an occupation that 100 percent matches your personality style. This is usually the case for the vast majority of career planners. If this should occur for you, do not consider this guidance system to be flawed, or that you have somehow failed in your career quest. The number of personality factors that you have listed about yourself, and the more unique they are as compared to other individuals, and whether any two or more of your factors conflict with each other will determine how many occupations exist that match your personality style and how well they match your personality style.

The important factor to remember is not whether you have identified occupations that 100 percent match your personality style, but which occupations *best* match your personality. Decision making is part science and part art—there are no hard and fast rules for this task.

This decision-making step is broken down into two phases. In Phase 1 you will compare the occupations on your Occupational Possibilities List to your known personality factors. This phase will help you identify an occupation that is suitable or occupations that are suitable as a career goal or goals. If you determine from completing Phase 1 that you are ready to select a specific career goal, then you may ignore Phase 2. However, if you end up with several seemingly equal career goals as a result of completing Phase 1, Phase 2 can help you narrow down your choice.

Caution! You should not attempt to complete this step if you have failed to adequately complete Steps 1, 2, and 3 in this program. Decision making without proper information to support your decisions is inviting disaster!

Expected Results. As a result of completing this step, you should be able to identify a specific career goal—an occupation that you feel best matches your personality style.

How to Complete Phase 1. To compare your personality style to occupations on your Occupational Possibilities List (page 26), follow these directions:

1. Describe your personality style: Refer to the Personality Profile Final Summary Chart (page 21) if you have difficulty answering these questions.

   1a. List your strongest interests on lines A1-A6 on the Decision-Making Chart, see page 37.

   1b. List your strongest skills/aptitudes on lines B1-B6 on the Decision-Making Chart, see page 37.

   1c. List your most important values/needs on lines C1-C6 on the Decision-Making Chart, see page 37.

   1d. List your most descriptive behavioral traits on lines D1-D6 on the Decision-Making Chart, see page 38.

   1e. Place a check mark to the left of any factor that you feel *must be satisfied by or be part of* your ultimate career direction.

2. On page 39 (Tally Sheet), write in the names, at the top of each column, of the occupations you want to evaluate as career goals. Refer to the occupations listed on your Occupational Possibilities List. Make and use additional sheets if you wish to evaluate more than 6 occupations.

3. Starting with occupational possibility #1 (page 39):

   3a. Compare your interests. Look at your first interest (line A1, page 37). Place a check mark on line A1 (page 39), if one of the main duties of this occupation is similar to your interest. Place two check marks if it is also one of your *must satisfy* interests.

   3b. Repeat this procedure for the rest of your interests.

   3c. Compare your skills/aptitudes. Look at your first skill/aptitude (line B1, page 37). Place a check mark on line B1 (page 39), if one of the main skills/aptitudes required for this occupation is similar to your skill/aptitude. Place two check marks if it is also one of your *must satisfy* skills/aptitudes.

   3d. Repeat this procedure for the rest of your skills/aptitudes.

3e. Compare your values/needs. Look at your first value/need (line C1, page 37). Place a check mark on line C1 (page 39), if the occupation will help you satisfy this value/need. Place two check marks if it will help you satisfy one of your *must satisfy* values/needs.

3f. Repeat this procedure for the rest of your values/needs.

3g. Compare your behavioral traits. Look at your first behavioral trait (line D1, page 38). Place a check mark on line D1 (page 38) if your trait is characteristic of people who work in this occupation, or if your trait will not interfere with completing the work assignments of this occupation. Place two check marks if the occupation can satisfy one of your *must satisfy* behavioral traits.

3h. Repeat this procedure for the rest of your behavioral traits.

3i. Total the number of check marks that you have recorded for this occupation at the bottom of the first column on page 39.

4. Repeat steps 3a through 3i for all other occupations listed on page 26.

5. Now, examine the results of Phase 1 of this decision-making step. Look at the total score for each occupation on page 40. For those occupations with the highest scores, carefully examine which personality factors were checked (matched) and which ones were not. Matching one's interests is generally considered the most important factor in career selection. Therefore, an occupation with a lower total score *may* be more appropriate if it better matches your interests then one with a higher total score that does not match your interests.

6. Determine if you are ready to select a specific career direction. If you feel that you have now identified an occupation that well matches your personality style, and are comfortable with your decision, move on to Step 5—Planning. If you find that you are faced with several seemingly equal options, continue on to Phase 2 of this step to (hopefully) narrow down your choice to a specific career goal.

How to Complete Phase 2. To evaluate and prioritize the occupations that seem most appealing, follow the directions below.

Rating Scores

10	= Very Desirable
5	= Desirable

0	= Neither Desirable nor Undesirable (Neutral)
-5	= Undesirable
-10	= Very Undesirable

1. On page 40, list the names of all occupations that at this point in the decision-making process seem to be equal career options (refer to the results of Phase 1).

2. Select one of the rating scores that best describes how desirable or undesirable Job Factor #1 is when evaluated in terms of the first occupation on your list. Record your score in column 1, line 1 on page 40.

Job Factors:

1. Duties and responsibilities

2. Entrance qualifications

3. Salary and fringe benefits

4. Necessary knowledge and skills

5. Advancement opportunities

6. Future job outlook

7. Location of work

8. Personal qualifications

9. Working conditions

10. Coworkers, clients, and customers

3. Repeat Step 2 for Factors 2-10 for the first occupation on page 40.

4. Add together the scores recorded for this first occupation and place this score at the bottom of column one, page 40.

5. Repeat Step 2 for all occupations on page 40.

6. Look at the results of Phase 2. Look at the total scores for each occupation. Carefully examine those factors that were rated as desirable and undesirable.

7. Determine if you are ready to select a specific career direction. If you feel

that you have now identified an occupation that well matches your personality style, and are comfortable with your decision, move on to Step 5—Planning.

If you find that you are unable to decide between various occupations, it is recommended that you discuss your options with a career counselor to gain an objective opinion regarding which option may be best for you to pursue.

Suggested Electronic Resources

To obtain a list of suggested electronic references useful in completing this step, refer to the Cross-Reference Table on page 245.

Step 5—Planning

Objective. The purpose of this step is to guide you in developing a step-by-step plan of action that you can follow to actually reach your newly chosen career goal. Considering the amount of work that you have invested into the program, and the positive impact an enjoyable career can have on your life, it would be a shame to fail to reach your career goal simply because you do not know how to get there. But this is exactly what happens to many individuals who fail to develop an effective career plan!

One of the most important steps in your career development is the preparation of a plan for determining how you will actually reach your career goal. Careful career planning is necessary if you expect to be able to progress from the point of career decision making to an actual job in an effective and efficient manner. Many individuals fail to realize their career dreams and goals simply because they have an inadequate plan, wrong plan, or no plan at all to follow. Time, money, personal drive, and motivation, and your own sense of well-being can be lost due to poor planning.

Imagine if you were to attempt for the first time a trip by car from New York City to San Francisco. One of the very first things you would do is obtain a detailed road map. Such a map could tell you in which direction you should drive, how fast you can or should go, where to avoid dangers and obstacles, where to take rests along the way, and how long it will take you to get to your destination. You would never think twice about the necessity for a good road map.

Consider your career development as a road untraveled. Having a map is as important when traveling down this road as on any long-distance highway. You are at one point on the road and wish to travel to some distant point (i.e., your new career goal), but since you have never been there before, you're unsure how best to get there.

Like any other long-distance trip through unknown territory, there are unknowns, dangers, wrong turns, and detours that await the first-time traveler. Reaching your destination is not guaranteed. However, by careful planning you can increase your chances that you will arrive at your desired destination safe, sound, and happy.

Expected Results. By completing this step, you will have a deeper understand regarding what steps you should take, in which order, when, where, and how to effectively realize your career goal. Specifically, your career plan will contain information regarding:

❑ The qualifications usually required or recommended for entrance into your chosen career field.

❑ What qualifications (if any) you need to develop to give yourself a competitive edge.

❑ What steps you can take to develop your missing qualifications.

❑ What obstacles you're bound to run into when attempting to develop your missing qualifications.

❑ What resources you can call upon when you need to resolve obstacles.

❑ When you should start and when you can expect to complete each step.

How to Complete. To develop your career plan, follow these directions:

1. Write in the job title of your career goal on the Normal Qualifications section of the Career Planning Guide, see page 43.

2. Based on your research into the field (Step 3—Occupational Profiling), write in the qualifications that are normally recommended or required under each of the following sections:

   ❑ Areas of knowledge

   ❑ Skills and aptitudes

   ❑ Personal characteristics, traits, and qualities

   ❑ Educational background

   ❑ Work experience

Write in your answers on page 43.

3. On the Self-Assessment section of the Career Planning Guide (see page 44), describe what qualifications, if any, you currently lack for each of the following areas:

   ❑ Areas of knowledge

   ❑ Skills and aptitudes

   ❑ Personal characteristics, traits, and qualities

Decision-Making Chart - Phase 1 Personality Factors

Must Satisfy INTERESTS (list only your strongest and only 1 per line)

_____ A1_____

_____ A2_____

_____ A3_____

_____ A4_____

_____ A5_____

_____ A6_____

Must Satisfy SKILLS/APTITUDES (list only your strongest and only 1 per line)

_____ B1_____

_____ B2_____

_____ B3_____

_____ B4_____

_____ B5_____

_____ B6_____

Must Satisfy VALUES/NEEDS (list only your most important and only 1 per line)

_____ C1_____

_____ C2_____

(*Continued on next page.*)

_____   C3_____

_____   C4_____

_____   C5_____

_____   C6_____

Must Satisfy   BEHAVIORAL TRAITS (list only your most descriptive and
     only 1 per line)

_____   D1_____

_____   D2_____

_____   D3_____

_____   D4_____

_____   D5_____

_____   D6_____

Tally Sheet (Occupational Possibilities—write in titles)

	Title 1:	Title 2:	Title 3:	Title 4:	Title 5:	Title 6:
A1						
A2						
A3						
A4						
A5						
A6						
B1						
B2						
B3						
B4						
B5						
B6						
C1						
C2						
C3						
C4						
C5						
C6						
D1						
D2						
D3						
D4						
D5						
D6						
Total Check Marks:						

Decision-Making Guide—Phase 2

10 = Very Desirable, 5 = Desirable, 0 = Neutral, -5 = Undesirable, -10 = Very Undesirable

Occupational Possibilities

	Title 1:	Title 2:	Title 3:	Title 4:	Title 5:	Title 6:
Duties & responsibilities						
Entrance qualifications						
Salary & fringe benefits						
Knowledge & skills						
Advancement opportunities						
Future job outlook						
Location of work						
Personal qualifications						
Working conditions						
Coworkers, customers, and clients						
Total scores						

❏ Educational background

❏ Work experience

Write in your answers on page 44. Be specific about your missing qualifications and identify as many qualifications as you can. If you do not lack any qualifications for a particular area, skip that area or label it as "None Missing."

4. On the Task-Analysis section of the Career Planning Guide (see page 45), describe what steps you can take to develop the missing qualifications for each of the following areas where you have indicated you do have missing qualifications:

❏ Areas of knowledge

❏ Skills and aptitudes

❏ Personal characteristics, traits and qualities

❏ Educational background

❏ Work experience

Write in your answers on page 45.

5. On the Trouble-Shooting and Problem-Solving section of the Career Planning Guide (see page 46), describe what you believe will be the main obstacles you will likely encounter in attempting to develop the missing qualifications. Indicate this information for only those sections where you have indicated you lack certain qualifications.

Directly below the area where you list obstacles, list the resources that you believe you can call on to overcome or resolve the obstacles, if encountered.

6. Review the information you have recorded in Steps 2 through 5. Of all the work that needs to be done to upgrade your qualifications, determine what step (task) should be completed first. On the Master Plan section of the Career Planning Guide (see page 48), indicate for Step 1, the following information:

❏ *Task*—describe briefly the nature of the task that needs to be completed.

❏ *Starting date*—state when you plan to begin the task.

❏ *Ending date*—determine when you anticipate completing the task.

❏ *Obstacles*—identify the problems you expect to encounter.

❏ *Resources*—point out what people, services, and so on will be called upon to solve the obstacles that are encountered.

7. Repeat the procedure for every step (task) that you believe must be taken to prepare your qualifications to the level where you can successfully compete for employment in your chosen career field.

The number of steps in your plan should be equal to the number of tasks you believe you need to complete. Arrange the steps in sequential order from first to last.

Once you have laid out your step-by-step plan, you should be ready to implement your plan. Soon you will be well on your way to realizing your new career goal.

Suggested Electronic Resources

To obtain a list of suggested electronic references useful in completing this step, refer to the Cross-Reference Table on page 245.

Career Planning Guide/Normal Qualifications

Career goal: _____

Directions: List the qualifications below that are normally recommended or required for each area.

Areas of knowledge ...

_____
_____
_____

Skills and aptitudes ...

_____
_____
_____

Personal characteristics, traits, and qualities ...

_____
_____
_____

Educational background ...

_____
_____
_____

Work experience ...

_____
_____
_____
_____
_____
_____

Career Planning Guide/Self-Assessment

Directions: Describe what qualifications, if any, you currently lack for each of the following areas.

Areas of knowledge ...

_____

_____

_____

Skills and aptitudes ...

_____

_____

_____

Personal characteristics, traits, and qualities ...

_____

_____

_____

Educational background ...

_____

_____

_____

Work experience ...

_____

_____

_____

_____

_____

_____

Career Planning Guide/Task Analysis

Directions: Describe what steps you can take to develop the missing qualifications for each of the following areas where you have indicated you do have missing qualifications..

Areas of knowledge ...

_____

_____

_____

Skills and aptitudes ...

_____

_____

_____

Personal characteristics, traits, and qualities ...

_____

_____

_____

Educational background ...

_____

_____

_____

Work experience ...

_____

_____

_____

_____

_____

_____

Career Planning Guide/Trouble Shooting and Problem Solving

Directions: Describe what you believe will be the main obstacles you will likely encounter in attempting to develop the missing qualifications. Indicate this information for only those sections where you have indicated you lack certain qualifications. Directly below the area where you list obstacles, list the resources that you believe you can call upon to overcome or resolve the obstacles, if encountered.

Areas of knowledge ...

_____

        Obstacles _____

        _____

        Resources _____

        _____

Skills and aptitudes ...

_____

        Obstacles _____

        _____

        Resources _____

        _____

Personal characteristics, traits, and qualities ...

_____

        Obstacles _____

        _____

        Resources _____

        _____

Educational background ...

_____

    Obstacles _____

    _____

    Resources _____

    _____

Work experience ...

_____

    Obstacles _____

    _____

    Resources _____

    _____

Career Planning Guide/Master Plan

Directions: Enter the information as called for below for each step of your plan. Create additional steps if your plan requires more than five steps.

Step 1—

      Task

      Starting date

      Ending date

      Obstacles

      Resources

Step 2—

      Task

      Starting date

      Ending date

      Obstacles

      Resources

Step 3—

>   Task
>
>   Starting date
>
>   Ending date
>
>   Obstacles
>
>   Resources

Step 4—

>   Task
>
>   Starting date
>
>   Ending date
>
>   Obstacles
>
>   Resources

Step 5—

Task

Starting date

Ending date

Obstacles

Resources

3

On-Line Education

The Learning Society—Learning as a Lifetime Job

Not too long ago you would have seen the word "terminal" applied to most forms of education. Community college, technical, and vocational programs were called "terminal" programs—and PhDs still are. When you finished one, you were supposed to be equipped for life—to pursue a career, earn a living, and fulfill your dreams.

Now, there are no terminal education programs. The knowledge we accumulated yesterday may be replaced by new knowledge learned today. The skills we learn today may become obsolete tomorrow, and those who don't or can't acquire new knowledge and new skills may find themselves obsolete and irrelevant, unable to work or function in a society that has become grounded in continual learning.

There is no graduation, no commencement any longer. Learning has become a lifetime job.

The Campus as a Place of Learning— Myths and Realities

For all the criticisms leveled against them, our colleges and universities are widely considered the finest in the world. Almost 500,000 foreigners now study in them each year, and millions more would come here if they could.

For many people, the word *college* brings to mind an image of the small residential institution, with its small classes featuring warm and close relations between professors and students, intense discussions in the dorm, more learning

Contributing authors: Dr. Steve Eskow and Sarah Haviland Blackmun, Electronic University Network (EUN).

in the extracurriculum as students debate and publish the college newspaper and put on plays.

That college does indeed still exist: small, communal, populated by full-time students for whom learning is the central preoccupation.

For most American students, however, the reality of the college experience is quite different. The majority are part-time students who must work to support their studies and perhaps a family. They sit in large classes, have little or no time for extracurricular activities, take part in no discussions in dormitories, and often have trouble registering for the courses they need because of schedule conflicts.

The ideal or traditional residential college is not for them. It was designed to be an intentional community of study and growth for the young, who would live together at a place called a campus. It was not designed to be a lifetime learning opportunity for adults who must balance study with work, family, and community obligations—adults whose responsibilities might not let them attend classes on 15 consecutive Tuesday evenings, or who live too far from the campus for easy travel. It was also not designed for would-be students with physical disabilities, for whom the trip to campus is difficult and painful, or who cannot hear the lecture or see the blackboard. Nor for people who need courses and resources not available at a local college, but available at a college in the next county, or in the next state, or 3000 miles away.

For all of its richness as a learning environment, the campus cannot serve the lifetime learning needs of a significant number of Americans. The issue before the gatekeepers of American education, then, is not whether face-to-face education is better than long-distance education, but whether we are willing to provide for those who cannot come to campus.

The New Vagabonds—Traveling the Information Highways

In the Middle Ages the vagabonds were the wandering scholars who traveled to where the teachers were who had the knowledge they desired. When a vagabond had learned from one teacher what that teacher had to impart, he would then move on to the next teacher, perhaps in another country.

The new vagabonds today are the growing numbers of Americans who can learn from teachers and trainers and libraries anywhere in the nation, and increasingly, anywhere in the world.

The information highways of old—correspondence study, for one—are quickly being replaced by the information superhighways of today made possible by the new communication technologies of radio, video, satellite technology, and computer conferencing.

No longer do the vagabonds have to pack their bags, leave their job, family, and friends, and set off in search of teachers, books, ideas, and dialogue. All of these things now come to them—electronically.

The New College—Moving Learning to Students, Not Students to Learning

All forms of long-distance education are based on the belief that learning can take place when learners are out of sight and out of earshot of the teacher.

Each type of long-distance learning, however, is based on a different analysis of what good learning and good teaching require; as a result, the administrators of long-distance learning programs incorporate different technologies to link learners and teachers, with each technology having advantages and deficits.

The prospective student should be aware of how each long-distance learning program under consideration is organized, what technology or combination of technologies is used, and what the technology and the program offer to the learner and demand of him or her in return. The technologies used for long-distance education include:

Correspondence Study. In the United States and around the world, correspondence study (i.e., study done through the mail) enrolls millions of students. Despite its limitations (i.e., it cannot create the conditions of student discussion, it is slow), it is dependable, low cost, and needs no batteries. And, of course, the book can be taken anywhere, so that students can study in their hotel rooms, or barracks, or workplace, as well as in their homes.

Audiocassettes. Widely used for language instruction, audiocassettes can bring much of the immediacy and warmth of the instructor and the classroom to the distant learner. Cassettes allow the student to choose when and where to study.

The Audio Bridge. Using the telephone system to create a voice-only class or seminar, this technology produces classes that are conducted in real time and provide a sense of live participation.

Satellite Technology. Typically the instructor's lecture, or a discussion, is uplinked to a satellite and from there downlinked to many receiving stations around the nation. Each downlink must have a dish to receive the program; these are most often found in companies, colleges, and hotels, or other sites that provide downlink service.

Programs occur in real time—that is, the students must be at the downlink when the instructor is delivering the lecture. This technology is often described as "one-way video, two-way audio," since students can often use telephones at the downlink to ask questions of the instructor.

Television. Television ranges from elaborate, professionally produced programs to "candid classrooms" featuring the instructor talking and students asking questions. Television courses are broadcast by cable, or microwave, ITFS (instructional television fixed service), and compressed video; some are broadcast first and then made available later on videocassettes.

Videotape. The VCR is increasingly a household fixture in American homes and makes it possible for students to study from video programs on their own schedules and at locations of their choosing. And videotape can be stopped and replayed so that a puzzling concept can be reconsidered.

The Computer and Modem. Perhaps 25 percent of American homes now have computers, and persons without computers in their homes often have access to computers in their workplaces.

The modem is a device that, when attached to a computer, allows the computer to communicate through the national and international telephone system with other computers located anywhere in the world.

The computer and modem have capacities that make them a powerful instrument for long-distance learning. They can create the conditions of the traditional seminar, where students may converse with each other as well as with the teacher; they can link students, teachers, and counselors together for mentoring and tutoring and counseling; and they can link the students to databases and other intellectual resources.

While many technologies are involved in providing today's long-distance education, the computer now plays a central role in what has become known as on-line education.

Combining the Technologies. Today, students at home can use books, videotapes, and laptop computers that can connect them to more faculty, more students, and a richer array of learning resources then what they could gain access to if they attended a single campus.

Which new college is right for you?

How do you choose a college, a program of study, a technology? The following lists a few factors you should consider. Which factors are most important, or which ones should you consider in your decision, will vary from learner to learner, but all might well be considered important before your decision is made.

We'll begin with a factor and a concept often overlooked:

Your Life Style. Study on the college campus is "structure, location, and time dependent." That jargon means, of course, that to study something you want or need to study at the college means that you have to go to a particular building in a particular town or city at certain fixed hours over a period of time.

Certain instructional delivery systems release you from one or two or these, but not three. You'll want to know exactly what each system requires of you, and how those requirements mesh with the routines and requirements of your life.

Suppose, for example, that a program you want or need is offered by satellite technology and correspondence study. You tend to believe that "one picture is worth a thousand words," and that you'll do better with the satellite technology version. You'll want to consider, however, that you'll have to be at the downlink—a fixed location in your town or city—for 15 consecutive Tuesdays at 9:30 a.m., and that might not be desirable or possible for you. You may, therefore, after considering the tradeoffs, choose the correspondence program.

Your Learning Style. Most of us believe we know ourselves quite well, and in particular that we know how we learn best: in groups or alone; from print or pictures; on a fixed schedule or at our own pace.

There is, surprisingly, substantial research evidence questioning whether students who are allowed to pick their own learning conditions choose those for which they are best suited. That is, students who think they need the structure of the fixed schedule do better in the conditions of self-scheduling, and vice versa.

Nevertheless, think hard about such things as your ability to get yourself to study without the pressure of scheduled class attendance, your ability to profit from studying alone, your ability to learn from the printed page, and your ability to learn from pictures transmitted via a television screen.

What and How Much You Need to Learn. Are you looking for credits, degrees, credentials, or the skill and the knowledge that can come from learning? Or all of these? Check out how much of what you want is available from the various colleges or agencies you are considering. Some colleges, for example, have "residency requirements" that require you to take substantial portions of their degree programs on campus. You might in such cases decide to take some or all of the courses offered and apply those courses to a degree at a local college where you will finish your studies.

Costs. Of course! Be sure you consider all the costs associated with a particular type of long-distance learning, and make sure you inquire about what financial aid, if any, is available through the institution you are considering.

What Learning Environment You Want and Need. Some of us are able to read a book, write a paper, think about an instructor's comments, and find the reading and the writing and tutoring to be all the stimulation and guidance we need. Some of us need, or think we need, more—we need to actually see the teacher, other students, and the blackboard to learn.

Some of us need even more. We need to be able to ask questions of the instructor, take part in dialog and discussion with other students, have a library available when we need to read more, have access to counselors when we have personal, academic, or career problems, or want help in finding a job.

Think about what you want, think about what you need. And look at the programs and the colleges and the technologies used to see whether what you want and need is provided.

A Case Study in Distance Learning

To aid you in determining if on-line education is right for you, we will examine an actual on-line educational program currently available on the America Online computer network service—a program sponsored and administered by the Electronic University Network.

The mission of the EUN is to provide an on-line "electronic campus" option to accredited colleges and universities that offer traditional long-distance learning degrees and courses. The EUN also offers support services such as course development and publishing, faculty orientation, on-line student registration, and technical support.

In our example, we'll look at an electronic campus, that has five main "buildings" (Fig. 3-1): Administration Building, Academic Center, Library, Student Union, and Continuing Education Center.

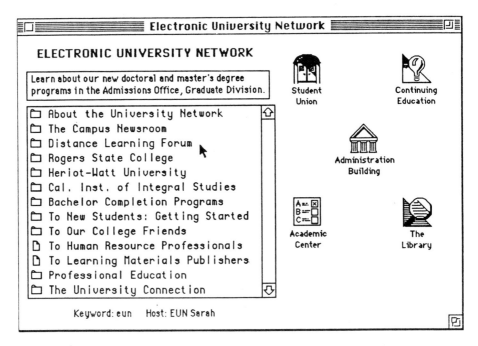

Figure 3-1

There is also a Campus Newsroom (Fig. 3-2), where visitors can get information on current and new programs; and a Long-distance Learning Forum (Fig. 3-3), where colleges that want to consider becoming long-distance learning providers, and individuals examining long-distance learning for their college study, can experience long-distance learning through a minicourse, "Long-distance Learning 101."

The Long-Distance Learning Forum. In Long-distance Learning 101, newcomers experience all aspects of long-distance learning on-line:

❑ Getting instructions on how to do the course work and attend the on-line sessions (Fig. 3-4).

❑ Downloading and reading articles posted in the library.

❑ Writing assignments using a word processor, and sending them to the instructor.

❑ Discussing the assignments, and getting to know each other, in the "seminar rooms" that provide spaces for "asynchronous" discussions (i.e., discussions

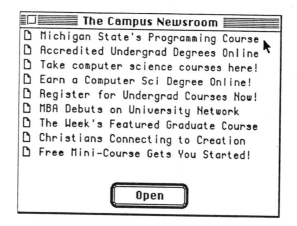

Figure 3-2

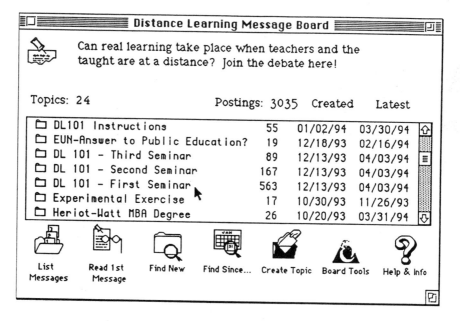

Figure 3-3

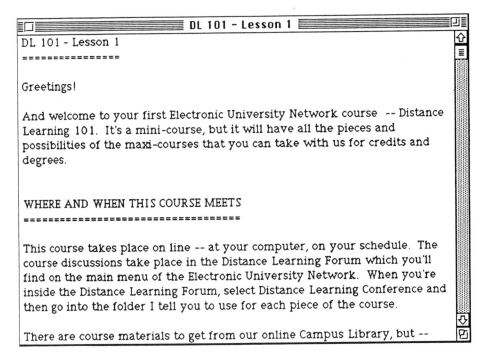

Figure 3-4

that don't take place in real time but to which participants add their comments at their convenience).

❏ Taking part in a real-time session.

Long-distance Learning 101 also teaches essential on-line skills: signing on, logging, creating and sending messages and files, uploading and downloading files, using the library, and creating a filing system.

Administration Building. This area (see Fig. 3-5) houses all the offices you would typically find in the same building on a traditional campus: Academic Counseling, Admissions, Finance, Registration, and the administration offices.

In Academic Counseling (see Fig. 3-6), students and prospective students receive on-line analysis of their prior learning, both formal and nonformal, and participate in an asynchronous conference designed to get their questions about distance learning answered.

Then, in the Admissions Office (see Fig. 3-7), they review the options and decide which program is most appropriate for them. All the information needed to enroll is provided, and students may apply for admission and enroll in courses on-line.

Figure 3-5

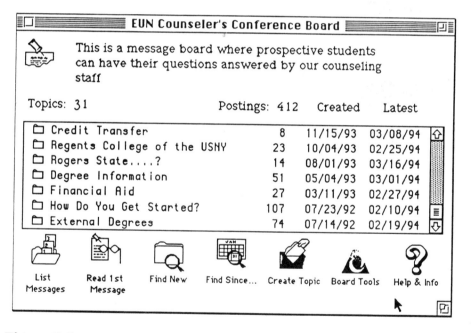

Figure 3-6

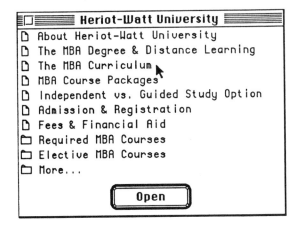

Figure 3-7

Academic Center. This is the heart of the electronic campus, the place where courses take place, where faculty and students meet and get to know each other, hold discussions, do problem solving and get course questions answered, and prepare for exams. Most seminars take place asynchronously (that is, not in real time) so that students can set their own schedules for participation (Fig. 3-8, 3-9, and 3-10). Some courses have optional real-time sessions.

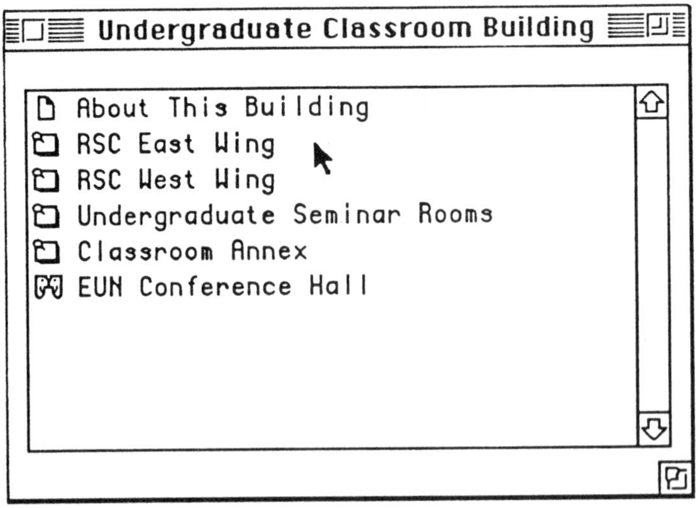

Figure 3-8

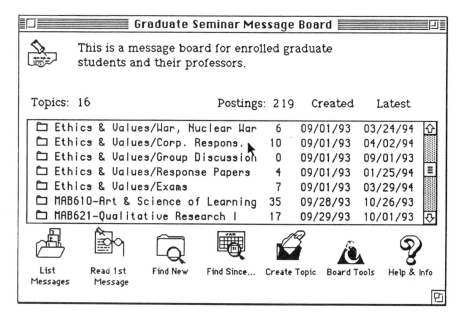

Figure 3-9

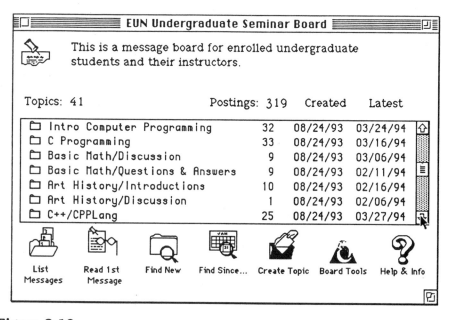

Figure 3-10

The course package that students receive typically includes a wide array of learning materials: a primary textbook, one or more supplemental texts or study guides, videocassettes, audiocassettes, software, and an Electronic University Network "teleguide" that provides the road map and all of the course instructions and assignments, as well as detailed instructions for navigating on the electronic campus.

Library. The library is an essential resource for any college program. The electronic campus provides library space to each college, each degree program, and each course being taught on-line (see Figs. 3-11 and 3-12). Here, faculty can post readings, assignments, and course archives (records of all on-line discussions for the course), and students can request bound books from college libraries.

Figure 3-11

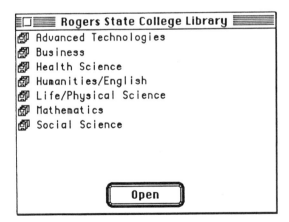

Figure 3-12

Student Union. This is just what you would expect: a student lounge, a campus store, and meeting rooms.

Continuing Education Center. Here, courses and seminars for professionals are offered (Fig. 3-13).

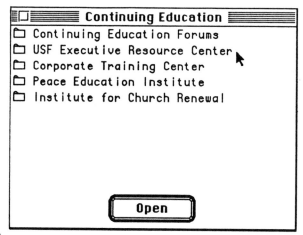

Figure 3-13

Learning About the Long-Distance Learning Colleges

If you want to learn about the long-distance learning programs open to you, there are several books and organizations that can help.

The National University Continuing Education Association (NUCEA) has prepared two comprehensive guides on long-distance learning, one dealing with correspondence programs, the other with programs delivered through various electronic media and formats. These guides are:

Peterson's Guide to Independent Study. Princeton, NJ: Peterson's Guides, 1992.

The Electronic University: A Guide to Long-distance Learning Programs. Princeton, NJ: Peterson's Guides, 1993.

In addition, the *Electronic University Network* is a member of a consortium of organizations that work with groups of colleges to provide long-distance learning programs. This consortium includes:

AG*SAT: The Agricultural Satellite Corporation
1800 N. 33rd Street
P.O. Box 83111
Lincoln, NE 68501
Randy Bretz, Director
402-472-3611

The Electronic University Network

1977 Colestin Road
Hornbrook, CA 96044
Ms. Sarah Blackmun, Director of Instruction
415-221-7061

International University Consortium

University of Maryland University College
University Blvd. at Adelphi Rd.
College Park, MD 20742-1660
John Strain, Director
301-985-7811

Michigan Information Technology Network, Inc.

4660 S. Hagedorn Road #230
East Lansing, MI 48823
Ms. Sarah Gozmanian, Director
517-336-1321

Mind Extension University

9697 East Mineral Ave
P.O. Box 3309
Englewood, CO 80155-3309
800-777-6463

National Technological University

700 Centre Ave
Fort Collins, CO 80526
Douglas Yeager, Marketing Vice-President
303-495-6400

National Universities Degree Consortium

Members use Mind Extension University
Contact: Mind Extension University

Tribal College Consortium

Rocky Mountain College
Billings, MT 59012
406-657-1000

Western Cooperative for Educational Telecommunications

P.O. Drawer P
Boulder, CO 80301-9752
Ms. Mollie McGill, Director
303-541-0233

About the Authors. Dr. Steve Eskow was president of Rockland Community College (State University of New York) for 20 years. He is now a professor in the School for Transformative Learning of the California Institute of Integral Studies, where he directs the on-line doctoral program. Sarah Haviland Blackmun is the president of Open Learning Systems, Inc., which she and Eskow founded in 1985, and cheif operating officer of its Electronic University Network. From 1973 to 1985 she was an executive of Harcourt Brace & Company and president of its Media Systems division.

For additional information see the *Electronic University Network* area in Learning and Reference on America Online, or send email to Sarah Haviland Blackmun at screen name "EUN Sarah." If you wish to write or call:

The Electronic University Network
Ms. Sarah Blackmun, Director of Instruction
1977 Colestin Road
Hornbrook, CA 96044
415-221-7061

In addition to offering the Electronic University Network (EUN) service, America Online also provides two other on-line educational options:

Interactive Education Services (IES). These are actual courses that America Online members may take and complete on-line. These courses are offered by certified teachers and professional experts. Most courses are eight weeks in length. Weekly on-line lecture and discussion groups are held, with supportive services including daily message boards, email support, and private libraries. Typical course areas include English, Languages, History, Sociology, Math, Science, Computer Science, and the Arts. No college credit or certificates are awarded for completion of these courses. Members usually enroll in these courses for educational enrichment purposes only.

For additional information, see the *Interactive Education Services* area in Learning and Reference on America Online, or send email to Mark Hulme at screen name "IESCoord."

International Correspondence School (ICS). ICS is the world's leader in correspondence-based career training, offering dozens of certificate and degree programs in a wide range of technical and business subject areas. While most instruction is still offered through the mail in the form of textbooks and other similar materials, ICS offers its students the opportunity—through America Online—to communicate directly, in real time, with instructors, other students, and ICS staff. In addition, a variety of course work information and library resources are available electronically to support the student's overall education. ICS and AOL together form a relationship that offers students the best traditional distance education with today's immediate electronic communications.

For additional information, see the *International Correspondence Services* area in Learning and Reference on America , or send email to Susan Wade at screen name "CorSchool."

4

Job Hunting the Electronic Way

This chapter outlines a number of well tested and proven activities (in the form of sequential steps) that can help you conduct a successful job search—using electronic resources to gain a competitive edge.

If you have made a decision regarding which career direction (i.e., job) you want to secure, and have the necessary qualifications, this chapter is for you!

This chapter is *not* appropriate if you are unsure of a career direction, or have not yet developed the qualifications normally required of the position you wish to secure. If you are unsure of which occupational direction would be best for you to pursue, please complete Chap. 2—Career Planning the Electronic Way. If you feel you lack the educational qualifications necessary for the position you desire, Chap. 3—On-Line Education—may help you find on-line programs that can provide you with the necessary training.

For millions of Americans, the task of hunting for work produces high levels of anxiety, frustration, a feeling of personal rejection, and a sense of helplessness. In today's job market, these outcomes are not uncommon, nor unexpected—they are, unfortunately for many, the norm. Upon a close examination of the causes underlying these conditions, one soon discovers two very important factors at play:

❏ The job market is highly competitive—there are simply more job seekers available than there are job openings, especially for the more desirable professions.

❏ The job search itself requires the use of a certain set of skills. Unfortunately, everyday life does not offer opportunities for the development of these skills. Therefore, most job seekers are ill prepared for the task of job hunting. While it's not your fault that you may lack these skills, you'll pay the price if you do not master them quickly when needed.

Place most people into a highly competitive job market unarmed with the right skills to compete and the outcome is predictable: Many will fail.

How then can you reach your employment goals? There is little that anyone can do to change the level of competition associated with today's job market. However, there is much that can be done to help you develop effective job seeking skills. Remember, as Tom Jackson states in *Guerrilla Tactics in the Job Market*, "It's not the most qualified persons who get the best jobs, it's those who are most skilled in job finding."

Few individuals would consider attempting to tune an automobile engine without prior training—the task is just too complex. However, many people assume that the job search is an easy task and can be accomplished merely by sending out copies of their resume to hundreds of employers. Nothing could be further from the truth!

The job search is a task, and like all tasks it can be learned and mastered. Certain professionals, including this author, have devoted their entire work life to the understanding of this task. As a result, an effective job search plan has been developed, used, and perfected by tens of thousands of individuals, and is now outlined in this chapter for your use.

What does it require to succeed in today's competitive job market? Several factors including:

❏ *A step-by-step plan that works*—one that can guide you in completing those steps proven to be most successful in obtaining employment.

❏ *A strong and positive self-concept*—you must constantly remind yourself that you are a worthwhile individual, one who can make a contribution to society, and one who is needed and valued in the workplace. By the very nature of the job search you will be rejected more often than offered employment. You should not take this rejection personally, or interpret it to mean that there are no suitable positions for you.

❏ *An unending dedication and commitment to succeed*—the job search will demand of you both time and energy. It is likely that you will have to work longer and harder than you anticipated to find your next job. If you allow yourself to be easily defeated, then you are doomed to failure by your own hand.

❏ *A resource team*—conducting a job search solely by yourself will result in a longer and more difficult job search. Soliciting help from both professional employment specialists and personal friends and family members can make the process easier, more enjoyable, and more successful. More about how to build a resource team later in this chapter.

❏ *Access to leading edge job search technology*—it has been said that information is power and access to information is the key to unleashing that power. At your disposal today are many services available through various technologies (e.g., computers, on-line databases and bulletin board services, and fax-back services) that can give you a competitive edge in securing employment. For example, with your personal computer, you can gain access to thousands of job listings in hundreds of career fields from companies all over America in a matter of minutes! For those who can take advantage of such technology, the search for employment will be easier and more productive. You will soon be introduced to many of today's most useful electronic job hunting technologies.

Getting a Job Is a Job in Itself!

As a professional career and employment counselor for over 20 years, I know the difficulties involved in finding employment. The expression "finding work is work itself," is more true today than ever before. It doesn't just seem to be more difficult to find work today, it *is* more difficult. Getting your next job will likely require you to spend more time and exert more effort than you may have imagined or experienced in your last job search.

The fact of the matter is this: American employers do not have enough jobs to employ all those who wish to work. While there are several factors that have brought about this condition, the one common factor is economics. American employers facing increased world competition are adopting policies designed to save money while improving productivity. Some common cost-cutting measures include downsizing and merging facilities, moving plants overseas, discharging senior-level executives, hiring part-time workers or subcontractors rather than full-time employees, and increasing the work load of those employees who are retained.

As Walter Cronkite pointed out in a recent television special, *Help Unwanted*, America is producing a permanent class of citizens who, while wishing to work, may not find employment. The end result of this is that you will need to use effective job hunting skills and resources—especially electronic resources—to find your next job.

Your Competitive Edge!

The job hunting guide outlined in this chapter has been used effectively by tens of thousands of job seekers and contains a unique strategy that can increase your success—especially when the techniques are supplemented with the use of electronic job hunting resources. If you follow this plan, your chances of finding employment can be improved.

As in Chap. 2, this chapter offers a self-directed approach to job hunting. A step-by-step system for finding and securing employment is outlined for your use. A wide variety of job hunting techniques have been tried and tested by tens of thousands of job seekers. The very best techniques have been assembled into the plan you are about to use. The job seeking expertise is built into the plan—your job is to implement each step at a pace and level that is most comfortable to you.

How Long Will It Take?

There are no hard and fast rules regarding how long it should take you to find employment. It may take you only days, or it could take you years. Landing a job depends on many factors, including:

❑ Your qualifications

❏ Your ability to find appropriate employers who need your help

❏ Your ability to "sell" yourself to employers

❏ The competition that you have to face

❏ The employment market conditions in the geographical area or areas where you hope to secure employment

Since any of these factors can change—and usually do—it is nearly impossible to predict how long it should take you to land your next job.

However, if we examine the time it takes most professionals in today's job market to find employment, we find that the average length of the job hunt is approximately six to nine months. Your job search could be the same, shorter, or longer.

A Full-Time Project!

It is expected that the job search program contained in this chapter will take longer to complete than the system found in Chap. 2—Career Planning the Electronic Way. If you are currently out of work, you should devote at least 6 to 8 hours each day, five days a week to your job search. By devoting full time to this task, you are more likely to secure employment sooner than later. The longer it takes you to find employment, the more likely you will compound the problems often associated with long periods of unemployment. Typical of these problems are limited finances, loss of self-respect and worth, and a growing sense of hopelessness. It is usually at such times that job seekers become desperate and take any job they can get, rather than getting the job they want. These problems can be avoided or reduced by bringing about a quick end to your job search, and that can be best accomplished by working full time at your search.

If you are currently employed, but looking to change jobs, you should set aside at least 10 to 15 hours per week to complete this task.

The demands of the job search in today's world are such that you must make it the center of your life for the time necessary to find employment. This may seem like a harsh requirement, or one unfair considering your other interests and responsibilities in life. However, the competition is keen, and since the benefits of working far outweigh those of being unemployed, the search for employment must become your number one priority.

Help Is Available When You Need It!

Finding and securing employment is usually not a one-person operation. If you desire assistance in some way to discuss your job search needs and problems, you are encouraged to email your questions to the author.

The job hunting steps outlined in this chapter include:

❏ Conducting an occupational self-assessment

❏ Setting employment goals (targets)

❏ Building a personal support team

❏ Building a professional support team

❏ Researching targets—identifying your employment value

❏ Communicating your value—shining your light

❏ Following up—setting the hook

❏ Interviewing—closing the deal

❏ Accepting/rejecting an offer

❏ Evaluating your job search strategy

For each step listed, you will find the following information:

❏ Objective

❏ Expected results

❏ How to complete

❏ Suggested electronic resources

It is recommended that you follow the plan outlined in this chapter, step-by-step, starting with Step 1 and progressing to Step 10.

Step 1—Conducting an Occupational Self-Assessment

Objective. The objective of this step is to examine what you know about your personality style, and then identify your *occupationally related* interests, skills/aptitudes, values/needs, and behavioral traits

If you completed Chap. 2—Career Planning the Electronic Way, you have already prepared a list of your *general* interests, skills/aptitudes, values/needs, and behavioral traits. Some of what you have discovered about yourself is important when selecting an occupational goal, other information is not. For example, you might have discovered that you have a deep interest in wildlife but have no desire to actually work with animals. Your "animal interest" is, therefore, considered to be nonvocational or avocational in nature. In this step, you will use only those factors that are related to, have a bearing on, can be matched to, or can be satisfied by certain occupational selections.

Job hunting involves searching for a particular type of employment. While this concept is easy to understand, it's amazing how many people fail to recognize the importance of having a specific goal in mind before starting to search for employment. Many job seekers make the mistake of believing that by getting involved in a job search, a direction will eventually become apparent. Either they believe that they will discover a direction, or worse yet, some generous, kind-hearted employer will take the time to examine their past and suggest a direction they should pursue. Neither option is likely to happen. The title of a book by David Campbell sums up this fallacy nicely—*"If you don't know where you're going, you'll probably end up somewhere else."*

Before you begin your job search, know what you're searching for. By doing so, you will decrease the amount of time and labor required to find the job you want. The search for the ideal job begins from within! The clues to which type of employment would be best for you can be found in your personality style.

Expected Results. By completing this step, you should be able to prepare of list of your occupational:

❏ Interests

❏ Skills/aptitudes

❏ Values/needs

❏ Behavioral traits

How to Complete. If you have not done so already, follow the directions contained in the *How to Complete* section of Step 1—Personality Assessment, found in Chap. 2—Career Planning the Electronic Way—to complete this step.

Once completed, review all the information you have gathered regarding your *general* personality style from the assessment options you used in Chap. 2. Now decide which factors best describe the *occupational* elements of your personality style. Go with your best judgment. Do not include information that you do not believe is true, and do not exclude information that you know to be true but dislike about yourself. Using the Occupational Personality Profile Chart (see page 73), list what you believe are your most important, or most descriptive, *occupational* interests, skills/aptitudes, values/needs, and behavioral traits.

After completing the Occupational Personality Profile Chart, move on to Step 2—Setting Employment Goals (Targets).

Step 2—Setting Employment Goals (Targets)

Objective. Armed with the information you collected in Step 1, your objective now is to determine the:

❏ Actual job positions that you wish to secure

❏ Names of companies for whom you wish to work

Caution! Do not assume that employers will help you determine which positions would be appropriate for you. They are too busy to provide you with career counseling. If you are uncertain as to which positions you want and are capable of handling, you are likely to be rejected or simply ignored by employers. Many employers interpret this lack of direction as a sign that you are unsure of your capabilities and, therefore, would be a poor choice as a new employee. Determining your career direction is your responsibility and should be completed *before* you start job hunting.

Occupational Personality Profile Chart

My main *occupational* interests are ...

1. _____
2. _____
3. _____
4. _____
5. _____
6. _____

My strongest *occupational* skills/aptitudes are ...

1. _____
2. _____
3. _____
4. _____
5. _____
6. _____

My most important *occupational* values/needs are ...

1. _____
2. _____
3. _____
4. _____
5. _____
6. _____

My most descriptive *behavioral* traits are ...

1. _____
2. _____
3. _____
4. _____
5. _____
6. _____

To further increase your chances of finding employment, you also need to identify (by name) those companies that you would like to work for—both those that have advertised job openings, and those who have not advertised but who do have positions available (i.e., the *hidden job market*).

How to Complete. Follow procedures 1 and 2 to accomplish this step. Procedure 1 will require you to first determine in which geographical areas you would like to work, and for which type of employer (e.g., bank, school, department store, hospital, or law office) you prefer to work. Procedure 2 will require that you specify companies by name within the areas that you have selected that you want to target as potential employers.

Procedure 1. Indicate on the following list the positions (by title) that you wish to secure. List only those positions that you are interested in and capable of performing. These positions should match or be in line with the information you gathered in Step 1 about your occupational interests, skills/aptitudes, values/needs, and behavioral traits.

Desired Position(s):

_____

_____

_____

_____

_____

If you have not done so already, refer to Step 2—Occupational Exploration in Chap. 2 for suggestions regarding how to identify positions related to your occupational interests.

If, after completing Chap. 2, you are still unsure as to which positions would be right for you, then career guidance or counseling is advised. There are several options for obtaining professional advice. For example, you could:

❑ Enroll in a career planning seminar, workshop, or course

❑ Complete an on-line career analysis inventory

❑ Talk privately on-line with a professional career counselor

Enrolling in a career planning seminar, workshop, or course usually involves some cost, but you have the advantage of being able to talk directly with a trained career guidance professional as you complete the program. The disadvantage of these programs is that they are not always available when you need them and may be expensive.

Talking privately—keyboard-to-keyboard—with a professional career counselor is one of the most inexpensive, fastest, and easiest to use options of those mentioned.

Whichever option you choose, the important thing to remember is to get some kind of assistance as soon as possible to select a direction that's right for you.

Procedure 2. Indicate on the following list the names of those companies that you would like to work for:

Desired Employers:

_____

_____

_____

_____

_____

_____

_____

_____

_____

Suggested Electronic Resources. How do you find the names of specific companies, especially if your targeted areas are far from your current location? Several options could be used, including the following:

❑ *Use the Help Wanted–USA* database of employment listings (see Chap. 8) to obtain information, updated weekly, on thousands of job openings in hundreds of professional career fields from employers across America.

❑ *Use the Select Phone CD-ROM employer directory (see Chap. 8).* This directory lists millions of employers (name, address, and phone number) according to industry type and geographical location.

❑ *Read several on-line electronic newspapers.* Monitor the help wanted classified ads to obtain names of local employers. See Chap. 6 for more information.

❑ *Use any of the on-line commercial mailing list services.* They can provide you—for a fee—with a list of employers, including address, phone number, names of key executives, and other information about each employer.

To obtain a list of suggested electronic references useful in completing this step, refer to the Cross-Reference Table on page 245.

❏ *Contact the Chamber of Commerce in the communities where you wish to seek employment.* They usually have lists of local employers available at no cost.

❏ *Several commercial software programs are also available that list employers by geographical area and industry type.*

To obtain a list of suggested electronic references useful in completing this step, refer to the Cross-Reference Table on page 245.

❏ *Contact the Office of Career Planning and Placement at any college or university within the area(s) you wish to research.* They often provide lists of employers at no cost.

When you have developed your list of employment objectives (job positions and employers), you are ready to move to Step 3—Building a Personal Support Team.

Step 3—Building a Personal Support Team

Objective. Considering that the job search may require considerable time and energy to complete, it is wise to pull together a small team of people who can assist you in carrying out many of the basic duties associated with job hunting. Simply stated, the more help you have at your disposal, the more successful your search is likely to be.

Your task at this point is to assemble of small team of people (5 to 10 individuals) who can help you complete some of the time-consuming tasks associated with finding employment, such as:

❏ Obtaining information from libraries

❏ Writing letters

❏ Photocopying resumes

❏ Making phone calls to obtain information

❏ Conducting research of employers

❏ Calling employment agencies and services

❏ Monitoring help wanted classified ads

❏ Mailing letters and other materials

❏ Reading articles for the purpose of gathering company background information

❏ Updating your status list of companies contacted for employment

In conducting a job search, your main responsibility should be to contact as many qualified companies as possible to inquire about employment. However, the more time you spend completing the clerical duties involved in this process, the less time you will have to actually seek out targets, conduct research, generate employment letters and letters of inquiry, process application forms, and participate in interviews. Therefore, to increase your job search productivity, assign as much of the clerical work as possible to your team members.

Who should be on your team? Anyone willing to help you out, or who needs to repay a favor. Consider asking your relatives, friends, or even hiring a few people to work for you on a part-time, temporary basis. Should you pay your team? Yes, by all means, offer each person some form of compensation. However, it is not necessary that the compensation always be in the form of money. Some members may wish to help because they simply want to, others because they're repaying a debt, still others may wish to barter with you for an even exchange of goods or services.

How to Complete. Assemble the team at least once per week for the purpose of delegating work assignments, discussing how each person is handling his or her responsibilities, and generally to manage the team's overall operation. Before you meet for the first time, have a clear idea of what assignments you wish to delegate, and then discuss with each team member his or her work assignments. Do not underestimate the value of this team! Over the years, it has shown itself to be one of the important factors of success in the job search.

Once you have assembled your support team, complete the Support Team Roster (see page 78) indicating the name of each member and his or her responsibilities, and then move ahead to the second phase of this step to build your network contacts.

Building Network Contacts

In addition to developing a support team, it is recommended that you also network. Networking involves using your personal and business contacts to identify employment opportunities or individuals who can connect you to information and potential employment opportunities. Here's how you can expand your network contacts:

❏ Prepare a list of the names and addresses of at least 100 people you know. Do not discount the value of any of your contacts—even the gas station attendant may be related to a company vice-president who could offer you a job!

❏ Send a brief note or letter to each person on your list. Indicate that you are looking for employment—indicate the type of employment and/or employer you desire. Ask each contact to call you with any information that they may obtain that may help you achieve your goals. Offer to accept any long-distance phone calls if the contact lives outside your local calling area.

❏ Continue to add names to your contact list and continue sending out your request for assistance on a monthly basis.

❏ Try to contact each person on your list at least once by phone to thank them for their assistance and to solicit new information that they may have recently collected.

❏ Use the membership directory services of the major commercial computer on-line network services to expand your list of contacts nationwide. The membership directory is a service available from each network where-

Support Team Roster

Directions: List the names below of each person who has agreed to become a member of your personal support team. Next to each individual indicate the responsibiliies that he or she has agreed to complete.

Name: _____

Responsibilities: _____

_____

_____

_____

Name: _____

Responsibilities: _____

_____

_____

_____

Name: _____

Responsibilities: _____

_____

_____

_____

Name: _____

Responsibilities: _____

_____

_____

_____

_____

Name: _____

Responsibilities: _____

_____

_____

_____

Name: _____

Responsibilities: _____

_____

_____

_____

Name:_____

Responsibilities: _____

_____

_____

_____

Name: _____

Responsibilities: _____

_____

_____

_____

by you can identify other members who have similar interests as you, or who live and work in certain geographical areas across the country

Each network's membership directory operates differently, but they all provide about the same kind of information. See the information below regarding how to access each directory

Don't be bashful about contacting strangers on-line. You'll be surprised at how many people love to chat on-line or via email. Just ask if they can share with you the names of any individuals or companies in your area that you might contact regarding employment.

To obtain a list of suggested electronic references useful in completing this step, refer to the Cross-Reference Table on page 245.

❑ Using your word processing program, prepare a profile similar to the sample profiles that follow for each person on your network contact list. Then, when you are in need of information or assistance from some individual—either well known or only recently introduced—you can easily search through your document (using your word processing search function) to identify individuals who may be able to provide the information or assistance you need.

Keep your contact file up to date. Every time you have a conversation, or send information to, or receive information from one of your contacts, update that contact's file to reflect this information. By doing so, you'll never be at a loss regarding what you did, when, for whom, and what was said.

When you have completed your list of network contacts, move on to Step 4—Building a Professional Support Team.

Sample Network Contact Profiles

Roberta E. Johnson
1234 Anywhere Drive
Manchester, NH 03104
603-123-4567—home
603-123-4567—work

Relationship:
Friend of cousin June. Referred by June.

Possible Employment Value:
Works for Metropolitan Life in Manchester, NH as an administrative assistant. May be able to help me obtain information regarding insurance opportunities in New Hampshire.

Thomas Barrington
America Online Screen Name: KoolKid

Relationship:
Discovered on-line from a search of the Membership Directory.

Possible Employment Value:
Tom and I have exchanged email messages on several occasions. Tom has indicated he works for a large newspaper in Detroit, Michigan, and has agreed to send me names of local employers in the Detroit area if requested.

Contact Dates:
January 20, 1994—1st email
January 26, 1994—2nd email—asked for list of employers
February 2, 1994—received list of 20 employers
February 3, 1994—sent "thank you" email

Cynthia Reed
CompuServe Address: 70154,186

Relationship:
Discovered on-line while searching the Bulletin Board messages in the Home Office Forum area.

Possible Employment Value:
Cynthia and I have exchanged email messages on several occasions. Cynthia works for Phoenix First, a major bank in Phoenix, Arizona. Cynthia's husband is a private employment recruiter in southwestern Arizona, and Cynthia has agreed to pass my resume on to her husband if requested.

Contact Dates:
February 7, 1994—1st email
February 9, 1994—sent resume via email
February 12, 1994—received confirmation that resume was received and would be passed on to her husband
February 13, 1994—sent email thanking her for her help

Hank Alison
123 Main Street
Hometown, PA 12345
215-555-5555—home

Relationship: Brother-in-law

Possible Employment Value:
Unsure at this time, but Hank says he'll help in any way he can.

Step 4—Building a Professional Support Team

Objective. The more people you have working for you (i.e., looking for work on your behalf), the greater your chances will be that you will find employment quickly and easily, and that you will find the kind of employment you desire.

Now that you have your personal support team assembled and network contacts working for you, your objective in this step is to list your credentials with several professional employment placement agencies (sometimes called headhunters, executive recruiters, executive search firms, etc.) to avail yourself of their employment placement services.

Before you list with any agency, make sure you fully understand their purpose. In many cases, recruiters do not work for you but are the agents of employers who have hired them to find employees on their behalf. Therefore, they owe their allegiance to those companies who pay them for their service, not to you. Because they do not work for you, they will naturally be more concerned about satisfying the needs of their paying clients. Understanding this condition will help you understand why you may not receive the attention and support that you believe you should.

Some recruiters are paid by their clients only when they have found an employee acceptable to the employer—these recruiters are usually called *contingency* agencies. Others are paid regardless of whether they find an acceptable employee—these recruiters are usually called *retained* agencies. Some experts believe that you may have better success with the retained agencies as they may have more time to spend with you since they are not under constant pressure to work only with those job seekers that they know they can quickly place.

How to Complete. How can you determine which agencies would be best for you? Several software-based and online directories of recruiters exist that help you identify appropriate services.

To obtain a list of suggested electronic references useful in completing this step, refer to the Cross-Reference Table on page 245.

Caution! Some recruiters require job seekers to pay for their service. Considering that there are plenty who do not charge, it is suggested that you seek out the free services before spending any money. Some recruiters will require your signature on a contract (usually those who charge a fee) before they will work with you. Be very certain you fully understand all terms before you sign as you could end up owing a great deal of money. Run, don't walk, from those recruiters who attempt to high pressure you into signing a contract, or who attempt to guarantee that they can find you a job!

Some recruiters will tell you that they will work with you only if you list exclusively with them. It is not suggested that you agree to such terms. Remember, each agency has many job seeking clients on their list. Therefore, only so much time can be devoted to your case.

It is suggested that you list with several agencies to increase the number of recruiters working on your behalf. If you do list with several agencies, it is not suggested that you mention this fact to any one of the agencies, as this may result in less effort on their part in finding you employment.

Finally, please understand that using a recruiting service is helpful in finding employment but is not always the most effective means of finding employment. Research has demonstrated that the direct approach (where you contact potential employers) is by far the most effective job hunting strategy. Using a placement agency should be considered as one of several strategies you will employ.

Use the Placement Agency Registration Form (page 84) to list those agencies that you have contacted and who have agreed to help you search for employment.

Once you are registered with several recruiting agencies, you are ready to move on to Step 5—Researching Targets: Identifying Your Employment Value.

Step 5—Researching Targets: Identifying Your Employment Value

Important! *This step outlines the most important task of the entire job search process. If you learn how to identify and use this information effectively, your chances of being offered employment can be greatly enhanced. If you fail to recognize the importance of this information, your chances of securing employment can be decreased.*

Objective. When you get right down to it, employers are mainly interested in one thing—what talent you have to offer and how it can be used to further their business success! It is imperative, therefore, that you clearly determine what your employment value is and then communicate your value to the right people.

What is your employment value? Your employment value is your talent (i.e., knowledge and skills) and how it can be used to further the success of those employers for whom you wish to work. To recognize your employment value requires that you (1) fully understand the knowledge and skills you possess, (2) understand the business objectives and needs of the companies where you wish to gain employment, and (3) understand how your talent can be used to aid employers in reaching their business goals.

How to Complete. A two-step procedure exists for identifying your employment value.

Procedure 1. The mechanics of how to identify your knowledge and skills was outlined in Step 1—Conducting an Occupational Self-Assessment (see page 73). If you are still unclear as to what talent you have to offer, it is strongly suggested that you return to Step 1 before you continue.

Procedure 2. Identifying the business objectives and needs of those companies where you wish to work is a more difficult task. However, by using a procedure similar to what a police detective might use to solve a crime, you can discover this information. By gathering a variety of information about a particular company, you can better understand what objectives they have set for themselves and, therefore, what needs they may have that you can satisfy with your talent.

The following lists several items that you should collect on each company:

❑ Copies of any and all brochures, sales flyers, etc.

❑ Copies of the company's annual report

❑ Company telephone directory

❑ Magazine articles about employees and/or the company itself

❑ Dun & Bradstreet reports

❑ Better Business Bureau reports

❑ Supply catalogs

❑ Articles in any trade journal

❑ Press releases

❑ The names of the key executives of the company, especially the name of the person that you would report to if offered the position you wish to secure

Placement Agency Registration Form

Directions: List below those agencies with which you have registered. Include the basic profile information, plus a record (log) of all conversations you have had with the contact person at each agency.

Agency:

Name _____

Address: _____

City/State/Zip: _____

Phone: _____

Contact: _____

Conversation Log:

_____

_____

_____

Agency:

Name _____

Address: _____

City/State/Zip: _____

Phone: _____

Contact: _____

Conversation Log:

_____

_____

Agency:

Name _____

Address: _____

City/State/Zip: _____

Phone: _____

Contact: _____

Conversation Log:

_____

_____

_____

Agency:

Name _____

Address: _____

City/State/Zip: _____

Phone: _____

Contact: _____

Conversation Log:

_____

_____

_____

Read anything and everything you can get your hands on regarding each company. In addition, talk to people who once worked or still work for the company, people such as:

❑ Sales Representatives

❑ Marketing and Advertising Executives

❑ Personnel Directors and/or Human Resource Managers

❑ Telephone Receptionists

❑ Company Librarian (if one exists)

❑ Past or retired employees (a major source of information)

When reading, your objective should be to identify information that describes the company's business objectives. In other words, what is the company attempting to do as a business? To whom? How? When? Where? Why? And most importantly, what obstacles, problems, or situations are they encountering as they attempt to reach their objectives?

When speaking to individuals, your questions should have the same objective, but you should be more discreet so as not to reveal your true objective. Never inform someone that you are looking for employment, as this will almost always cause the person to end the conversation. Your reason for inquiring should be more along the lines of an interested party who wishes to know more about the company, its services, and/or its product line.

Prepare a one- or two-page Employment Value Report for each company on your target list, indicating the following information:

❑ Paragraph 1—The overall objectives of the company

❑ Paragraph 2—The overall objectives of the position you wish to secure

❑ Paragraph 3—How the position you wish to secure is related to the overall success of the company

❑ Paragraph 4—How you, if hired, can help the company achieve its business goals. Include the objectives you would set for yourself, the methods or strategies you would employ to reach those objectives, the obstacles you expect to encounter, the resources you would employ to overcome those obstacles, and a general time schedule you believe would be required in order to reach your objectives.

Note: Paragraph 4 is the definition of your employment value—it is what you have to offer the company. If you have done your homework well, it should be of great interest to the company. After all, what could be more important to any company than reaching their business goals?

A clear and concise description of your employment value, coupled with an equally clear and concise description of the company and its objectives is the most powerful job seeking tool you can employ—far more powerful than the traditional resume! The value of your personal support team should be more evident now, as you can see how they can help you collect the information necessary for the preparation of your reports.

To obtain a list of suggested electronic references useful in completing this step, refer to the Cross-Reference Table on page 245.

A sample Employment Value Report (see page 88) is included to illustrate how one may be written. This sample is basic in nature—your report may or may not need more detail. You should be able to state your case in 2 to 5 pages. Avoid longer reports, as they are less likely to be read.

There are no hard and fast rules about how to write such a report. Feel free to vary the page layout design to suit your needs. However, certain information should be included, such as the preceeding information outlined in Paragraphs 1 to 4.

Once you have prepared your Employment Value Report for each company on your list, you are ready to move to Step 6—Communicating Your Value: Shining Your Light.

Step 6—Communicating Your Value: Shining Your Light

Objective. Now that you have determined how and why you can be of value to each employer on your list, it's time to communicate your value to the right people. Your objective in this step is to let each employer on your target list know that you are available and ready to help them reach their business goals.

In physics, nothing can be seen without the presence of light, and only those objects that can radiate or reflect light can be seen by the human eye. There exists a similar condition in the job seeking world—employers cannot see you until you first shine your light in their direction. You've got to tell them you're available and what value you have to offer before they can offer you a job. Actually, you hold the key to your own job hunting success if you learn how to effectively advertise your talent.

Within each company, there exists an individual who has the *power to hire.* These individuals are responsible for various departments or functions, and have the authority to make decisions, including the authority to hire new employees. It is to these people that you must now communicate your employment value. The people with the power to hire are not usually the Personnel Director or Human Resource Manager. While these individuals are involved in the hiring process, they usually carry out the hiring orders made by the people with the power to hire.

For example, the decision to hire a new Marketing Assistant is not usually made by personnel. It is usually made by the Director of Marketing, and then conveyed to the Personnel Director whose responsibility it is then to find appropriate candidates and then to turn that information over to the Director for final selection.

The golden rule in gaining employment is this: *If an employer can clearly see how he or she can gain (financially or otherwise) by hiring you, even if it requires creating a new position, he or she will do it more times than not!* Business people are in the

Sample Employment Value Report

Prepared by: John Doe
123 Main St.
Hometown, NH 12345

Prepared for: Thomas Smith
Dean of Continuing Education
City College
Hometown, NH 12345

Date: January 6, 1993

Introduction: The following report has been prepared for Dean Thomas Smith by John Doe for the purpose of illustrating how Mr. Doe can be of value to City College in the capacity of Director of Alternate Education.

Mission Objectives: From research conducted by Mr. Doe over the last several weeks, it seems apparent that one of the main goals of City College for the 1993-1994 academic year is to develop and implement alternate methods of providing continuing education courses and degrees to nontraditional adult students who wish to pursue courses or a degree program. This conclusion is the result of conversations held between Mr. Doe and Dean.

Smith, Dean Roberts, several faculty members, and a review of the 1993-1994 Mission Statement as prepared by the City College Board of Directors (on file in College Library), as well as from the fact that City College has recently advertised an employment opening for a Director of Alternate Education.

College has recently advertised an employment opening for a Director of Alternate Education.

Objectives of the Director of Alternate Education: To achieve the goals as set forth by the college to bring in an increasing number of nontraditional adult students—students who desire additional education, but who cannot participate in traditional methods of learning, the Director of Alternate Education must be able to:

(1) Conduct a survey of nontraditional adults in the greater Hometown, NH, area to identify their educational needs, desires, and concerns;

(2) Conduct an assessment of services and programs available at City College to identify those existing services that will be needed, as well as new services that must be developed;

(3) Formulate in writing a comprehensive implementation plan illustrating how best to establish an alternate education program for nontraditional adult students; and

(4) Convey the objectives of City College to administrative staff members, faculty, students, and to community leaders for the purpose of securing their cooperation and assistance in realizing the objectives of the division.

The relationship of the Director of Alternate Education to the overall success of City College: The Director of Alternate Education is one of 10 administrative officers of the college, with full voting rights and responsibilities as a member of the President's Council. The Director shall report to the Dean of Academic Affairs. In this capacity, the Director shall be the one individual who is primarily and mainly responsible for the design and implementation of the alternate education program. Considering that this new venture has been established as one of the two top mission objectives of the Division of Continuing Education, the success of the individual who holds this position will have a direct impact on the operational success of the Division of Continuing Education at City College.

How John Doe can be of value to City College: As someone with over 15 years of experience designing and developing educational training programs and services—often using nontraditional methods and techniques, I believe I am uniquely qualified to carry out the objectives of this position. A copy of my personal resume is enclosed outlining my past qualifications and experiences. The following scenario illustrates how I would manage this new venture during the first six months of operation.

I would first create a seven-member steering committee of college and community leaders who would be charged with the responsibility of advising me regarding the design, content, objectives, procedures, resources, and staffing of the new alternate education division.

The committee would conduct its work in two phases. Phase 1 would involve the preparation and delivery of a preliminary committee report outlining the above information. This report would then be reviewed by college officials and a summary report developed outlining questions and concerns that need to be further addressed by the steering committee. Phase 2 would consist of a second report prepared by the steering committee addressing all concerns and questions as outlined in the summary report. The revised and completed second report would then be used as a plan of action for creating the alternate education division.

Special emphasis will be placed on incorporating the use of technology (computers, on-line bulletin board services, videotape programs, teleconferencing, and satellite services) to enable adult students to complete course work when and where it is most convenient, especially from their home or office. One of the steering committee members will be someone with in-depth knowledge of the field of technology and education.

I believe my experience in managing various departments, conducting budget reviews and allocations, hiring and training of staff members, public relations, marketing, and advertising of services would enable me to effectively manage the overall operation of the Office of Alternate Education.

Monthly progress reports would be prepared by myself and forwarded to the Dean of Academic Affairs to monitor the development of the program. A more comprehensive six-month and annual report would also be prepared.

A close working relationship would be immediately established between my office and the on-campus offices of marketing, personnel, budget and finance, and faculty affairs to ensure a smooth and effective development of the program's objectives.

A staff of one director, two assistant directors, and two administrative aids is anticipated to be needed during the first year of operation. A total budget for year one of $120,500 is also expected to be necessary to reach the objectives of this division.

Conclusion: If given the opportunity to become the first Director of Alternate Education, I will devote my full talent and energies to implementing the mission objectives of the college and of the position—nothing less will be acceptable. I pledge my full cooperation and untiring dedication to work closely with all members of the Administrative Team, as well as the Dean of Continuing Education, College President, and other appropriate individuals to ensure that the outstanding reputation associated with City College is ensured for the future.

business of creating profit—show them how you can increase their profit and you can become an indispensable commodity.

If you have not yet identified from your research the names of those individuals within each company who have the power to hire, please complete this task before completing this step.

How to Complete. How do you best communicate your employment value? Three items are necessary for communicating your value (in order of importance):

❏ A well written Employment Value Report outlining your value

❏ A well written cover letter to introduce yourself and your value

❏ A well written resume outlining your qualifications

Note: Many job seekers believe the resume is the most important item or factor in gaining employment—many individuals build their entire job search strategy around the distribution of resumes. While traditionally this was the case, the role and importance of the resume in today's society has changed. Today, a resume is still an important tool, but it should not be seen as the main or central strategy. Rather, the resume is necessary to provide *background* information to employers *after* you have interested them in your candidacy. How you get them interested is through the use of an Employment Value Report!

Understand that it is the Employment Value Report that is of most interest to employers, as it contains information regarding what you can do for each company. Resumes are documents that outline your past life (i.e., schooling, work history, etc.). Since most people do not have a consistent theme to their life, a good deal of the information contained in your resume *may have no bearing on or value to* the job you are now seeking. For example, your schooling may not match all the jobs you have held, or not all the jobs you have held may be similar in nature.

Another disadvantage of the resume is the fact that the reader (i.e., employer) may misinterpret what is written on your resume, thereby disqualifying you from further consideration. The only way to ensure that the employer becomes aware of your employment value is to clearly state it in the form of an Employment Value Report.

Many job seekers place an unwarranted amount of emphasis on a resume simply because they are not aware of what truly is important and how best to present what is important. Do not waste a great deal of time trying to create the perfect resume or cover letter, or trying to write a resume that's right for all employers (both of which are nearly impossible to do). Put your time and energy where it can pay off—into your Employment Value Reports!

Your cover letter should be one page in length, and should simply introduce yourself and briefly summarize how you can be of value to the company. It should refer the reader to your Employment Value Report and resume (both should be included) and finally indicate that you will contact the reader to further discuss how you can be of value.

The subject of what should be contained in a resume and/or cover letter and how these items should be written has been covered by hundreds of books and software programs. In addition, there exist thousands of real resumes that can be downloaded from computer on-line services and databases and used as guides for creating your own resume. Therefore, there is no need to provide information here regarding how to create a resume. If you are unsure as to how to write a resume or cover letter, please refer to the following electronic resources.

Make sure your written communications are professional in nature—no handwritten letters; no spelling errors, typos, or crossouts; make sure they are typewritten or computer printed with a good quality typewriter or laser printer; and use only top quality white bond paper. Send all letters first class (or overnight express if you wish). Do not email or fax your materials unless you have been granted permission by the intended reader.

To obtain a list of suggested electronic references useful in completing this step, refer to the Cross-Reference Table on page 245.

Once you have started forwarding your Employment Value Reports to employers on your target list, you are ready to move to Step 7—Following Up: Setting the Hook.

Step 7—Following Up: Setting the Hook

As any good salesperson will tell you, it often takes several contacts with a potential customer before the sale is accomplished. Selling is often a process of overcoming objections, or of convincing the buyer that he or she will benefit from purchasing what you have to offer. This is definitely the case in seeking employment. You must follow up each and every application or inquiry. Many employers purposely do not respond to letters mailed in by job seekers preferring to wait and see who follows up. Such a practice is an excellent means of determining who is most dedicated and, therefore, most motivated for the position.

Also, most sales are not made during the initial contact between the seller and buyer. Human behavior is such that buyers often prefer to think a bit about the purchase, to mull it over, or to sleep on it to ensure that it will be a wise decision. Impulse buying can be dangerous and expensive! This same behavior can be seen with employers as they too prefer to slowly consider the possibility of hiring you to ensure that they don't make a decision they will later regret. Hiring the wrong individual can cost the company thousands of dollars and lost customer confidence, not to mention the job of the person who hired you!

A good salesperson understands this phenomenon and will at first attempt to identify the buyer's main reasons for considering the sale, as well as any objections that the buyer may have about the sale. Then, slowly at first, and more forcefully as time goes on, the salesperson will continue to address why the sale is wise (i.e., why the product or service can meet the buyer's needs), and how the product or service can overcome and satisfy any and all of the buyer's objections.

Because this process is also similar to how an expert angler catches fish, it is often referred to as *setting the hook*. An experienced fly fisher, for example, will not attempt to catch the fish on the first nibble. This often results in the fish spitting out the bait and escaping, since the hook has not yet been fully set into the fish's jaw. A good angler will allow the fish to swallow more and more of the hook and then yank the line only after the hook is firmly in place.

In job hunting, don't expect to secure an offer of employment on the first encounter. Your employment value may not yet be fully understood by the employer and may be missed if you push for a job offer at this point. Your objective should be to convey your value, and then over the next few encounters push home more strongly how you can be of value to the employer. Only when you sense that the employer fully understands and appreciates your value should you then ask for employment.

Your objective in this step is to set the hook—to get each employer on your target list to agree to a meeting (a.k.a. interview) where you can fully discuss how you can be of value.

How to Complete. Wait approximately one week after you have sent in your Employment Value Report and then place a phone call to the person who received your letter. In today's busy world, you may have to call back several times to personally reach the right person. Once you reach your party, ask if they had time to review your recent correspondence. If not, schedule another time to call back to give your party time to review your materials. Send a second copy of your letter if the party claims not to have seen your first letter.

During your phone call, stress your interest in the company and briefly outline your ideas regarding how you can help the company reach its business objectives. Ask for an opportunity to personally meet (i.e., interview) to further discuss your employment value. Schedule a date, time, and location. *Note:* You still have not asked for a job!

If you are responding to a position that has actually been advertised and is still open, and if you do not seem to be getting anywhere, then it is safe to assume that the employer does not see you as the most qualified candidate. Regardless of whether you do or do not have the necessary qualifications, one thing that is true is that you may not have presented yourself adequately or properly for the employer to understand your value.

Ask the employer what he or she believes are the most important qualifications for the position. Then, prepare a second letter outlining how you can satisfy these qualifications, forward the letter immediately (even by fax), and follow up a second time. Continue to stress your employment value and identify and overcome any obstacles or objections that are presented to you—persistence is often the key to success.

If you are proposing that you be hired when no position has been advertised, and if you do not seem to be getting anywhere, then it is safe to assume that the employer does not see your value. Ask the employer what additional information you could provide that would convince him or her that hiring you would be beneficial to the company. Prepare a second letter outlining how you can satisfy these additional conditions, forward the letter immediately (even by fax), and follow up a second time. Again, continue to overcome any obstacles or objections that are presented to you.

If after several repeated contacts you still are getting nowhere, it is suggested that you back off to avoid alienating the employer by too much persistence. At this point, a brief (one page) letter mailed once a month would be appropriate to keep your letter of inquiry, application, or Employment Value Report fresh in the employer's mind. Continue to emphasize how you can be of value, especially as it relates to anything the company is involved with at the current time.

The Bottom Line. In all the conversations and communications you have with potential employers, make sure you continue to stress your Employment Value and its relationship to the employer's business success.

Once you have completed your follow-up calls, you are ready for Step 8—Interviewing: Closing the Deal.

Step 8—Interviewing: Closing the Deal

Objective. In survey after survey of job seekers, the interview is reported to be the most fearful and anxiety-producing step in searching for employment. Two reasons are given as the cause for such distress. First, having to *sell* yourself to strangers with the possibility of personal rejection is a very uncomfortable prospect. Job seekers often compare this situation to asking for a date only to be rudely rejected. Second, knowing that the interviewer will be asking questions designed to test and evaluate your suitability for employment and not knowing what those questions will be, creates a situation fraught with anxiety and possible errors. And if errors are made, rejection or disqualification will often follow.

To prepare for the interview, most job seekers adopt the attitude that the best strategy is to attempt to sell their background (i.e., experiences, knowledge, and skills) to the employer. In short, job seekers must convince the employer through the use of a discussion of past situations where they have been successful that they are the best suited candidate for the job. Unfortunately, while this strategy is not inappropriate in itself, it is usually conducted in a vacuum of knowledge. Specifically, most job seekers fail to research the company prior to the interview and, therefore, fail to have a good understanding of (1) what the company is attempting to do as a business, and (2) how the job seekers with their talent can be of value to the company. Not knowing the latter prohibits you from "selling" those specific aspects of your talent that are truly needed by the employer—aspects that will otherwise cause the employer to conclude that he or she should hire you.

Your objective in the interview is to get the employer to agree that you are the best qualified person for the job. And this can be accomplished only if the employer first believes that your talent can be used to reach the objectives of the position you wish to secure. If you can demonstrate the latter, you can accomplish the former.

How to Complete. What then should be the best way to prepare for and conduct an interview? Keeping in mind that the employer is most interested in business objectives and has at least tentatively concluded that you may be able to help advance these objectives, your objectives for the interview should be as follows:

❏ To discuss your Employment Value Report to further convince the employer of your value to the company.

❏ To discuss other ways (not outlined in your report) that you may be able to contribute to helping the employer reach his or her business objectives. *Note:* By discussing the employer's objectives, it is likely that you and the interviewer will be able to brainstorm other possible ways in which you can be of value.

❏ To demonstrate your ability to help the employer reach his or her business objectives by citing evidence from your past where you have accomplished similar tasks.

❏ To ask the employer if he or she would like to make you an offer of employment, and then to discuss the terms of employment, such as salary, benefits, starting date, and so on.

It should be evident to you by now that if you have conducted the proper research to determine what the employer has established as business objectives, and if you have determined how you can be of value, then you should be able to more easily and effectively handle and succeed in the job interview.

Always remember the following: By preparing an Employment Value Report, you have demonstrated to the employer your willingness to "go the extra mile" to help him or her reach the company's business objectives. If you're willing to do this *before* you are hired, just imagine how dedicated and helpful you can be *after* you're hired when you have easier access to company information, procedures, objectives, and resources.

When asked by the employer, "Why should I hire you?" Your answer should be (1) because I can be of value to your company (i.e., see my Employment Value Report), and (2) I am more willing to dedicate myself to your company's success as compared to other applicants as evidenced by my willingness to prepare this report for you.

If the interview ends with an offer of employment, you should discuss the terms of employment and then inform the interviewer that you tentatively accept the position, but wish to evaluate the terms overnight and that you will call tomorrow with your final answer. It is not considered wise to immediately accept an offer. While it would be appropriate to indicate that you believe the offer is acceptable, it's considered professional to "sleep on the offer" until the next day.

How you conduct yourself in the interview, and especially the information you present in response to the interviewer's questions is of prime importance. It is not recommended that you go cold into the interview. It is recommended that you role play the interview with a trained professional counselor, so that you can practice responding to questions that are typically presented. A review of your answers can reveal weaknesses and areas where additional or different information should be presented. Remember, practice makes perfect!

You can engage in a mock interview by scheduling an on-line counseling session with one of the professional counselors in the Career Center on America Online. See Chap. 10 for more information.

If this step ends with no suitable offer of employment and neither a clear indication that the employer is seriously considering your offer, nor an indication that he or she will get back to you soon with an answer, then you need to continue pursuing other employment targets on your list.

If this steps ends with a suitable offer of employment, you are now ready to move on to Step 9—Accepting/Rejecting an Offer.

Step 9—Accepting/Rejecting an Offer

Objective. Your objective in this step is to officially notify the employer of your decision regarding the offer of employment.

How to Complete. If you were offered employment during the interview, your next step should be to call the employer the next day and inform him or her of your final decision. If your decision is to accept the offer, then you should verbally confirm the terms and follow up your phone call with a letter or fax formally accepting the position and terms. If you feel different terms are necessary, then you should call the employer and indicate that you wish to discuss changes to the terms outlined during the interview. If your decision is to reject the offer, then you should call the employer, indicate that you are unable to accept the position, and why, and then follow up your phone call with a letter or fax graciously declining the offer.

If you were informed that someone would soon get back to you regarding your application, you should forward a fax or letter (within a day or two after the interview) thanking the interviewer for his or her time, briefly restating your strong interest in the position and clearly summarizing how you can be of value. If additional information about the company and its objectives was disclosed during the interview that was not in your Employment Value Report, be sure to indicate how you can help to achieve these new objectives.

If after one week (or after the time stated by the interviewer) you still have not heard from the employer regarding the status of your application, you should call the employer and ask if any action has been taken on your application.

If you now have the job you set out to achieve, or one similar in nature, your job search is over. Congratulations on a job well done! Enjoy your new position, work hard and prosper!

If you have not yet secured a position, then you should move on to Step 10—Evaluating Your Job Search Strategy.

Step 10—Evaluating Your Job Search Strategy

Objective. The objective of this step is to determine if your lack of success in your job search up to this point is due to your actions, or lack of actions, and if you are responsible, what can be done to improve your chances of success.

Now that you have applied for a position or positions, and have not been offered employment, it is important to evaluate what you have done (and perhaps have not done) in conducting your search.

Do not automatically assume you are at fault if you have not secured employment. It is very common for job seekers to conduct a *textbook perfect* job search and still not gain employment. Remember, it all comes down to someone deciding if they believe you are the best candidate for the position. Their perception of your qualifications may or may not be accurate or the same as yours, plus they may have some hidden agenda that causes them to vote for a different candidate. While you should not blame yourself, you should take the time to evaluate your job search system to ensure that you are doing everything as effectively as possible.

At this point, ask yourself the following questions:

❏ Do I fully understand my personality style—my occupational interests, skills/aptitudes, values/needs, and behavioral traits?

❏ Have I identified an occupational direction or directions that is in line with my personality style—a direction that employers won't question once they understand my background?

❏ Have I researched the geographical area or areas in which I would like to work to identify all possible target employers?

❏ Have I assembled a personal support team to help me conduct a job search, and have I effectively used this resource to help me secure employment? Should I select new members or use the same members in the future?

❏ Have I registered with several executive recruiters as a means of expanding my job search effort? Should I register with additional recruiters?

❏ Am I able (through research) to clearly identify what my employment value is at the locations where I would like to work? Do I need to improve my research efforts to better and more accurately obtain this information?

❏ Have I clearly and effectively communicated my employment value through the use of my Employment Value Reports, cover letters, resumes, and other forms of communication?

❏ Am I able to interview effectively? Am I able to anticipate the interests and needs and, therefore, the questions of employers? Am I able to effectively convince interviewers during the interview that my employment value is appropriate for their needs, and that I am the best qualified candidate?

❏ Have I professionally and properly followed up all applications for employment, as well as all interview sessions in a manner that emphasizes my employment value and how it can be of benefit and use to the employer?

❏ Is my dedication to the job search strong, positive, consistent, and ongoing?

❏ Have I used all the electronic resources that I am aware of that can help me identify even more employment opportunities?

An answer of "no" to any of these questions may reveal where the fault lies in your job search. Return to the section of this book associated with any item where you answered with a "no" and review that section. Then determine how you can improve that particular task, and repeat those steps again.

Above all else, remember this: One of the most important keys to your success is dedication. There is no normal or set time that dictates when you should or will secure employment. It may take you only a few weeks, several months, or a year or two. A consistent and persistent professionally developed strategy will result in success!

5
The Internet

This chapter provides basic information regarding the Internet—the world's electronic *information superhighway*, and its value to career planners and job seekers. Simply put, of all the resources that can help you advance your career, none is more valuable than access to the Internet! For career planners and job seekers, Internet offers a *relatively* easy, quick, and inexpensive means of accessing, through your personal computer, millions of individuals nationwide and around the world, hundreds of thousands of companies, thousands of employment listings and a vast array of data and services. Gaining access to the Internet, and learning how to navigate once on-line are not easy tasks to accomplish, but the rewards once mastered are well worth the labor. For career planners and job seekers who wish to arm themselves with the best resources to gain the highest possible competitive edge now and in the future, understanding how to use the Internet is mandatory.

Large and Getting Larger!

"Twenty million strong and adding a million new users a month, the Internet is suddenly the place to be," according to *TIME Magazine*.

College students are queuing up at universities nationwide. Elementary students in Indiana are communicating regularly and exchanging research projects with their peers in Australia. American industry is moving large amounts of information around the globe quickly and cheaply. Executives are ordering business cards that show off their Internet address—even the president, vice-president, and top government officials have their own Internet accounts.

The Internet is a "network of computer networks" spanning the globe. Today more than 20 million people use this worldwide web of interconnected computer networks to exchange electronic mail, transfer computer files, search databases, and "chat" in real time with other on-line users.

Internet is the world's largest collective computer network, connecting people on every continent on the globe including teachers, students, librarians,

Contributing author: William Warren, Executive Director, Online Career Center.

researchers, business executives and professionals, science fiction readers, venture capitalists, world policy makers, programmers, and many, many more.

This mother network-of-all-networks has evolved from a government funded national research and defense system to the electronic underpinning of the rapidly emerging "global village." Although not yet the 500-channel, 100-lane data superhighway envisioned by many, there is no network in existence approaching its scope or potential.

Karl Tate, Assistant Art Director for the Associated Press, has depicted the Internet as a "cloud" because its structure is unimportant to the user. There is no physical location for the Internet, and there is no master computer that people dial into; it is simply a web of millions of interconnected computers scattered around the world.

Internet is the sum of all the diverse computer networks that are tied together—from corporate networks that link personal computers in single offices to networks that span continents with fiber-optic cable and satellite links.

While more than half of the Internet-connected computers are in the United States, Internet is available in over 100 countries, with a strong presence in Canada, Europe, Asia, Australia, and the Pacific Rim.

According to U.S. Department of Commerce statistics the current new-user rate of growth is a phenomenal 7 to 10 percent per month. Kevin M. Savetz, writing in the January/February 1994 issue of *INTERNET WORLD* stated, ". . . if the Internet were to continue to grow at its current rate, by the year 2005 the number of users on Internet would equal the total human population."

Through a variety of tools, the Internet gives its users access to a mind-boggling universe of information resources and services. Most of all, the Internet has become a community (actually, a community of communities) and a global way of working and living.

Business executives and professionals are one of the fastest growing user groups on the Internet. Companies of all shapes and sizes are finding that the Internet provides new opportunities for competitive advantage.

How the Internet Is Often Used

Many activities that companies currently perform by phone, with a fax machine, or via overnight express can be done more effectively and a lot less expensively over the Internet. For example, you can send a 100-page document full of graphs and charts to Japan and be confident it will arrive immediately. You can also find new employees quickly, often on the same day that you conduct a search of various resume databases or announce your employment needs through a Newsgroup. Through the Internet, you can track the daily progress of federal and state legislation and read the latest Supreme Court decisions. You can also download any of thousands of photo-quality space images from NASA or actively assist earthquake victims in California.

Want to send a message to your son, daughter, or friend who's in college in another state and have it arrive in just seconds? How about being able to send a message just as quickly to a friend, family member, or business associate in England? Want to follow the stock market, find the latest government reports on the country's economic performance, or search the Library of Congress on-line service for Congressional or foreign legislation? It's all on the Internet!

Internet can also provide you with current weather reports for major U.S. and foreign cities; files updated hourly containing North American satellite weather images and radar maps, and color radar maps of the United States that show severe weather patterns, fronts and current temperatures just to name a few of the common types of information that is as close as your computer keyboard. The Internet can do all this and much, much more.

Many companies connect to the Internet because of its global communications power. Once linked up, they often find the network can contribute to every business function from research and development to marketing, sales, and customer support. While email remains the most widespread application, more companies are venturing beyond communications into using the Internet for strategic business purposes.

Government use of the Internet is expanding so quickly that it is difficult to say just how many agencies are now on-line. But a quick survey shows that tens of thousands of databases, documents, graphics files, and other services are available to the average citizen from many federal agencies—information that simply is not as accessible without the use of computers and network services.

Only in the last few years have private individuals joined the Internet in large numbers, and the growth of individual users is skyrocketing. The number of commercial Internet connection providers has also exploded from a handful only two years ago to well over 100 today; more are being added daily. These connectivity providers provide individual users with a means of getting connected to the Internet. By some estimates, the percentage of private users connecting through company connections and commercial service providers now exceeds over one-half of all Internet usage.

How Do You Connect to the Internet?

Connecting to the Internet used to be difficult and expensive. If you had lots of money to spend, could afford buying a superfast main frame computer system (not a personal computer) as well as an expensive fast phone line, then you could set up a system through which your main frame computer (often referred to as a server) was connected directly to the Internet. Because of the high cost, this option was and still is not practical for most private citizens. It is the option, however, that most colleges, universities, federal and state government agencies, and major corporations still use to access the Internet.

For private individuals, connecting to the Internet is done by first connecting one's personal computer through the regular phone line to some main frame computer system owned by someone who is already connected to the Internet. Consider the other person's main frame to be a gateway to the Internet. This can often be accomplished by agreement with a local college, university, government agency, large corporation, or commercial service. There usually is a fee required to access the Internet by this option, but most fees are reasonable.

One option growing in popularity is to subscribe to a commercial computer on-line network, such as America Online, BIX, CompuServe, Delphi, GEnie, or Prodigy. They all provide access to the Internet. Each of these services is available to anyone wishing to become a member. Each service charges a monthly subscription fee (usually around $10/month), plus per hour charges than can range from less than $5.00 per hour to over $20 per hour depending on which service you use and which Internet location you want to access.

With your copy of America Online, you have full access to the Internet. See Chap. 10 for more information regarding how to gain access to America Online. Once on-line, use the keyword "Internet" to access the Internet area. While most readers will find America Online more than sufficient to access the Internet, other access options are presented in the following pages.

You can also access the Internet through a commercial connection service—a private company that will sell you an access number. These companies install a main frame system and then sell access numbers to the general public. The fees for these services are similar to the fees charged by the commercial computer network services. However, these commercial connection services usually provide full access to the Internet, which is not the case for most of the commercial computer on-line network services.

If you happen to live in a community that offers a "freenet" service, count yourself lucky. Some individuals and organizations believe that access to the Internet should be made available to everyone at no cost. These are people who are part of a new movement who believe strongly in the right of every individual to have access to information. If you have a freenet service in your area, you can connect to the Internet without paying a single penny!

The access route you elect will determine how much you can do on the Internet. If you are connected through a main frame, anything that is happening on the Internet is potentially within your grasp. Some of the commercial computer network services provide only email exchange. Most commercial connection services allow full access.

What Can You Do on the Internet?

You can essentially do five things:

1. Send and Receive Email

The most common way for individuals to communicate with each other on the Internet is by sending and receiving email—the electronic version of postal mail, but much faster. Each individual who has access to the Internet has a unique email address, just as each person who uses the postal service has a unique address. The email address actually identifies the computer that has access to the Internet and the user who has access to the computer. When you send email out into the

Internet it travels to all computers connected in the network until it finds the computer with the matching email address, then it waits for the intended recipient to view the message and, if desired, respond to the sender. This can all happen worldwide in a matter of seconds to minutes as the message travels through the telephone infrastructure system built around the world.

For example, assume you wanted to reach the author of *The On-Line Job Search Companion* email from the Internet. Since the author uses the America Online system as his means of connecting with the Internet, you need to send email to his America Online address—which is *careerdoc@aol.com.* The "careerdoc" part of the address identifies the person associated with the address, in this case, James Gonyea. The "@aol" section indicates that the message is to be sent to the America Online computer (which is in Vienna, Virginia). Finally, the "com" section simply indicates that the America Online computer is a commercial account, rather than an educational or government account. If you were to send email to careerdoc@aol.com, it would be like telling the Internet to send your message to the computer at America Online, and then to direct it internally to careerdoc (or James Gonyea).

Conversely, if you were to receive email from careerdoc@aol.com, you would know that the message is coming from the America Online computer, which is a commercial account, and that it was written by "careerdoc."

2. Participate in Discussion Groups Through Mailing Lists and Usenet Newsgroups

Mailing Lists. Groups of individuals who share a common interest can have their Internet address name added to a central mailing list, by sending it to a person who is responsible for the management of the list. Anytime that someone has anything of interest to say related to the topic of a particular mailing list, that person can simply send comments to the appropriate mailing list manager. Copies of that message are then routed to everyone on the mailing list. You can add your name to as many lists as you like. Thousands of mailing lists exist. Then all you have to do is sit back and wait for the mail to arrive—and arrive it will!

Usenet Newsgroups (Sometimes Known as "Net News" or "News"). Similar to Mailing Lists, Newsgroups exist as a means of sharing information. Thousands of different Newsgroup topics exist from A to Z. You name it, and there's probably a Newsgroup that covers your topic. Unlike mailing lists, you cannot just turn on your computer and receive messages related to your interests.

First, you need to be connected to a main frame computer (often referred to as a server) and the server must accept Newsgroup broadcasts—most do, some don't. You then need a special software program to capture the Newsgroups in which you are interested. The person or persons responsible for running the main frame system has the right to decide which Newsgroups will be received and made available to people connected to the server. This is similar to the power your local TV cable company has regarding what programs you get to watch and which ones you do not. If the server does provide access to Newsgroups, then it usually offers the necessary software (as downloadable files) for receiving Newsgroups.

With the appropriate software program, and depending on the selections made by the server, you can then download articles of information related to any subject in which you are interested.

3. Transfer Files

One of the most popular uses of the Internet is to transfer files from one person to another. You can transfer just about any type of electronic file, including word processing documents, database files, graphics, pictures, and video clips. With Internet you can say goodbye to sending files on diskette using the regular mail.

4. Search for Information

Just about any information you may want can be found somewhere on someone's computer system, and more than likely it can be accessed from your computer and downloaded to your system. The federal government alone maintains thousands of databases that can be accessed by your personal computer. The world is rich in electronic information just waiting for your call!

5. Talk to Other Internet Folks

Internet allows you to talk keyboard-to-keyboard in real time with other individuals, either one-to-one or in groups.

It's good, but not perfect . . . yet!

In the past the Internet has often been described as "hard-to-use" or "mostly for hackers" with advanced technical skills and knowledge. Finding your way around on the Internet at one time called for nerves of steel and high levels of patience. While this is still true, it has changed dramatically during the past few years with the introduction of several easy-to-use navigational software programs. Search software programs such as *Gopher*, developed at the University of Minnesota, provide simple keyword searches and standardized menus for quick information retrieval.

A more recent and advanced information retrieval software program rapidly becoming the most popular and widely used Internet access tool is called Mosaic. It combines graphical images and the benefits of the printed page (headings and subheadings that let you quickly find your way around) with the benefits of the Internet. With a single mouse click you can travel around the world to access a database or down the street to retrieve the latest weather report (plus a satellite picture) in a matter of minutes.

With improved access and navigational software, and with a dramatic increase in the number of available public access services and locations, and with the resultant trend toward increased commercial and private use of the Internet, the Internet provides the business community with a resource of unparalleled value. Bankers, lawyers, doctors, educators, engineers, researchers, and other professionals are quickly recognizing the importance of being connected to the Internet. For some businesses, their very existence depends upon the ability to use the Internet profitably! Foremost in this group of business leaders to get on board are employment and recruitment professionals. The Internet now provides employers and executive recruiters with a new and effective resource for the recruitment of new employees—all at large cost savings over traditional means of recruitment advertising.

In the past, corporate use of the Internet for recruitment and employment was traditionally limited to posting employment ads to Usenet Newsgroups such as "misc.jobs.offered" for technical or systems-type jobs or scrolling through resumes posted by Internet users to the "misc.jobs.resumes" Newsgroup. This procedure produced limited success for both employers and job seekers.

The problem was caused by two factors. First, the Usenet Newsgroups at that time had limited distribution (the distribution is much better today and improving daily). Brian Reid of DEC Network Systems Laboratory in Palo Alto, California, maintains an information service on the Internet which ranks the top 40 Newsgroups in order of popularity. He estimated the total number of individuals who subscribed to employment-related Newsgroups to be at one time less than 2 percent of the Internet user population worldwide. The second problem was the lack of effective search software to quickly find the information you need from the sea of information available on the Internet.

The limited distribution of the Usenet Newsgroups and the lack of effective search software for managing Newsgroup information has in the past frustrated both employers and job seekers in trying to use the vast resources of the Internet. But all this is changing rapidly!

In late 1992, a group of U.S. corporations formed a nonprofit association of employers (called the Online Career Center [OCC]) for the purpose of developing an employment database and effective, yet easy-to-use search software for both corporate recruiters and job seekers who wish to recruit or find employment on the Internet. Today the Online Career Center functions as a central Internet recruitment and human resource management service and is available at no cost to job seekers. The OCC is considered by many to be one of the prime "locations" on the Internet where employers can place employment help wanted ads and review resumes of job seekers, and where job seekers can find employment opportunities and place their resume on-line.

In 1993, Online Career Center and Gonyea & Associates, Inc. agreed to join forces to share their respective database services. Gonyea & Associates specializes in distributing employment listings and candidate resumes through several commercial computer network services, including America Online and National Videotex. Under a joint arrangement, Gonyea & Associates agreed to provide employment listings drawn from its Help Wanted-USA employment database to OCC for distribution via the Internet. In exchange, OCC agreed to provide its employment listings drawn from the Internet to Help Wanted-USA for distribution through various commercial computer network services that carry the Help

Wanted-USA data. Together, OCC and Help Wanted-USA offer one of the largest collections of employment ads and candidate resumes available anywhere in the world. The OCC provides keyword search software and other tools on-line to help employers and recruiters find appropriate candidates and to help job seekers to quickly and easily find employment opportunities.

The OCC is sponsored by member corporations ranging from large multinational companies such as AT&T, GTE, Kraft General Foods, Hallmark Cards, Bank of America, MCI, ALCOA, and DuPont to smaller regional or local employers with 100 or fewer employees.

The Future of the Internet

Look for rapidly increasing amounts of on-line information as access by private individuals increases and both government and business discover the cost effectiveness of using the Internet as a vehicle for distributing information, products, services, and documents—plus finding highly qualified employees.

Even the current administration in Washington is betting on the *information superhighway* as a means of improving the productivity of government, education, business, industry, and commerce. It is developing executive programs with serious financial funding to bring the *information superhighway* into your homes and offices.

Major television and cable companies in collaboration with some of America's entertainment giants are developing plans, systems, and equipment to deliver a wide range of information and services to you through the *information superhighway* and your computer and television set. Stay tuned!

How Can You Learn More About the Internet?

If you are new to the Internet, or are curious about the Internet, wondering how to access it and what it can do for you, the InterNIC information center can help. The InterNIC is the Internet's information center and may be reached at (800) 444-4345. This voice response selection menu will direct your call to the appropriate InterNIC department. The information services' referral desk hours are Monday through Friday 8:00 a.m. to 4:00 p.m. (EST). If you have email to the Internet, you can send messages to info@internic.net. Queries sent to this mailbox will be forwarded to the InterNIC referral desk staff for response.

If you wish to gain access to the Internet through a commercial computer network, contact any of the following:

❏ America Online

❏ BIX

❏ CompuServe

❏ Delphi

❏ GEnie

❏ Prodigy

See Chap. 6 for phone numbers and addresses for the preceding services. Also, contact your local colleges and universities to inquire if you can gain access to the Internet through their computer system. Some federal or state departments or agencies in your area may provide access—check your local phone directory under federal and state government.

To discover if you're one of the lucky few communities with "freenet" access, contact local computer stores, the Chamber of Commerce, and local computer user groups and inquire if a freenet exists in your community.

The following lists a number of commercial companies that provide access— for a fee—to the Internet and the areas (i.e., area codes) from which access to the Internet is possible. You may want to contact several to inquire about how you can use their service:

For each service listed, the following information is provided:

Service—the name of the service provider.

Modem—the phone number(s) you may call (once registered) with your computer to connect to the service.

Area Codes Served—the phone calling area(s) serviced by the service provider.

Local Access—general locations where the service is available.

Email—the service provider's email address.

Voice—the service provider's voice telephone number.

Internet Access Providers

Service: a2i communications
Modem: 408-293-9010, 415-364-5652, 408-293-9020—login as "guest"
Area Codes Served: 408, 415
Local Access: CA: West and South SF Bay Area
Email: info@rahul.net
Voice: 408-293-8078

Service: University of Alaska Southeast, Tundra Services
Modem: 907-789-1314
Area Codes Served: 907
Local Access: All Alaskan sites with local UACN access Anchorage, Barrow, Fairbanks, Homer, Juneau, Keni, Ketchikan, Kodiak, Kotzebue, Nome, Palmer, Sitka, Valdez
Email: JNJMB@acad1.alaska.edu
Voice: 907-465-6453

Service: Anomaly Rhode Island's Gateway to the Internet
Modem: 401-331-3706 or 401-455-0347
Area Codes Served: 401, 508
Local Access: RI: Providence/Seekonk Zone
Email: info@anomaly.sbs.risc.net
Voice: 401-273-4669

Service: APK
Modem: 216-481-9436
Area Codes Served: 216
Local Access: OH: Cleveland
Email: zbig@wariat.org
Voice: 216-481-9428

Service: The Black Box
Modem: 713-480-2686
Area Codes Served: 713
Local Access: TX: Houston
Email: info@blkbox.com
Voice: 713-480-2684

Service: CAPCON Library Network
Modem: contact for number
Area Codes Served: 202, 301, 410, 703
Local Access: Washington, DC; MD: Suburban MD; VA: Northern VA
Email: capcon@capcon.net
Voice: 202-331-5771

Service: Clark Internet Services, Inc. ClarkNet
Modem: 410-730-9786, 410-995-0271, 301-596-1626, 301-854-0446, 301-621-5216;
    login as "guest"
Area Codes Served: 202, 301, 410, 703
Local Access: MD: Baltimore; Washington, DC; VA: Northern VA
Email: info@clark.net
Voice: Call 800-735-2258

Service: Community News Service
Modem: 719-520-1700 id "new", password "newuser"
Area Codes Served: 303, 719, 800
Local Access: CO: Colorado Springs, Denver; continental US/800
Email: service@cscns.com
Voice: 719-592-1240

Service: CONCERTCONNECT
Modem: contact for number
Area Codes Served: 704, 919
Local Access: NC: Asheville, Chapel Hill, Charlotte, Durham, Greensboro,
    Greenville, Raleigh, Winston Salem, Research Triangle Park
Email: info@concert.net
Voice: 919-248-1999

Service: CRIS

Modem: contact for local number
Area Codes Served: Nationwide
Local Access: Nationwide
Email: criscs@cris.com
Voice: 800-745-2747

Service: CTS Network Services CTSNET

Modem: contact
Area Codes Served: 619
Local Access: CA: San Diego, Pt. Loma, La Jolla, La Mesa, El Cajon, Poway,
    Ramona, Chula Vista, National City, Mira Mesa, Alpine, East County, new
    North County numbers, Escondido, Oceanside, Vista
Email: support@crash.cts.com
Voice: 619-637-3637

Service: CR Laboratories Modem: Internet Access

Modem: 415-389-UNIX
Area Codes Served: 213, 310, 404, 415, 510, 602, 707, 800
Local Access: CA: San Francisco Bay area and San Rafael, Santa Rosa, Los
    Angeles, Orange County; AZ: Phoenix, Scottsdale, Tempe, and Glendale; GA:
    Atlanta metro area; continental US/800
Email: info@crl.com
Voice: 415-381-2800

Service: Colorado SuperNet, Inc.

Modem: contact for number
Area Codes Served: 303, 719, 800
Local Access: CO: Alamosa, Boulder/Denver, Colorado Springs, Durango, Fort
    Collins, Frisco, Glenwood Springs/Aspen, Grand Junction, Greeley,
    Gunnison, Pueblo, Telluride; 800 service available
Email: info@csn.org
Voice: 303-273-3471

Service: The Cyberspace Station

Modem: 619-634-1376; login as "guest"
Area Codes Served: 619
Local Access: CA: San Diego
Email: help@cyber.net
Voice: n/a

Service: DELPHI

Modem: 800-365-4636 login as "JOINDELPHI" password: "INTERNETSIG"
Area Codes Served: 617
Local Access: MA: Boston; KS: Kansas City
Email: walthowe@delphi.com
Voice: 800-544-4005

Service: DIAL n' CERF or DIAL n' CERF AYC

Modem: contact for number
Area Codes Served: 213, 310, 415, 510, 619, 714, 818
Local Access: CA: Los Angeles, Oakland, San Diego, Irvine, Pasadena, Palo Alto
Email: help@cerf.net
Voice: 800-876-2373 or 619-455-3900

Service: DIAL n' CERF USA

Modem: contact for number
Area Codes Served: 800
Local Access: 800 service is available
Email: help@cerf.net
Voice: 800-876-2373 or 619-455-3900

Service: Echo Communications

Modem: 212-989-8411; login as "newuser"
Area Codes Served: 212
Local Access: NY: Manhattan
Email: horn@echonyc.com
Voice: 212-255-3839

Service: Eskimo North

Modem: contact for number
Area Codes Served: 206
Local Access: WA: Seattle, Everett
Email: nanook@eskimo.com
Voice: 206-367-7457

Service: Evergreen Communications

Modem: 602-955-8444
Area Codes Served: 602
Local Access: Arizona
Email: evergreen@libre.com
Voice: 602-955-8315

Service: Express Access: A Service of Digital Express Group

Modem: 301-220-0462, 410-766-1855, 703-281-7997, 714-377-9784, 908-937-9481;
    login as "new"
Area Codes Served: 202, 301, 410, 703, 714, 908
Local Access: Northern VA; Baltimore MD; Washington DC; New Brunswick NJ;
    Orange County CA
Email: info@digex.net
Voice: 800-969-9090, 301-220-2020

Service: Freelance Systems Programming

Modem: 513-258-7745
Area Codes Served: 513
Local Access: OH: Dayton
Email: fsp@dayton.fsp.com
Voice: 513-258-7246

Service: Halcyon
Modem: 206-382-6245; login as "new"
Area Codes Served: 206
Local Access: Seattle, WA
Email: info@halcyon.com
Voice: 206-955-1050

Service: HoloNet
Modem: 510-704-1058
Area Codes Served: 510
Local Access: Berkeley, CA
Email: info@holonet.net
Voice: 510-704-0160

Service: HookUp Communication Corporation
Modem: contact for number
Area Codes Served: 800, 416, 519
Local Access: Ontario, Canada
Email: info@hookup.net
Voice: 519-747-4110

Service: The IDS World Network
Modem: 401-884-9002, 401-785-1067
Area Codes Served: 401
Local Access: East Greenwich, RI; northern RI
Email: sysadmin@ids.net
Voice: 401-884-7856

Service: Institute for Global Communications/IGC Networks
Modem: 415-322-0284 N81, login as "new"
Area Codes Served: 415, 800
Local Access: CA: Palo Alto, San Francisco
Email: support@igc.apc.org
Voice: 415-442-0220

Service: Internet Direct, Inc.
Modem: 602-274-9600 Phoenix; 602-321-9600 Tucson; login as "guest"
Area Codes Served: 602
Local Access: AZ: Phoenix, Tucson
Email: info@indirect.com automated; support@indirect.com human
Voice: 602-274-0100 Phoenix, 602-324-0100 Tucson

Service: KAIWAN Public Access Internet Online Services
Modem: 714-539-5726, 310-527-7358
Area Codes Served: 213, 310, 714
Local Access: CA: Los Angeles, Orange County
Email: info@kaiwan.com
Voice: 714-638-2139

Service: Maestro

Modem: 212-240-9700; login as "newuser"
Area Codes Served: 212, 718
Local Access: NY: New York City
Voice: 212-240-9600

Service: MCSNet

Modem: 312-248-0900 follow prompts
Area Codes Served: 312, 708, 815
Local Access: IL: Chicago
Email: info@genesis.mcs.com
Voice: 312-248-UNIX

Service: Merit Network, Inc. MichNet project

Modem: contact for number
Area Codes Served: 313, 517, 616, 906
Local Access: Michigan; Boston, MA; Washington, DC
Email: info@merit.edu
Voice: 313-764-9430

Service: MSen

Modem: contact for number
Area Codes Served: 313
Local Access: All of SE Michigan 313
Email: info@msen.com
Voice: 313-998-4562

Service: MV Communications, Inc.

Modem: contact for numbers
Area Codes Served: 603
Local Access: Many NH communities
Email: info@mv.com
Voice: 603-429-2223

Service: NEARnet

Modem: contact for numbers
Area Codes Served: 508, 603, 617
Local Access: Boston, MA; Nashua, NH
Email: nearnetjoin@nic.near.net
Voice: 617-873-8730

Service: NeoSoft's Sugar Land Unix

Modem: 713-684-5900
Area Codes Served: 504, 713
Local Access: TX: Houston metro area; LA: New Orleans
Email: info@NeoSoft.com
Voice: 713-438-4964

Service: Netcom Online Communication Services

Modem: 206-547-5992, 214-753-0045, 303-758-0101, 310-842-8835, 312-380-0340, 404-303-9765, 408-241-9760, 408-459-9851, 415-328-9940, 415-985-5650, 503-626-6833, 510-274-2900, 510-426-6610, 510-865-9004, 617-237-8600, 619-234-0524, 703-255-5951, 714-708-3800, 818-585-3400, 916-965-1371
Area Codes Served: 206, 213, 214, 303, 310, 312, 404, 408, 415, 503, 510, 617, 619, 703, 714, 718, 818, 916
Local Access: CA: Alameda, Irvine, Los Angeles, Palo Alto, Pasadena, Sacramento, San Diego, San Francisco, San Jose, Santa Cruz, Walnut Creek; CO: Denver; DC: Washington; GA: Atlanta; IL: Chicago; MA: Boston; OR: Portland; TX: Dallas; WA: Seattle
Email: info@netcom.com
Voice: 408-554-8649, 800-501-8649

Service: Northwest Nexus Inc.

Modem: contact for numbers
Area Codes Served: 206
Local Access: WA: Seattle
Email: info@nwnexus.wa.com
Voice: 206-455-3505

Service: North Shore Access

Modem: 617-593-4557; login as "new"
Area Codes Served: 617, 508
Local Access: MA: Wakefield, Lynnfield, Lynn, Saugus, Revere, Peabody, Salem, Marblehead, Swampscott
Email: info@northshore.ecosoft.com
Voice: 617-593-3110 voicemail

Service: NovaLink

Modem: 800-937-7644; login as "new" or "info", 508-754-4009
Area Codes Served: 508, 617
Local Access: MA: Worcester, Cambridge, Marlboro, Boston
Email: info@novalink.com
Voice: 800-274-2814

Service: Nuance Network Services

Modem: contact for number
Area Codes Served: 205
Local Access: AL: Huntsville
Email: staff@nuance.com
Voice: 205-533-4296 voice/recording

Service: OARnet

Modem: send email to nic@oar.net
Area Codes Served: 614, 513, 419, 216, 800
Local Access: OH: Columbus, Cincinnati, Cleveland, Dayton
Email: nic@oar.net
Voice: 614-292-8100

Service: Old Colorado City Communications
Modem: 719-632-4111; login as "newuser"
Area Codes Served: 719
Local Access: CO: Colorado Springs
Email: dave@oldcolo.com / thefox@oldcolo.com
Voice: 719-632-4848, 719-593-7575 or 719-636-2040

Service: Olympus
Modem: contact for number
Area Codes Served: 206
Local Access: WA:Olympic Peninsula/Eastern Jefferson County
Email: info@pt.olympus.net
Voice: 206-385-0464

Service: PANIX Public Access Unix
Modem: 212-787-3100; login as "newuser"
Area Codes Served: 212, 718
Local Access: New York City, NY
Email: alexis@panix.com, jsb@panix.com
Voice: 212-877-4854, 212-691-1526

Service: The Pipeline
Modem: 212-267-8606; login as "guest"
Area Codes Served: 212, 718
Local Access: NY: New York City
Email: info@pipeline.com, staff@pipeline.com
Voice: 212-267-3636

Service: The Portal System
Modem: 408-973-8091 highspeed, 408-725-0561 2400bps; login as "info"
Area Codes Served: 408, 415
Local Access: CA: Cupertino, Mountain View, San Jose
Email: cs@cup.portal.com, info@portal.com
Voice: 408-973-9111

Service: Prairienet Freenet
Modem: 217-255-9000; login as "visitor"
Area Codes Served: 217
Local Access: IL: Champaign/Urbana
Email: jayg@uiuc.edu
Voice: 217-244-1962

Service: PREPnet
Modem: contact for numbers
Area Codes Served: 215, 412, 717, 814
Local Assess: PA: Philadelphia, Pittsburgh, Harrisburg
Email: prepnet@cmu.edu
Voice: 412-268-7870

Service: PSI's WorldDial Service

Modem: send *Email:* to numbersinfo@psi.com
Area Codes Served: Most major cities. Contact PSI for information
Local Access: Most major cities. Contact PSI for information
Email: allinfo@psi.com, worlddialinfo@psi.com
Voice: 703-620-6651

Service: PUCnet Computer Connections

Modem: 403-484-5640 v.32 bis; login as "guest"
Area Codes Served: 403
Local Access: Edmonton
Email: pwilson@PUCnet.com
Voice: 403-448-1901

Service: RainDrop Laboratories

Modem: 503-293-1772, 503-293-2059; login as "apply"
Area Codes Served: 503
Local Access: OR: Portland, Beaverton, Hillsboro, Forest Grove, Gresham, Tigard,
   Lake Oswego, Oregon City, Tualatin, Wilsonville
Email: info@agora.rain.com

Service: RealTime Communications

Modem: 512-459-4391; login as "new"
Area Codes Served: 512
Local Access: TX: Austin
Email: hosts@wixer.bga.com
Voice: 512-451-0046

Service: South Coast Computing Services, Inc.

Modem: 713-661-8593, 713-661-8595
Area Codes Served: 713
Local Access: TX: Houston metro area
Email: info@sccsi.com
Voice: 713-661-3301

Service: Telerama Public Access Internet

Modem: 412-481-5302; login as "new"
Area Codes Served: 412
Local Access: PA: Pittsburgh
Email: info@telerama.pgh.pa.us
Voice: 412-481-3505

Service: TelLink Networking

Modem: 408-247-8444 v32bis; login as "guest"
Area Codes Served: 408, 415
Local Access: CA: San Jose, Sunnyvale, Los Altos, Mountain View, Campbell,
   Cupertino, Los Gatos, Santa Clara, Saratoga
Email: info@tellink.net
Voice: 408-247-8445

Service: Texas Metronet
Modem: 214-705-2902 9600bps, 214-705-2917 2400bps
Area Codes Served: 214
Local Access: TX: Dallas
Email: srl@metronet.com
Voice: 214-401-2800

Service: The Meta Network
Modem: contact for numbers
Area Codes Served: 703, 202, 301
Local Access: Washington, DC metro area
Email: info@tmn.com
Voice: 703-243-6622

Service: Vnet Internet Access, Inc.
Modem: 704-347-8839; login as "new"
Area Codes Served: 704
Local Access: NC: Charlotte; RTP, Raleigh, Durham
Email: info@char.vnet.net
Voice: 704-374-0779

Service: The Whole Earth 'Lectronic Link
Modem: 415-332-6106; login as "newuser"
Area Codes Served: 415
Local Access: Sausalito, CA
Email: info@well.sf.ca.us
Voice: 415-332-4335

Service: The World
Modem: 617-739-9753; login as "new"
Area Codes Served: 617
Local Access: Boston, MA
Email: office@world.std.com
Voice: 617-739-0202

Service: Wyvern Technologies, Inc.
Modem: 804-627-1828; Norfolk, 804-886-0662 Peninsula
Area Codes Served: 804
Local Access: VA: Norfolk, Virginia Beach, Portsmouth, Chesapeake, Newport
   News, Hampton, Williamsburg
Email: system@wyvern.com
Voice: 804-622-4289

When evaluating local Internet access service providers or commercial computer network service for access to the Internet, make sure the services provide the proper type of access to meet your needs. For instance, the ability to "telnet" to remote locations or to access a "gopher" server is required to access many databases on the Internet. File Transfer Protocol (FTP) is required for file transfers of large amounts of data. You might also want access to the Usernet Newsgroups—Internet's global bulletin board system.

How to Gain Access to the Online Career Center

The Online Career Center database of employment ads, candidate resumes, and other career-related information is available to all 20 million Internet users through a variety of access methods. OCC is available on *Gopher*, the World Wide Web (WWW), Mosaic, WAIS, and email in addition to the traditional Usenet Newsgroups.

You may connect directly to the Online Career Center database through *Gopher* at *gopher.msen.com*; from the main Internet *gopher* menu; or via telnet to a public *gopher* site such as *gopher.msu.edu*. Additional access information may be obtained by sending an email message to *occ-info@msen.com* if you have Internet email capability. Otherwise, you may contact OCC at:

Online Career Center
William Warren, Executive Director
3125 Dandy Trail
Indianapolis, IN 46214
317-293-6499

In the following list, you will find a *small sample* of electronic resources available through the Internet to help you with your career planning and job seeking needs. These services are accessible as Newsgroups. Considering that the Internet offers thousands of Newsgroups with new ones being created daily, you might wish to consider purchasing a directory of Newsgroups, such as *The Internet Directory* by Eric Braun (see the following). The services listed here are to illustrate the vast diversity of information available through the Internet.

Newsgroup	Content
ab.jobs	jobs in Alberta, Canada
atl.jobs	jobs in Atlanta, Georgia
aus.jobs	jobs available and wanted in Australia
ba.jobs.misc	discussion of the job market in San Francisco Bay area
ba.jobs.offered	job postings in the San Francisco Bay area
bionet.jobs	scientific job opportunities
biz.jobs.offered	help wanted ads
can.jobs	jobs in Canada
fl.jobs	jobs in Florida

Newsgroup	Content
kw.jobs	help wanted ads
mi.wanted	jobs and products, wanted and offered for sale
milw.jobs	jobs available and wanted in Milwaukee, Wisconsin area
misc.jobs.contract	discussions about contract labor
misc.jobs.misc	discussions about employment, workplaces, careers
misc.jobs.offered	announcements of positions available
misc.jobs.resumes	postings of resumes and help wanted articles
ne.jobs	New England job listings
ont.jobs	jobs in Ontario, Canada
sdnet.jobs	jobs in San Diego, California
slac.jobs	job openings
stl.jobs	St. Louis job openings
su.jobs	jobs wanted or available
swnet.jobs	help wanted notices
tor.jobs	jobs in Toronto, Canada
triangle.jobs	jobs available in the Research Triangle area of North Carolina
tx.jobs	jobs in Texas
ucb.jobs	help wanted announcements
uiuc.cs.jobs	computer science job openings
uiuc.jobs.offered	job openings for people interested in UIUC
ut.jobs	job openings and positions wanted at University of Texas
utcs.jobs	job announcements from University of Texas for computer science specialists
vmsnet.employment	jobs available and wanted, and workplace and employment related issues

Suggested Books on the Internet

The 1994 Internet White Pages: Instant Access to Over 100000 Internet Addresses
Seth Godin & James S. McBride
IDG Books
Beginner to Advanced Levels
812 pages—$29.95

Connecting to the Internet
Susan Estrada
O'Reilly & Associates, Inc.
170 pages—$15.95

Doing Business on the Internet
Mary J. Cronin
Van Nostrand Reinhold
308 pages—$29.95

A DOS User's Guide to the Internet
James Gardner
Prentice Hall
Software included for use in sending email, accessing Net news, and file
transfer with UUCP
308 pages—$34.95

Hands on Internet: A Beginning Guide for PC Users
David Sachs & Henry Stair
PTR Prentice Hall
Beginner Level
DOS software included to access the Internet
273 pages—$27.95

The Instant Internet Guide
Brent Heslop & David Angell
Addison-Wesley
209 pages—$14.95

*Internet Basics—Your On-line Access to the Global Electronic
Superhighway*
Steve Lambert & Walt Howe
Random House Electronic Publishing
All levels
495 pages—$27.00

The Internet Companion: A Beginners Guide to Global Networking
Tracey LaQuey with Jeanne C. Ryer, Foreword by Vice President Al Gore
Addison-Wesley
196 pages—$12.95

*The Internet Companion Plus a Beginners Start-up Kit for Global
Networking*
Tracey LaQuey with Jeanne C. Ryer, Foreword by Vice President Al Gore
Addison-Wesley
PC software included to access the Internet—Mac software available
upon request
198 pages—$19.95

The Internet Complete Reference
Harley Hahn & Rick Stout

Osborne McGraw-Hill
All Levels
817 pages—$29.95

The Internet Directory
Eric Braun
Faucett Columbine / Ballantine Books
704 pages—$25.00

The Internet for Dummies
John R. Levine & Carol Baroudi
IDG Books Worldwide, Inc.
Beginner / Intermediate Level
355 pages—$19.95

Internet Getting Started
April Marine, Susan Kirkpatrick, Vivian Neou, Carol Ward
Prentice Hall
390 pages—$28.00

The Internet Guide for New Users
Daniel P. Dern
McGraw-Hill
Beginner Level
570 pages—$27.95

Internet: Instant Reference
Paul E. Hoffman
Sybex, Inc.
All levels
317 pages—$12.99

Internet: Mailing Lists
T. L. Hardie & Vivian Neou
Prentice Hall
582 pages—$29.75

The Internet Navigator
Paul Gilster
John Wiley & Sons, Inc.
470 pages—$24.95

The Internet Roadmap
Binnett Falk
Sybex, Inc.
Beginner / Experienced Level
263 pages—$12.99

The Internet Starter Kit for Macintosh
Adam C. Engest
Hayden Books
Software included:

Mac TCP—Your key to the Internet
Eudora—A Macintosh mail reader
InterSLIP—What you need for great connections
Fetch 2.1.1 & TurboGopher—the best ways to find the newest info
Stuffit Expander—The Universal File unpacker
641 pages—$29.95

Internet System Handbook
Daniel C. Lynch & Marshall T. Rose
Addison-Wesley
790 pages—$62.75

The Internet Yellow Pages
Harley Hahn & Rick Stout
Osborne McGraw-Hill
447 pages—$27.95

The Mac Internet Tour Guide
Michael Fraase
Ventana Press
Software included—For Mac TCP, Interslip, Eudora, Fetch, Turbogopher,
and Stuffit Expander
290 pages—$27.95

Navigating the Internet
Mark Gibbs & Richard Smith
Sams Publishing
Beginner/Intermediate Level
500 pages—$24.95

New and Improved Zen and the Art of the Internet:
A Beginner's Guide
Brendan P. Kehoe
Prentice Hall
Beginner Level
193 pages—$23.95

The PC Internet Tour Guide
Michael Fraase
Ventana Press
Beginner/Intermediate Level
Includes software to access the Internet
284 pages—$24.95

Pocket Guides to the Internet
Mark Veljkov & George Hartnell
Mecklermedia Publishing
    Volume 1—Telenetting (42 pages)
    Volume 2—Transferring Files with File Transfer Protocol (54 pages)
    Volume 3—Using & Navigating Usenet (68 pages)

Volume 4—The Internet Email System (58 pages)
Volume 5—Basic Internet Utilities (68 pages)
Volume 6—Terminal Connections
$7.00 each

Riding the Internet Highway
Sharon Fisher
New Riders Publishing
Beginner/Intermediate Level
266 pages—$16.95

Using the Internet
William A. Tolhurst, Mary Ann Pike, Keith A. Blanton, with legal contri-
bution by John R. Harris
Que Corporation
All Levels
Software included to access the Internet, plus an index of over 3000
Internet resources.
1188 pages—$39.95

Welcome to . . . Internet: From Mystery to Mastery
Tom Badgett & Corey Sandler
MIS Press
Beginner/Intermediate Level
324 pages—$19.95

The Windows Internet Tour Guide
Michael Fraase
Ventana Press
Beginner / Intermediate Level
Includes software to access the Internet
344 pages—$24.95

The Whole Internet: Users Guide and Catalog
Ed Kroll
O'Rielly and Associates, Inc.
376 pages—$24.95

6

Commercial On-Line Network Services

This chapter contains a sample listing of career planning and job hunting resources available from many of the most popular commercial computer on-line network services, including:

❏ America Online

❏ CompuServe

❏ GEnie

❏ Prodigy

Together with the Internet and the thousands of Bulletin Board Services (BBS) that exist today, these commercial computer network services form what has become known as the *information superhighway*.

Over the last few years, commercial computer network services have quickly become one of the most convenient, quick, and inexpensive means of obtaining information and services. An estimated 5 million people are registered users of the on-line network services. When you consider that for each registered user, there are approximately five additional people who use the same account, the number of actual users climbs to 25 million people!

From the convenience of their office, home, or portable computer—day and night, weekdays and weekends, 365 days of the year—on-liners travel the electronic information highways stopping here and there for entertainment, education, access to information and services, to chat across town or coast to coast, to finish work taken home from the office, to send and receive email, and even to start and run a small business from home or from a traditional office location. All this is possible because of the computer!

In the years prior to the introduction of network services, obtaining information required that you physically travel to some location, have the information mailed to you, or, in some cases, you could call to obtain assistance over the phone. Most everyone agrees, getting information that way is usually slow! But that was yesterday. Today, businesses; federal, state, and city governments; organizations; educational institutions; entertainment providers; and private individuals are getting on-line to make information and services available to others, as well as to gain access to information and services—all in a matter of minutes.

Even some cities are getting on-line. From home, you can actually dial up any one of several city government offices, many businesses and professional services, the city library, and schools to find out what's going on in town, to chat with electronic neighbors, read or post classifieds, get medical information, or download information of various sorts from favorite food recipes to what's playing at the local movie theaters. While some of these services are pioneering to say the least, they highlight the trend currently growing within the communications industry. Look at the television commercials from such communication giants as AT&T and you'll hear and see what marvelous resources you'll have access to through your computer in the very near future.

Your computer will do a lot more than allow you to play games, type letters, calculate your bank balance, and store data—it is your gateway to information and services within your community, across the country, and around the globe. And commercial computer networks are providing you with that gateway.

Imagine for a moment how convenient it would be if you could take all the shopping centers in your community and group them together with all the professional business services, educational services, government agencies, and culture and civic institutions and plant them directly outside your front door. Almost anything you wanted or needed would be only a few feet from your easy chair. Well, that's exactly what's happening today, but rather than move all those facilities to your yard, you can gain access to them electronically and within minutes of flipping the switch on your computer. That's what the commercial network service are scrambling to do—put the world of information on your desk accessible through your computer.

To access any of these services, all you need is a personal computer, modem, phone line, and a special communications software program—usually provided at a small cost by the commercial network service you wish to join. For example, if you want to join America Online, CompuServe, or Prodigy, each company makes available proprietary software that can be purchased from most software stores. While you can use any general purpose communications software program to access GEnie, you do need to contact GEnie before hand to obtain the necessary modem settings and access identification number and password.

Use of these network services is on a subscription basis. As a member, you will be required to pay a monthly fee, and in most cases, a per hour fee. With little exception, both fees from all services are modest and fit within the budget of most individuals. Members may continue their service for as long as they wish, or cancel at any time.

The number and type of services and information available on-line is extensive and growing daily. CompuServe continues to offer the largest number of on-line databases and forum areas (special areas created where individuals who share similar interests may communicate with each other on-line). Prodigy and America Online are close behind CompuServe in terms of on-line databases and forum areas. America Online's easy-to-use interface and on-line chat capability are two of the reasons for its popularity.

To list all forum areas and databases available from all network services would fill a book of its own. The following list is a sample of what can be accessed on-line. Please note that new services and databases are added daily, while others that are of narrow appeal are removed frequently. Therefore, you can expect to find more services of value to career planners and job seekers then those listed below. You are encouraged to get on-line and roam to your heart's delight—you'll be surprised at the amount of information and services you have access to through your computer!

The electronic resources listed in this chapter are organized according to the career development steps found in Chap. 2—Career Planning the Electronic Way, and Chap. 4—Job Hunting the Electronic Way. By using these resources, you may easily identify those that may help you accomplish those steps important to your career development.

Note: As a whole, the commercial network services do not offer sufficient resources to assist you with each and every career development step outlined in this book.

If you wish to contact any of the commercial computer network services, you may do so by calling or writing:

America Online

8619 Westwood Center Drive
Vienna, VA 22182
800-827-6364

Monthly membership: $9.95
Hourly on-line charge: $3.50 (5 hours available each month)
First month membership is free with up to 10 free hours of connect time.

CompuServe

5000 Arlington Centre Blvd.
PO Box 20212
Columbus, OH 43220
800-848-8199

Monthly membership: $8.95 (basic package—other services available for additional fees)
Hourly on-line charges: None for basic package (from $6.00 to $16.00 for additional services)

GEnie

c/o GE Information Services
PO Box 6403
Rockville, MD 20850
800-638-9636

Monthly membership: $8.95 nonprime time; $9.50 prime time
Up to 4 hours of credit granted each month based on usage
Hourly on-line charges: $3.00 nonprime time

Prodigy Services

445 Hamilton Avenue
White Plains, NY 10601
800- PRODIGY

Monthly membership: Options range from $7.95, $14.95, $19.95 up to $29.95—depending on how many services you wish to access.
Some plans offer some free connect hours.
Hourly on-line charges: If applicable = $3.60

Career Development Resources Available from *America Online*

To quickly access any service or database from the following list, use the keyword listed below any item. Once on-line, press and hold down the Control key. While doing so, press the "k" key to display the keyword search dialog box. Then, type in the keyword and select the OK button. You will be taken immediately to the area where the resource can be found. You may need to hunt around within the resource area to actually find the specific resource you have chosen.

Career Planning Steps:

Personality Assessment
   Resource: Career Focus 2000

   Keyword: Career

Occupational Exploration
   Resource: Occupational Profiles Database

   Keyword: Career

   Business and Job Postings

   Keyword: Classified

   Keyword: Career

   Home Office Computing Magazine

   Keyword: Home Office

   Macintosh Desktop Publishing Forum

   Keyword: MDP

   Career Focus 2000 Directory

   Keyword: Career

Occupational Profiling
   Occupational Profiles Database

Keyword: Career

College Board

Keyword: College Board

Financial Aid Service

Keyword: Career

Educational Resources Information Center

Keyword: ERIC

National Education Association

Keyword: NEA

National Library Service for the Blind

Keyword: Library

Association of Supervision and Curriculum Development

Keyword: ASCD

Decision Making

Career Focus 2000

Keyword: Career

Career Analysis Service

Keyword: Career

Career Counseling

Keyword: Career

Planning

Career Focus 2000

Keyword: Career

Career Counseling

Keyword: Career

Career Resources Library

Keyword: Career

College Board

Keyword: College Board

Programmer U

Keyword: Programming

Interactive Education Service

Keyword: IES

Electronic University Network

Keyword: EUN

Technology Education and Training Forum

Keyword: Learning

Bachelor Completion Programs

Keyword: EUN

International Correspondence Schools

Keyword: ICS

Job Hunting Steps:

Conducting an Occupational Self-Assessment
(see Personality Assessment)

Setting Employment Goals (Targets)
Help Wanted-USA

Keyword: Career

E-Span

Keyword: Career

Hoover's Handbook

Keyword: Hoover

Federal Career Opportunities

Keyword: Career

Building a Personal Support Team
Membership Directory

Keyword: Membership

Talent Bank

Keyword: Career

Building a Professional Support Team
Membership Directory

Keyword: Membership

Employment Agency Database

Keyword: Career

Researching Targets
Hoover's Handbook

Keyword: Hoover

Executive Desk Register of Publicly Held Corporations

Keyword: Career

Federal Career Opportunities

Keyword: Career

Communicating Your Value
Resume Templates

Keyword: Career

Talent Bank

Keyword: Career

Cover Letter Library

Keyword: Career

Interviewing
Career Counseling

Keyword: Career

Career Resource Library

Keyword: Career

Accepting/Rejecting an Offer
Cover Letter Library

Keyword: Career

Evaluating Your Job Search Strategy
Career Counseling

Keyword: Career

Career Development Resources Available from *CompuServe*

To quickly access any service or database from the following list, use the "Go ..." keyword listed below any item. Once on-line, select the "Go ..." item from the Services Menu. This will display the "Go to" dialog box. Type in the "Go ..." word and select the OK button. You will be taken immediately to the area where the resource can be found. You may need to hunt around within the resource area to actually find the specific resource you have chosen.

Career Planning Steps:

Occupational Exploration and Occupational Profiling

AMIA (American Medical Information Association) Medical Forum
Go: MEDSIG

Labor Today Magazine
Go: MDP

Accountants Index
Go: IQUEST

ABA Banking Journal Magazine
Go: BUSDB

Labor Law—Legal Database
Go: IQUEST

Occupational Outlook Quarterly Magazine
Go: MDP

Occupational Safety and Health—Database
Go: IQUEST

Aquatic Sciences and Fisheries Abstract
Go: IQUEST

Society of Automotive Engineers Meetings
Go: IQUEST

Audio Engineering Society
Go: AESNET

United States Banker
Go: BUSDB

Broadcasters and Broadcast Engineers Forum
Go: BPFORUM

Professional Builder and Remodeler Magazine
Go: BUSDB

Professional Builder Magazine
Go: BUSDB

Academic Index—Database
Go: IQUEST

Careers and the Workplace
Go: INFOUSA

A-V On-line
Go: IQUEST

Classified Service—Employment/Education
Go: CLASSIFIEDS

Classroom Computer Learning Magazine
Go: COMPLIB

Peterson's College Database
Go: PETERSON

Computer Training Forum
Go: DPTRAINING

Grolier's Academic American Encyclopedia
Go: ENCYCLOPEDIA

Dissertation Abstracts
Go: DISSERTATION

Education Forum
Go: EDFORUM

Education Research Forum
Go: EDRESEARCH

Foreign Language Forum
Go: FLEFO

Science/Math Forum
Go: SCIENCE

Student's Forum
Go: STUFORUM

Education Daily—Database
Go: IQUEST

Education Index—Database
Go: IQUEST

Educational Directory—Database
Go: IQUEST

Educational Resources Information Center
ERIC—Database

Education Testing Service Test Collection—Database
Go: IQUEST

Exceptional Child Education Resources—Database
Go: IQUEST

Gradline—Education Database
Go: IQUEST

Linguistics and Language Behavior Abstracts—Database
Go: IQUEST

MLA Bibliography—Database
Go: IQUEST

Ontario Educational Resources Information—Database
Go: IQUEST

Rehabdata—Education Database
Go: IQUEST

Report on Literacy Programs—Database
Go: IQUEST

Resources in Vocational Education—Database
Go: IQUEST

Vocational Education Curriculum Materials—Database
Go: IQUEST

Educational Technology Magazine
Go: COMPLIB

Electronic Learning Magazine
Go: MDP

Planning

Encyclopedia of Associations—Database
Go: IQUEST

Educational Directory—Database
Go: IQUEST

Peterson's College Database
Go: PETERSON

Computer Training Forum
Go: DPTRAINING

Job Hunting Steps

Researching Targets

ABC Europe—Business Database
Go: IQUEST

Career Placement Registry—Database
Go: IQUEST

ABI/INFORM—Business Database
Go: MKTGAC

Affluent Markets Alert
Go: IQUEST

Airline Financial News
Go: IQUEST

Alaska Business Monthly
Go: BUSDB

Albany (NY) Times Union Newspaper
Go: NPL

Alberta Business—Database
Go: BUSDB

Air Conditioning, Heating and Refrigeration News
Go: BUSDB

Allentown (PA) Morning Call Newspaper
Go: NPL

Anchorage (AK) Daily News
Go: NPL

Andrew Seybold's Outlook on Professional Computing
Go: COMPLIB

Annapolis (MD) Capital
Go: NPL

Appraisal Journal
Go: BUSDB

Arizona Republic/Phoenix Gazette
Go: NPL

Arkansas Business
Go: BUSDB

Asahi News Service
Go: IQUEST

Asia-Pacific
Go: IQUEST

Asian Political News
Go: IQUEST

Atlanta Business Chronicle
Go: BUSDB

Business Atlanta
Go: BUSDB

Atlanta Constitution/Atlanta

Atlantic Business
Go: BUSDB

Atlantic Economic Journal
Go: BUSDB

Austin Business Journal
Go: BUSDB

Report on the Austrian Economy
Go: BUSDB

Business and Commercial Aviation
Go: BUSDB

Commuter—Regional Airline News
Go: BUSDB

Avionics Report
Go: BUSDB

Bakery Productions and Marketing
Go: BUSDB

Baltimore Business Journal
Go: BUSDB

Bank Management
Go: BUSDB

Bank Marketing
Go: BUSDB

Career Development Resources Available from *GEnie*

Follow the directions on-line to access the resources from the following list. To access any resource, select the appropriate menu item.

Career Development Steps

Occupational Exploration and Occupational Profiling

The WorkPlace RoundTable—Jobs in the Year 2005
Business Resource Directory

Job Hunting Steps

Setting Employment Goals (Targets)

E-Span Job Listings
Business Resource Directory
Thomas Register
Dun & Bradstreet Company Profiles
Dialog Database Center
Law Center

Building a Personal Support Team

Resume Directory

Interviewing

The WorkPlace RoundTable—Job Interviews

Career Development Resources Available from *Prodigy*

To quickly access any service or database from the following list, use the "jump" feature. Once on-line, select the "J" item on the Tool Bar to display the "jump" dialog box. Then, type in the name of the resource you would like to access and select the OK button. You will be taken immediately to the area where the resource can be found. You may need to hunt around within the resource area to actually find the specific resource you have chosen.

You may also select the main menu heading from the Welcome screen to access any resource.

Career Planning Steps

Occupational Exploration and Occupational Profiling

Heading:	News/Weather	
Resources:	Business News	Jump: Business News
	Health News	Jump: Health News
	Science News	Jump: Science News
	Politics	Jump: Politics
	Sports News	Jump: Sports News
Heading:	Business/Finance	
Resources:	More News	Jump: More News
	Markets	Jump: Markets
	Research	Jump: Research
	The Office	Jump: Office
Heading:	Communications	
Resource:	Classifieds	Jump: Classifieds
Heading:	Reference	
Resources:	Encyclopedia	Jump: Encyclopedia
	Consumer Reports	Jump: Consumer Reports

Job Hunting Steps

Researching Targets

Heading:	News/Weather	
Resources:	Business News	Jump: Business News
	Health News	Jump: Health News
	Science News	Jump: Science News
	Politics	Jump: Politics
	Sports News	Jump: Sports News
Heading:	Business/Finance	
Resources:	More News	Jump: More News
	Markets	Jump: Markets
	Research	Jump: Research
Heading:	Reference	
Resources:	Consumer Reports	Jump: Consumer Reports

Building a Personal Support Team

Heading:	Member Services	
Resource:	Member ID List	Jump: Member ID

7
Bulletin Board Systems (BBS)

This chapter will introduce you to Bulletin Board Systems (BBSs) and explain what they are, and how you can use them to electronically enhance your career planning and accelerate your search for employment.

What Is a BBS?

A computer Bulletin Board System, otherwise referred to as BBS, is an electronic information service offered by private individuals, organizations, companies, government agencies, civic groups, and others where you may post and review messages while connected online and download files from the BBS computer (referred to as the host computer) to your computer for use at a later time.

Think of the traditional bulletin board that you've used so often in schools, colleges, and at your place of employment. It's located where most people can see it, and attached to it are all kinds of notices. The purpose of the bulletin board is to allow for the exchange of information without requiring both the provider and reader to be at the same location at the same time. Notices may be posted by anyone at any time and may be reviewed by anyone at any later time. Sometimes the information that is posted is of such value to the reader that the information is often "taken down" and kept for use at a later time.

Another way of understanding this concept is to consider the following scenario that has been played out millions of times over the course of history. The year is 1950 and you (as a private individual, member of some organization, or as an employee of a company) have decided (or were asked) to collect certain information. What type of information you are about to collect is irrelevant. What is important is the fact that you will more than likely compile your pile of information into some type of printed format to make it easy to review at a later time. Considering that there are millions of individuals who live in your world, and that they also compile information (and will save it in print format), the number of information piles and the diversity of the topics of those piles is easily in the millions.

Contributing author: Ward Christman, Executive Director, Online Opportunities.

At some point you would find it advantageous to sell, exchange, or give away your data to help other individuals learn what you now know. And it's equally certain that you would eventually want to secure data from others to add to your pile so that you can learn what they know. Since information exchanged verbally is soon forgotten, you conclude that you will provide and ask for *printed* copies of the information.

How you exchange information is usually determined by the location of the person providing or the person requesting the information. If you both live or work close to each other, you may exchange it in person, hand-to-hand. Otherwise, you may mail the information to the person requesting a copy, or request that the information be mailed to you. Still there will be other times when you find it better to print copies in advance so that your information is available soon after it is requested.

As more and more people become aware of your information, the requests will come in from locations around the globe. Also, you soon discover that vast numbers of information piles exist around the world all for the asking. Now, sending and receiving information can take days, weeks, months, and even years to accomplish due to the distances involved. As critical as that information may be to your personal or business needs, it is subject to time—specifically, how quickly you can get it out your door or in from some other source.

Well, that was yesterday's scenario—today it's totally different! Today, the global exchange of information can occur in only a matter of minutes. Rather than putting your information into print format and then posting it on a cork bulletin board or in some other print format, you can now store it electronically in the form of files in your computer. Using any one of a number of special software programs—all generically referred to as BBS programs—your files can be accessed electronically by anyone with a computer who's connected to your computer by a modem and the phone line. Your data are now accessible to anyone living and working anywhere in the world—at any time you specify—all in a matter of minutes.

With the use of a BBS software program, you can turn your computer into a electronic library of information. In addition, you can use your computer and any one of several communication software programs to access information stored on other BBS systems scattered around the world.

Not only can you access information immediately from anywhere in the world, or let others access your data when they want it, but you (as a private individual, as a member of an organization, or as an employee of a company) can compile as large a library of information as you wish and share it all with the world!

Where It All Began

The first BBS was started in February 1978 by Ward Christensen, also known as the inventor of X-Modem—a special software program used to exchange messages and data from one computer to another.

A BBS service typically allows you the option of posting or accessing:

❏ Bulletins (announcements)

❏ Data files or computer programs

❏ Messages

❏ Surveys or questionnaires

Bulletins and data files may be posted on the host computer (the computer that is being called) by you or the owner of the BBS, and may be read on-line or downloaded to your computer for viewing and use at a later time. A BBS usually has a main menu with options for accessing various information files, computer programs, pictures, and other data.

For example, if you were to call the Online Opportunities BBS in Eaton, PA., you would be presented with a variety of menu options—one allowing you to download to your computer a file of information on job opportunities in the Philadelphia, Pennsylvania, area.

A second area found on most BBSs is a "message or conference section" where you can communicate with other users of the BBS system. Sometimes the message topics areas are broken into Special Interest Groups (SIGs). This allows a single BBS to respond to the needs and interests of a wide variety of individuals.

Most BBSs also have on-line questionnaires to solicit input from callers as a means of better serving the needs of those individuals who use the BBS.

Who Runs Each BBS?

Each BBS is managed and maintained by a "system operator" usually referred to as a SYSOP. The SYSOP is responsible for installing files, managing the messages, responding to questions from callers, and other tasks required to keep a BBS in working order. Should you ever have any questions or comments about a particular BBS, you should contact the SYSOP in charge of the board.

How Many BBSs Are There in the United States?

Experts estimate that there are well over 100,000 BBSs (70,000 public and 30,000 private) on-line today, and this number is growing and changing daily! Some BBSs have been around for years, while others are brand new. It is not uncommon to find many BBSs here today and gone tomorrow. Considering that anyone with a personal computer, modem, phone line, and BBS software program can set up a BBS, the number of BBSs is expected to continue to rise at an impressive rate.

Why Are BBSs So Popular?

Most BBSs specialize in a particular topic—often one that is of interest to only a select group of individuals. People who are interested in the topic can then learn and share information with other people with similar interests from locations around the nation and around the globe. For example, if you were interested in the processing of leather into consumer products, it's not likely that you will find many books written on the subject. Because this topic is not of interest to the masses, few publishers, if any, would release a book knowing that sales would probably be low. However, you could obtain a great deal of information and keep up with the industry by calling a BBS that specializes in this information. Some BBSs are created as a means of electronically publishing and distributing information.

Later in this chapter, you will find a sample list of BBSs that are of interest to many career planners and job seekers. More than likely you will want to call some of these BBSs to share and obtain information about your career or job search needs.

Another reason BBSs are popular is because of the convenience in terms of accessing information. Most BBSs work automatically and require little or no monitoring. Therefore, you can call and post or access and download information anytime, regardless of the time of day.

Who May Create or Set Up a BBS?

As previously stated, anyone with a computer, modem, and phone line, who is willing to purchase a BBS software program can create a BBS system. Several computer programs exist costing only a few hundred dollars that can enable you to set up a leading-edge BBS system with all the "bells and whistles." One of the most popular programs on the market today is called *The Major BBS* by Galacticomm. This DOS-based program has been used by thousands of individuals and organizations to share information electronically. Other BBS programs include TBBS, Wildcat, and PCBoard. Yes, even you, with your computer, can become an electronic library and welcome calls from down the street, or from the far corners of the globe.

Many of the general communication software programs on the market today, such as *ProComPlus* and *CrossTalk* have a function called Host Mode. This function enables you to set up your computer and modem to receive incoming phone calls, and then allows callers access to certain data files stored on your computer system. Some communication software programs also offer a function whereby callers may leave email or on-line messages. However, while these general communication software programs are designed primarily to allow you to "call out" to a BBS service with your computer, they do allow some level of "calling in" to your system. However, to offer a true BBS environment and service, software designed specially to run as a BBS should be installed and used.

What Do You Need to Access a BBS?

To reach any of the 100,000 BBSs available today, you need the following:

❑ Computer
❑ Modem

❑ Phone line

❑ Communications software program

Note: If you do not already own a communications software program, you may download a copy of any one of the several programs available free of charge from America Online. To download a copy, launch America Online and once on-line go to the Computer & Software area, and then select the Software Center. You may then search the database of thousands of free software programs. Use the search word "communications" to find programs suitable to your system (PC or Macintosh). Most programs are free of charge and include user documentation. Follow the directions on-line for downloading and using the programs you wish to obtain.

If you own Microsoft Windows, you can use the Terminal communications program that comes with Windows. It's usually found in the Accessories Group folder.

Essentially, to reach a BBS, all you need to do is start your communications program and enter the telephone number of the BBS you wish to reach. If the BBS is located outside of your local calling area, then you will be charged for a long distance call by your phone company at the same rate as if you had placed a regular long distance voice call. You may also need to select certain settings (see the following section) within your communications software program to enable your computer to "talk" to the host computer. Once done, your computer will then call the host computer to make the connection. You should then see the main menu of the BBS on your screen. From there you can select the various menu options you wish to use depending on what information you wish to access.

Note: If you have call waiting service installed on your phone line, you must disable it before making a phone call to a BBS. Otherwise, if a call comes in while you are connected to the BBS, the incoming call will cause you to become disconnected from the BBS. To keep an incoming call from disconnecting your session, you need to enter a special command into your communications package (as a prefix to the BBS number) prior to placing the call. In most communities across the country, the prefix command is *70. If this does not work, check with your local phone company for an alternate command.

BBS Settings

Most BBSs require that you configure your communication package with the following settings:

❑ No parity

❑ 8 data bits

❑ 1 stop bit

These settings are often represented as: N81. A few mainframe-based systems like CompuServe require the parity to be even and the data bits to be set to 7 or

E71. It's not necessary to understand the technical meaning of these settings. All you need to learn is how to set your communications software to these settings—usually an easy task to do.

How fast data and files can move from the BBS to your computer and vice versa is determined by the modem attached to each computer. Obviously, the faster you can communicate, the shorter the phone call, and, therefore, the less money you have to pay for phone charges. Modem speeds are referred to as "baud" rates or bps (bits per second). The slower modems operate at 1200 or 2400 bps. The faster modems operate at 9600, 14,400 bps, or higher. Most BBSs can support modems between 2400 bps and 9600 bps. Many will support modems that are slower or faster. The actual connection between your computer and the BBS computer will operate at the speed of the slowest modem. If the BBS can handle any speed, but you can communicate only at 9600, then the link is made at 9600 bps.

In today's technology, if you are buying a new modem, it is recommended that you purchase one that operates at least at 14.4 bps. Also, modems may be internal or external. *Internal* means the modem is built onto a "card" that can be inserted into one of your computer's internal card slots. Internal modems derive their power from within your computer's power system. *External* modems are self-contained units that plug both into your computer and into the wall electric outlet. If you have no free card slots, then you should consider buying an external modem. If you do purchase an external modem, make sure you purchase a serial port card with 16550 UART chips installed. This is necessary for your modem card to help your computer keep pace with other fast modems. Internal modems do not require such assistance. Finally, if you're buying a modem and do not have a fax machine, you should consider paying a little extra to obtain a fax/modem, which will enable you also to send and receive fax messages.

Due to the different BBS software programs that are available on the market today, BBSs will operate differently. You can expect that the main menus and commands will be different from one BBS to another, especially considering that many of the most popular BBS software programs allow the SYSOP to customize the program to his or her needs and preferences. However, once you experience a few systems, you'll find using a new BBS is not that difficult to do.

What Can You Expect When You First Get Online with a New BBS?

After making connection, a general welcome screen should appear with the name of the BBS, a brief description of what to expect on-line, and possibly additional access numbers and the name of the SYSOP.

Many BBSs are free and offer open access to all stored information. However, many BBSs require a subscription fee for access to special areas or information. In most cases, fees are modest. If a fee is required, payment is usually done by credit card. A few BBSs will not allow access until the caller first enters his or her phone number. Then the BBS will call the number back to verify that the caller is actually from that number. This is usually required to prevent unauthorized individuals from accessing certain information.

When calling for the first time, some BBSs will allow you to log on anonymously, without having to indicate your name or phone number. This will provide you an opportunity to look around to ensure that you want to use the service before divulging your name and other personal information. If the main screen does not offer a guest or visitor option, you will then be prompted to enter your name. By doing so, an account will be established on the system. The next time you call, you will be allowed in without having to set up a new account again. In most cases, you will need a password to access the BBS. This is to prevent unauthorized individuals (those who have not registered to use the service) from gaining access to the data. If the system does not issue you a password, you will be asked to create one yourself.

On many BBSs, after signing on for the first time, you will be asked to respond to a number of survey questions. For example, how you heard about the BBS, where you are calling from, your mother's maiden name (this is used to identify you when you call again), and other similar questions. These questions will be asked only during your first call. After the SYSOP reviews your answers and then verifies your name and phone number, an account will be established under your name giving you immediate access to the board the next time you call.

After completing the new user survey, and upon future calls, you will immediately have access to the main menu of the system. From the menu area it will be possible to navigate through the entire BBS by selecting menu entries. Be sure to read the menu options thoroughly! In their haste, many callers have missed the very information they were looking for.

If calling a BBS that requires payment for access to information, make sure the information is of value before providing the service with your credit card number.

How Can You Determine Which of the Over 100,000 BBSs Can Meet Your Needs?

This is no easy task considering the number of BBSs that exist! However, one option is to call several local BBSs. Look around on-line in the bulletins or file sections for listings of other BBSs in your geographical area. Often, a BBS will list the numbers of other similar BBSs to help users identify other sources of similar information and service.

There are several magazines that list BBSs including the numbers of each BBS. *Boardwatch Magazine, Online Access, BBS Magazine, Computer User Magazine,* and even *Computer Shopper* are several of the better options. These magazines can be obtained at most newsstands and bookstores.

The following lists a sample number of BBSs that may be appropriate for your career planning and/or job seeking needs. Remember, there are over 100,000 services—with new ones coming on-line daily. Whatever your need or interest, there's more than likely a board for your use!

BBS: Access America
SYSOP: Not available
MODEM: 918-747-2542 (OK)
VOICE: Not available
PURPOSE: Employment issues

BBS: Ad Connection
SYSOP: Not available
MODEM: 804-978-3927 (VA)
VOICE: Not available
PURPOSE: Classified advertisements

BBS: Aerospace Test Technologies
SYSOP: Aerospace Test Technologies/Paul Sniffen
MODEM: 908-741-9460 (NJ)
VOICE: Not available
PURPOSE: Employment opportunities for Aerospace Test technologists, and hardware/software/systems engineers, technicians, programmers, and drafts people.

BBS: American Building Design Exchange
SYSOP: Ted Fritzmeyer
MODEM: 617-665-0048 (MA)
VOICE: Not available
PURPOSE: Dedicated to the building design/construction professional with a construction products database.

BBS: Automation Insight
SYSOP: Not available
MODEM: 201-335-7202 (NJ)
VOICE: Not available
PURPOSE: Automation, process control, and instrumentation professionals

BBS: AVADS-BBS (DoI)
SYSOP: Department of Interior Job Announcements
MODEM: 800-368-3321 (DC)
VOICE: Not available
PURPOSE: The Automated Vacancy Announcement Information Center provides information on job vacancies from 10 bureaus at the Department of Interior. No fee. Also accessible through FedWorld BBS Gateway (DD132).

BBS: AXCESS—Emergency Medicine Online System
SYSOP: Not available
MODEM: 412-363-7510 (PA)
VOICE: Not available
PURPOSE: Emergency medicine job opportunity BBS created for EM physicians—other specialties to be added.

BBS: Bizopps Connection
SYSOP: Lawrence C. Toliver
MODEM: 310-677-7034 (CA)
VOICE: Not available
PURPOSE: Provides listings of business and franchise opportunities, venture capital sources, business opportunity seekers, and money-making opportunities.

BBS: Black Bag
SYSOP: Edward Delgrosso

MODEM: 302-994-3772 (DE)
VOICE: Not available
PURPOSE: Dedicated to the use of microcomputers in medicine—with megabytes of information. Also the latest AIDS statistics, MMWR, and the American Physical Society bulletin. On-line interactive medical doors, messages.

BBS: Boston Gas BBS
SYSOP: Jon Anderson
MODEM: 617-235-6303 (MA)
VOICE: Not available
PURPOSE: Topics covering anesthesia, medicine, science, and engineering.

BBS: Brain Storm Learning
SYSOP: Not available
MODEM: 713-550-8105 (TX)
VOICE: Not available
PURPOSE: Educational, free software application lessons, jobs, missing children forum.

BBS: Bust Out BBS
SYSOP: Not available
MODEM: 510-888-1443 (CA)
VOICE: Not available
PURPOSE: Job listings and information nationwide. Fee required.

BBS: Career Board
SYSOP: Nick Riccione and Penelope Clayton-Smith
MODEM: 214-931-5792 (TX)
VOICE: Not available
PURPOSE: Job listings with focus in southwest USA and national. Includes job tips. Free public BBS. "Employment Personals" for a nominal cost.

BBS: Career Connection BBS
SYSOP: Not available
MODEM: 214-247-0675 (TX)
VOICE: Not available
PURPOSE: Job listings nationwide in 14 different categories, including engineering, administrative, manufacturing, sales/marketing, data processing.

BBS: Career Connection BBS
SYSOP: Gregory Forster
MODEM: 414-258-0164 (WI)
VOICE: Not available
PURPOSE: Employment alternatives for job seekers and employers.

BBS: Career Connections
SYSOP: Not available
MODEM: 415-917-2129 (CA)
VOICE: Not available
PURPOSE: Worldwide job listings. No fee required. Internet: Telnet to CAREER.COM.

BBS: Career Decisions BBS
SYSOP: Ralph Schlender
MODEM: 909-864-8287 (CA)
VOICE: Not available
PURPOSE: Free access to employment ads, book reviews, recruiter directory, resume service, job profiles, and many other features.

BBS: Career-Link
SYSOP: Not available
MODEM: 714-952-1431 (CA)
VOICE: Not available
PURPOSE: An on-line bank of resumes accessible to hundreds of Southern
California employers.

BBS: Career Systems Online
SYSOP: Systems Personnel/Ed Carroll
MODEM: 413-592-9208 (MA)
VOICE: 413-592-4069
PURPOSE: Free of charge access to job listings for experienced professionals in the fields
of MIS and software engineering/development. Jobs are located nationwide.

BBS: Careers BBS
SYSOP: Jesus Dacal
MODEM: 305-828-5697 (FL)
VOICE: Not available
PURPOSE: JobNet node 100:1260/100, National Echo Conferences, On-line Forums,
NetMail access, Latino Echo, Local/national areas for posting/reading employment clas-
sifieds.

BBS: Careers First of N.J. (CFIN)
SYSOP: Gail Duncan
MODEM: 609-786-2666 (NJ)
VOICE: 609-786-0004
PURPOSE: Employment opportunities updated weekly. Resume upload option avail-
able. Job hunting tips on-line.

BBS: Careers Online
SYSOP: Not available
MODEM: 508-879-4700 (MA)
VOICE: Not available
PURPOSE: Computer World newspaper's BBS with listings of data processing jobs
nationwide. No fee required.

BBS: Careers Online
SYSOP: W&W Communications
MODEM: 408-248-7029 (CA)
VOICE: 408-248-0944
PURPOSE: On-line job listings and resume fax service. No fee required.

BBS: Census Personnel Board
SYSOP: U.S. Dept. of Commerce Bureau of the Census; Nevins Frankel
MODEM: 301-763-4574 (MD)
VOICE: Not available
PURPOSE: Job listings for Suitland, Maryland, only. No fee required.

BBS: Chicago Syslink
SYSOP: George Matyaszek
MODEM: 708-795-4442 (IL)
VOICE: Not available
PURPOSE: Employment listings from the Help Wanted-USA employment listing service.

BBS: **Classifieds BBS**
SYSOP: Not available
MODEM: 415-665-7918 (CA)
VOICE: Not available
PURPOSE: Help wanted advertisements.

BBS: **CloneBd**
SYSOP: Greg Smith
MODEM: 805-527-8704 (CA)
VOICE: Not available
PURPOSE: Employment information.

BBS: **Club House**
SYSOP: Not available
MODEM: 908-276-2581 (NJ)
VOICE: Not available
PURPOSE: Classified advertisements.

BBS: **Comp-U-Sell**
SYSOP: Not available
MODEM: 801-944-8786 (UT)
VOICE: Not available
PURPOSE: Classified advertisements.

BBS: **Computer Careers**
SYSOP: EDP Professionals, Inc.; Pat Luttrell
MODEM: 704-554-1102 (NC)
VOICE: Not available
PURPOSE: Specializes in data processing jobs nationwide. No fee required.

BBS: **Computer Department EIC**
SYSOP: Not available
MODEM: 310-421-6089 (CA)
VOICE: Not available
PURPOSE: Computer consulting topics and general business issues.

BBS: **Computer Jobs BBS**
SYSOP: Data Processing Careers, Inc.
MODEM: 817-268-2193 (TX)
VOICE: 817-268-1530
PURPOSE: Job listing service for Dallas/Fort Worth area since 1988. For experienced computer professionals. ALL fees are assumed by the employer. There is no fee for job seekers.

BBS: **Computer Plumber BBS**
SYSOP: Art Petrzelka
MODEM: 319/337-6723 (IA)
VOICE: Not available
PURPOSE: Maintains a list of engineering related BBSs.

BBS: **Connection**
SYSOP: Not available
MODEM: 415-686-6489 (CA)
VOICE: Not available

PURPOSE: General employment information and resources, such as resume writing tips, questions that can help you handle the job interview, job hunting methods, as well as a listing of companies that offer work-at-home opportunities.

BBS: Construction Hotline
SYSOP: Tracy Pengilly
MODEM: 209-982-1297 (CA)
VOICE: 209-982-1299
PURPOSE: Information for northern California construction jobs. State of California Progress Payments to contractors, license information, general discussions. Architectural/engineering jobs out to bid. Computer-related jobs out to bid.

BBS: Contractors Exchange
SYSOP: Not available
MODEM: 415-334-7393 (CA)
VOICE: Not available
PURPOSE: Construction-related issues in the San Francisco, California area, including contractor positions. Updated daily. No fee required.

BBS: Data Dimension PCBoard
SYSOP: Ricky Lacy
MODEM: 404-921-1186 (GA)
VOICE: Not available
PURPOSE: Local employment listings and resume writing conferences.

BBS: Delight The Customer
SYSOP: Dennis Hauser
MODEM: 517-797-3740 (MI)
VOICE: Not available
PURPOSE: Focus on customer service, training, and help desk professional issues. Maintains the National Business/Professional BBS List. Provides networking service to enhance your career development.

BBS: Department of Labor
SYSOP: Not available
MODEM: 202-219-4784 (DC)
VOICE: Not available
PURPOSE: Employment listings with the Department of Labor. Download jobs from every city listed in the JOBS Library for free.

BBS: Detroit Service Center
SYSOP: Office of Personnel Management (OPM)
MODEM: 313-226-4423 (MI)
VOICE: Not available
PURPOSE: Contains Federal Job Opportunity lists and information for the Detroit region. No fee required.

BBS: D.I.C.E. National Network
SYSOP: D&L Online, Inc.; Diane Rickert and Lloyd Linn
MODEM: 515-280-3423 (IA)
VOICE: 515-280-1144
PURPOSE: Nationwide contract and permanent job listings. Job postings from over 80 agencies. No fee required.

BBS: **Digital X-Connect BBS**
SYSOP: Andrew Walding
MODEM: 214-517-8443 (TX)
VOICE: 214-517-3717
PURPOSE: Serves as the home base for JobNet (the jobs network) echoed internationally utilizing the QWK packet specification. Hundreds of jobs listings in 16 message bases. Over 70 nodes.

BBS: **Doc's Place**
SYSOP: Not available
MODEM: 309-682-6560 (IL)
VOICE: Not available
PURPOSE: Employment opportunities in various medical fields including medical technology areas.

BBS: **DP Careers**
SYSOP: Data Processing Careers, Inc.; Gary Penn
MODEM: 817-268-2193 (TX)
VOICE: Not available
PURPOSE: Job listings for Texas only. No fee required.

BBS: **DP Job Works BBS**
SYSOP: Not available
MODEM: 813-495-1801 (FL)
VOICE: Not available
PURPOSE: Good source of DP/MIS jobs nationwide. No fee required. Downloadable files for viewing offline.

BBS: **DP NETwork (Toner Corp.)**
SYSOP: Not available
MODEM: 415-788-8663 (CA)
VOICE: Not available
PURPOSE: Data processing jobs for the San Francisco/Sacramento, California, area. Also, the JOBS-NOW echo in the Information Services section has listings of data processing jobs nationwide. Updated daily. No fee required.

BBS: **ECCO***
SYSOP: Not available
MODEM: 415-331-7227 (CA)
VOICE: Not available
PURPOSE: National permanent and contract job listings. No fee required.

BBS: **Economic BBS**
SYSOP: U.S. Department Of Commerce
MODEM: 202-377-3870 (DC)
VOICE: Not available
PURPOSE: Free access. Economic statistics—GNP/CPI/Employment, trade opportunities.

BBS: **EDP Professionals**
SYSOP: Not available
MODEM: 704-554-1102 (NC)
VOICE: 704-554-1101
PURPOSE: Data processing search and placement services.

BBS: Elf's Den BBS
SYSOP: Elvin Rosaly
MODEM: 212-402-1382 (NY)
VOICE: Not available
PURPOSE: Technical and administrative positions in radiologic sciences, EMT, and the medical field in general. Subboards include a placement area with matching professionals and positions.

BBS: Employer's Network
SYSOP: Dave McCoy and P. Spencer
MODEM: 206-475-0665 (WA)
VOICE: Not available
PURPOSE: Job announcements, federal job listings, resume programs, resume database.

BBS: Employment Board
SYSOP: Not available
MODEM: 619-689-1348 (CA)
VOICE: Not available
PURPOSE: JOBS-NOW echo and employment information for the San Diego, California, area. No fee required.

BBS: Employment Connection
SYSOP: Philip Oliver
MODEM: 508-537-1862 (MA)
VOICE: Not available
PURPOSE: Over 1000 new jobs postings.

BBS: Employment Line
SYSOP: Ed Rose
MODEM: 219-485-3551 (IN)
VOICE: Not available
PURPOSE: Job listings and resume databases.

BBS: Employment Line BBS
SYSOP: Bob Carbon
MODEM: 508-865-7928 (MA)
VOICE: Not available
PURPOSE: Job listings and resume databases.

BBS: Engineer's Connection
SYSOP: Denis Desharnais
MODEM: 603-497-4381 (NH)
VOICE: 603-497-4866
PURPOSE: Subscription based with validation required. Was established with a wide selection of message forums covering many technologies.

BBS: Enginet
SYSOP: Steve A. Witters, P.E.
MODEM: 513-858-2688 (OH)
VOICE: Not available
PURPOSE: An on-line job placement system (contract and direct) that aids engineers and employers in meeting job needs.

BBS: Entrenet
SYSOP: Greg Legacki

MODEM: 908-647-2202 (NJ)
VOICE: Not available
PURPOSE: Focuses on issues of interest to business owners.

BBS: Environet
SYSOP: Dick Dillman
MODEM: 415-512-9108 (CA)
VOICE: Not available
PURPOSE: Job openings with Greenpeace. Updated daily. Most positions are in the United States with a few in other countries. No fee.

BBS: Exec-PC BBS
SYSOP: Not available
MODEM: 414-789-4210 (WI)
VOICE: Not available
PURPOSE: E-Span Job Search access. No fee required to access Job Search door. Large variety of job listings in all areas.

BBS: Executive Connection Information System
SYSOP: George Smith
MODEM: 214-306-3393 (TX)
VOICE: Not available
PURPOSE: Focuses on careers, employment, and business management. Assistance for job seekers, or business owners. View, search, and download information on thousands of local and national openings in all industries and occupations.

BBS: Federal Jobline
SYSOP: Office of Personnel Management
MODEM: 818-575-6521 (CA)
VOICE: Not available
PURPOSE: Federal Job Information Center contains federal job listings and information for the western region. No fee required.

BBS: Federal Job Network
SYSOP: Scott Keen
MODEM: 703-715-1016 (VA)
VOICE: 703-264-7883
PURPOSE: Subscription-based BBS with federal job openings, specialized search program, national and oversees listings.

BBS: FedWorld
SYSOP: Not available
MODEM: 703-321-8020 (VA)
VOICE: Not available
PURPOSE: Federal employment opportunities worldwide. Also has Gateway service to over 100 other government BBSs. No fee required.

BBS: Fifth Estate BBS
SYSOP: Darrell Lowe
MODEM: 702-898-9684 (NV)
VOICE: Not available
PURPOSE: Broadcast/media-oriented issues and information.

BBS: FJOB
SYSOP: U.S. Office of Personnel Management

MODEM: 912-471-3771 (GA)
VOICE: Not available
PURPOSE: Provides information on jobs available with the federal government.

BBS: FJOB BBS
SYSOP: Office of Personnel Management
MODEM: 912-757-3100 (GA)
VOICE: Not available
PURPOSE: Federal Job Information Center contains federal job listings and information for all U.S. locations. No Fee required.

BBS: Geofuel Geoscience
SYSOP: Dr. Dieter
MODEM: 416-829-4097 (Canada)
VOICE: 416-829-2716
PURPOSE: Subscription service—first month free; phone validation or give geoscience society I.D.; Canada-based Geoscience BBS for earth science professionals and students. File database includes specialist programs (academia, Geological Surveys of Canada, Ontario) scientific graphics, etc.

BBS: Georgia Online
SYSOP: Paul E. Foster; Foster Employment Services
MODEM: 404-591-0777 (GA)
VOICE: 404-591-8448
PURPOSE: Job listings, resume database, Help Wanted-USA services.

BBS: Global Trade Net
SYSOP: Not available
MODEM: 415-668-0422 (CA)
VOICE: Not available
PURPOSE: International trade forum for both theory and practice. Help for starting new businesses. Bid and selling areas. International marketing forums. Job listing center.

BBS: Grapevine Job Network
SYSOP: Ray Osborne
MODEM: 404-924-8414 (GA)
VOICE: Not available
PURPOSE: Job seekers helping one another find opportunities. Free listings of high-tech jobs, files of job hotlines to find unadvertised jobs, and job listings shared by job seekers. Software to help job seekers.

BBS: Horseman's BBS
SYSOP: Brad Settles
MODEM: 517-596-3233 (MI)
VOICE: Not available
PURPOSE: For horse lovers or business people interested in the horse industry. Also includes an extensive classified ad section.

BBS: I-NET BBS
SYSOP: Not available
MODEM: 301-564-6749 (MD)
VOICE: Not available
PURPOSE: On-line resumes.

BBS: Infodata
SYSOP: Paul Reeves

MODEM: 404-621-0804 (GA)
VOICE: Not available
PURPOSE: Computer classified ad service listing employment opportunities.

BBS: InfoMat BBS
SYSOP: Not available
MODEM: 714-492-8727 (CA)
VOICE: Not available
PURPOSE: Job opportunity and franchise information. Carries several echoes such as
JobNet, Laran Communications, Rime, and Intelec job forums. No fee required.

BBS: Job and Opportunity Link
SYSOP: Larry Spiegel; Laran Communications
MODEM: 708-690-9860 (IL)
VOICE: Employment listings. Home of JOB-LINK and RESUME-LINK. All ads may
be downloaded.

BBS: JOBBS
SYSOP: Charles Sillery
MODEM: 504-851-0274 (LA)
VOICE: Not available
PURPOSE: Free access to nationwide job listings for various positions.

BBS: JOBBS
SYSOP: Alpha Systems, Inc.; Bill Griffin
MODEM: 404-992-8937 (GA)
VOICE: Not available
PURPOSE: Contains job listings for many employment areas. Also has listings of recruit-
ing firms and companies. No fee required.

BBS: JOBS-BBS
SYSOP: Ken Zwaschka
MODEM: 503-281-6808 (OR)
VOICE: 503-248-0734
PURPOSE: All varieties of jobs available nationwide. Home of the moderator of the
JOBS-NOW echo. No fee required.

BBS: Job Search Board
SYSOP: The Master Programmer Group/Job Search
MODEM: 416-588-3821 (Canada)
VOICE: 416-588-1111
PURPOSE: Job and resume postings and help wanted postings. Basic membership is free.
Additional services/time etc. available for a small membership fee. Home of Trans-
Canada jobs conference.

BBS: Jobs in America
SYSOP: John Wright
MODEM: 619-462-JOBS (CA)
VOICE: 619-469-3841
PURPOSE: A nationwide listing of help wanted ads. Authorized representative for Help
Wanted-USA employment listings.

BBS: Job Trac BBS
SYSOP: Kerry Goodsin; KLG & Associates
MODEM: 214-349-0527 (TX)
VOICE: Not available

PURPOSE: Job listings, resume uploads, and job forums in many areas for the Dallas/Ft. Worth, Texas, area. No fee required.

BBS: Kasta, James and Associates Career Assistance
SYSOP: Kasta, James and Associates
MODEM: 612-536-0533 (MN)
VOICE: 612-929-4202
PURPOSE: Resume uploads and a comprehensive collection of nationwide and international jobs listings. Also provides job hunting information and interviewing tips. No fee required.

BBS: Lee Johnson International
SYSOP: Lee Johnson
MODEM: 510-787-3191 (CA)
VOICE: 510-787-2110
PURPOSE: A small search firm established in 1974 specializing exclusively in employer-paid-fee recruiting and placement of software engineering professionals. Home of EasyResume ™, a resume composition system.

BBS: Legal Genius
SYSOP: Marc Bragg
MODEM: 610-695-9689
VOICE: Not available
PURPOSE: Legal files, law school outlines, and message areas.

BBS: Logikal Career Connection
SYSOP: Logikal Solutions
MODEM: 708-420-0424 (IL)
VOICE: 708-420-0210
PURPOSE: Data Processing Professionals on W2 or 1099 status. Special software is required to communicate with this service, which can be downloaded on first call.

BBS: Med-Talk
SYSOP: Steve Bernstein
MODEM: 305-749-2395 (FL)
VOICE: Not available
PURPOSE: Nursing continuing education credits on-line, medical news, including 13,500 files.

BBS: The Meeting Works
SYSOP: John K. Mackenzie
MODEM: 212-737-6932 (NY)
VOICE: 212-737-8910
PURPOSE: Assisting those who need a meeting theme or product introduction idea or a unique staging or exhibit concept. Also offers expert advice on interactive meeting technology or speech preparation.

BBS: Multi-Tech Support
SYSOP: Juan Martinez
MODEM: 305-596-6841 (FL)
VOICE: 305-342-9667
PURPOSE: Subscription available with validation. Support for X-RAY service and sales, also job posting in the medical field, and biomedicine.

BBS: Music Network USA
SYSOP: Vic Pettenuzzi

MODEM: 310-312-8753 (CA)
VOICE: Not available
PURPOSE: Midi music service and musicians referral service.

BBS: NABE
SYSOP: Dave Williams; National Association of Business Economists
MODEM: 216-464-1757 (OH)
VOICE: Not available
PURPOSE: Board of general interest to Business Economists. Coded resumes of members are listed, with any registered caller being able to view the (coded) resumes. Resumes are kept on file for 3 months.

BBS: National Technical Search
SYSOP: Allen Davis & Associates
MODEM: 413-549-8136 (MA)
VOICE: Not available
PURPOSE: Has national job listings plus forums and career guides. No fee required.

BBS: Nationserv Network
SYSOP: Ben Nation
MODEM: 812-426-9968 (IN)
VOICE: Not available
PURPOSE: USA Listings, Job Service, Shopping Mall. Has bulletins containing job openings and profiles of individuals seeking employment. Membership fee; charge for posting job listings and/or individual profile.

BBS: Network
SYSOP: Lee; (Run by a human resource consulting firm.)
MODEM: 301-681-5331 (MD)
VOICE: Not available
PURPOSE: Employment-related information files and conferences that contain job and applicant postings. Positions include technical, financial, engineering, medical and others. Also an area that lists employment-related services as well as a conference for new graduates.

BBS: Networking Careers On-line
SYSOP: Network World Magazine, Bill Reinstein
MODEM: 508-620-1178 (MA)
VOICE: Not available
PURPOSE: Advertised job openings. Information and advice about career and job related issues.

BBS: Olai
SYSOP: Not available
MODEM: 703-450-1790 (VA)
VOICE: Not available
PURPOSE: Job listings in accounting, business/management, engineering, data processing, medical, and sales/marketing which are searchable. Most positions are located in the MD-VA-DC area, nonsubscribers get limited access; subscribers get full access with features.

BBS: On-line Career Fair
SYSOP: Response Technologies Corporation
MODEM: 603-726-3344 (NH)

VOICE: 603-726-4800
PURPOSE: Provide direct access to career opportunities. Identify actual job openings. Apply for any of the positions by faxing 603-726-3909 or mailing your resume. Password is: newjob.

BBS: **Online Job Service of America**
SYSOP: Not available
MODEM: 813-237-8257 (FL)
VOICE: Not available
PURPOSE: Employment listings and resumes.

BBS: **Online Opportunities**
SYSOP: Ward Christman
MODEM: 610-873-7170 (PA)
VOICE: 610-873-2168
PURPOSE: Thousands of job listings on-line. Internet and Philadelphia area want ads are *free* after uploading your resume (at no cost) for area employers to view. Help Wanted-USA services available on-line. Career and job search programs and help files.

BBS: **OPM Atlanta**
SYSOP: Office of Personnel Management
MODEM: 404-730-2370 (GA)
VOICE: Not available
PURPOSE: Federal Job Information Center has on-line job search facility and download-able files for all regions. No fee required.

BBS: **OPM Express**
SYSOP: The Office of Personnel Management
MODEM: 214-767-0565 (TX)
VOICE: 214-767-0561
PURPOSE: An electronic bulletin board for federal personnel agencies.

BBS: **OPM FEDJOBS**
SYSOP: June Summers
MODEM: 201-645-3887 (NJ)
VOICE: Not available
PURPOSE: Job and personnel related federal government information; federal job listings, and employment applications.

BBS: **OPM FEDJOBS—Philadelphia**
SYSOP: U.S. Office of Personnel Management
MODEM: 215-580-2216 (PA)
VOICE: Not available
PURPOSE: Source for open federal government jobs and training schedules for all of United States. No fee required. Updated daily.

BBS: **Opportunity**
SYSOP: Patrick Jordan
MODEM: 804-588-4031 (VA)
VOICE: Not available
PURPOSE: Conferences, national, federal, private sector, state and local job openings, on-line resumes, business advertising, job search and business files. Free to job seekers.

BBS: **Opportunity Network**
SYSOP: Kathleen McMahon
MODEM: 415-673-4080 (CA)

VOICE: Not available

PURPOSE: Listings of technical jobs and candidates. Access to bulletins, resume writing suggestions, selected conferences, some files and a demonstration of the search system. Access to the jobs and resume databases and consultants involve a fee. Individuals can post resumes for free. Others are charged fees according to services desired.

BBS: Opportunity Network

SYSOP: Not available

MODEM: 404-578-0544 (GA)

VOICE: Not available

PURPOSE: A job computer network in Atlanta for high tech jobs.

BBS: ouT therE

SYSOP: Not available

MODEM: 408-263-2248 (CA)

VOICE: Not available

PURPOSE: Contract and permanent job listings for San Francisco, California area. No fee required. Updated every two days.

BBS: Pacific Teleconnect

SYSOP: Ken Summerville

MODEM: 310-986-0154 (CA)

VOICE: Not available

PURPOSE: Business networking.

BBS: PCAD User Group

SYSOP: Jak Olson

MODEM: 714-625-2679 (CA)

VOICE: 714-625-1080 (Tammy)

PURPOSE: For those interested in circuit board design. No subscription or ratios, instant validation; full access on first call. New job shop (employment) area.

BBS: P.C. CompoNet

SYSOP: Not available

MODEM: 213-943-0367 (CA)

VOICE: Not available

PURPOSE: Job opportunities.

BBS: PenCycle

SYSOP: Pennsylvania Resources Council; Russ Whetherill

MODEM: 215-892-9940 (PA)

VOICE: 215-565-9131

PURPOSE: The interactive recycling bulletin board system with information and job listings for environmental specialists.

BBS: POSH (Policy, Operations, & Staffing Headquarters)

SYSOP: Not available

MODEM: 912-757-3155 (GA)

VOICE: Not available

PURPOSE: Conferences, staffing/recruiting, and OPM/Agency/SYSOP.

BBS: Praedo

SYSOP: Unicus Advertising

MODEM: 609-953-0769 (NJ)

VOICE: Not available

PURPOSE: Local access to FJOLPJ job listings as a service to New Jersey residents who live outside the 201 area code. Also features tips on resume writing and on-line listings of job openings for senior executives and CEOs.

BBS: Psychonominal
SYSOP: Sam Hutchinson
MODEM: 318-254-0274 (LA)
VOICE: Not available
PURPOSE: Focuses on the science of psychology for professionals and any one who is interested in the field.

BBS: PWTG
SYSOP: Alternatives PLUS, Inc./James Buckland
MODEM: 302-328-0381 (DE)
VOICE: 302-328-8776
PURPOSE: Job Opportunities, uploading of resumes, open jobs/contracts, job applications, and write messages to JoBBS.

BBS: Resume Data Services
SYSOP: Steven J. Berry
MODEM: Not available
VOICE: 515-288-4067 (IA)
PURPOSE: A $5 per resume, per six-month period on-line, with a $1 charge for any changes to be made during that time, will get you exposure to all of Des Moines largest employers.

BBS: Resume Exchange
SYSOP: Not available
MODEM: 602-947-4283 (AZ)
VOICE: Not available
PURPOSE: Interactive communications network, legal network, and pioneer net international.

BBS: Resume File
SYSOP: Steve Hawley
MODEM: 805-581-6210 (CA)
VOICE: Not available
PURPOSE: A comprehensive collection of nationwide job listings. No fee required. Also has job related areas with job hunting information and tips. SBA and federal government job information.

BBS: Reunions USA
SYSOP: Not available
MODEM: 908-741-9460 (NJ)
VOICE: Not available
PURPOSE: Employment issues.

BBS: RHost
SYSOP: Ron Wills
MODEM: 404-392-9164
VOICE: Not available
PURPOSE: A data processing recruitment service of Robert Half of Atlanta.

BBS: $ales Force
SYSOP: Ronnie Oldham

MODEM: 817-847-9211 (TX)
VOICE: 817-847-7300
PURPOSE: Support for business and sales professionals. A selection of Windows, business, and contact management, as well as on-line magazines, information, and sales material.

BBS: SBA-Online
SYSOP: Not available
MODEM: 800-697-4636 (DC)
VOICE: Not available
PURPOSE: Small Business Administration BBS. Loaded with information of interest to individuals wishing to start or who have started a small business. No fee required.

BBS: Search
SYSOP: Bill Sawvel
MODEM: 206-253-5213 (WA)
VOICE: Not available
PURPOSE: Free access to high tech company profile database and data processing job listings.

BBS: Society For Technical Communications
SYSOP: Society For Technical Communications
MODEM: 703-522-3299 (DC)
VOICE: Not available
PURPOSE: For technical writers only. Job service and freelance registry. Job listings available only to verified STC members. No fee required.

BBS: Sourcery
SYSOP: Teresa Schoen
MODEM: 702-256-6050 (NV)
VOICE: Not available
PURPOSE: Free access. For purchasing professionals. Career and professional development opportunities.

BBS: State of Nebraska
SYSOP: Not available
MODEM: 800-392-7932 (NE)
VOICE: Not available
PURPOSE: A list of State of Nebraska jobs.

BBS: Streamline Design
SYSOP: Not available
MODEM: 905-793-1411 (NM)
VOICE: Not available
PURPOSE: General conferences in music careers, music education, songwriters, and copyright and general music law.

BBS: Strickly Business!
SYSOP: Bruce Kullberg
MODEM: 614-538-9250 (OH)
VOICE: Not available
PURPOSE: Information exchange for entrepreneurs, managers, and business professionals.

BBS: Systems Personnel
SYSOP: Donna M. Frappier

MODEM: 413-592-9208 (MA)
VOICE: 413-592-4069
PURPOSE: For professionals experienced in MIS/Software Engineering areas. Internal jobs listed in our 24-hour job listings BBS. No contract or entry level positions available.

BBS: TAG On-line Career Bank
SYSOP: Not available
MODEM: 215-969-3845 (PA)
VOICE: Not available
PURPOSE: Over 40 job-oriented conferences and joblistings from the United States and Japan, employment help, resume areas, and more. QWK off-line reader facility. Fee required.

BBS: Tech Pro
SYSOP: Al Gordon
MODEM: 619-755-7357 (CA)
VOICE: 619-755-7357
PURPOSE: No subscription needed. Free access to San Diego, California, technology jobs.

BBS: Texas Education Agency
SYSOP: Texas Education Agency HR Division
MODEM: 512-475-3689 (TX)
VOICE: Not available
PURPOSE: Contains Texas state government job listings in Austin, Texas. No fee required.

BBS: Traders Connection
SYSOP: Carol Hanrahan
MODEM: 317-359-5199 (IN)
VOICE: Not available
PURPOSE: Classified job postings from various newspapers.

BBS: Transnet, Inc.
SYSOP: Not available
MODEM: 217-384-5101 (IL)
VOICE: Not available
PURPOSE: Database of translators and translating firms as well as products for language specialists and jobs. Browsing is free. Annual membership for listing a resume.

BBS: Triangle Fraternity
SYSOP: Merle Newlon
MODEM: 317-872-4305 (IN)
VOICE: 317-872-4305
PURPOSE: Serves alumni members who may access the service to view employment listings. Membership is limited to students in the engineering, physical sciences, or architecture studies.

BBS: Turning Point
SYSOP: Not available
MODEM: 512-219-7848 (TX)
VOICE: Not available
PURPOSE: Employment listings.

BBS: Vanguard Chronicle Network
SYSOP: Angela Pope
MODEM: 305-524-4411 (FL)
VOICE: Not available
PURPOSE: Jobs in Florida.

BBS: Walt Disney Imagineering
SYSOP: Not available
MODEM: 800-959-3725 (FL)
VOICE: Not available
PURPOSE: The Disney Applicant Information System (DAISY), is for scientists and engineers. To be considered for positions in WDI's RandD Division in California, Florida, or New York, upload your resume. No fee required.

BBS: Wall / Resume Exchange
SYSOP: Not available
MODEM: 601-825-2820 (MS)
VOICE: Not available
PURPOSE: Users can read or post resumes and employment opportunities and services in a variety of categories and disciplines. New users get 10 minutes a day; subscription available for $1 a month for more time.

BBS: Washington Area Service Network (WASNET)
SYSOP: Bill Robinson
MODEM: 202-606-1113 (WA)
VOICE: 202-606-1848
PURPOSE: Free BBS and telecommunications service for federal job information and other recruitment-related matters. Call voice number first, leave first and last name, plus a password of up to 8 characters (upper case).

BBS: Ward Christman
America Online screen name is: "PAPHILLY2"
PURPOSE: Employment information and services designed for job seekers, recruiters, and employers. You may reach his board by calling 1-610-873-7170. To reach Ward by phone, mail, or email (on America Online):

Online Opportunities
PO Box 17
Downingtown, PA 19335
610-873-6811

8

Job Seeker's PowerPak

This chapter describes four electronic services that collectively represent one of the most powerful (hence the term PowerPak) job hunting strategies that you can employ. These resources can turbocharge your job search to its highest level of productivity. The four services include:

❏ Help Wanted-USA

❏ ClassiFACTS

❏ Select Phone

❏ Worldwide Resume/Talent Bank

Together, these resources can provide you with direct access to:

❏ Over 135,000 actual help wanted ads—updated weekly—covering most professional career fields from employers coast-to-coast

❏ 8,000,000 "hidden job markets" with American employers nationwide

❏ 20,000,000 plus potential readers of your resume

The ultimate job search strategy!

If you were to examine the job hunting strategies postulated by many of today's leading career guidance experts, you would soon discover that most of the strategists recommend the use of any one of three techniques for securing employment. While different in how each technique may be implemented, experts generally agree that to find employment, you should:

❏ Monitor as many help wanted ads as possible, and respond to as many ads as you can in a timely manner that match your qualifications and career goals.

❏ Forward a letter of introduction and a copy of your resume to as many "hidden job market" employers as possible that you have determined have a real need for your expertise. "Hidden job market" employers are those employers who have not yet advertised their personnel needs, but nonetheless have, or will have, job openings, or would be willing to create new positions for the right individuals.

❏ Distribute a copy of your resume to as many professional contacts (i.e., people on your networking list) and employers as possible to draw attention to your availability for employment.

If you are like most job seekers, you probably agree that the previous recommendations are clearly important to your job search success. However, due to constraints imposed upon you—as is the case with most job seekers—by your limited time and resources, it is possible to monitor only a select number of help wanted ads each week, identify and contact only a select number of hidden job markets, and distribute only a select number of resumes. In years past, if you were able to monitor a few hundred help wanted ads, or send out a few hundred letters of introduction and/or resumes each month you were doing well. However, in terms of what must be done today to secure employment, the traditional numbers are insufficient.

It's a numbers game!

Few individuals would disagree that the "numbers game" is operational in the job search process. If you were known to 1000 companies as an experienced professional in your career field, you would have a much better chance of securing employment than if you were known to only 10 companies. The question is not *"should* I contact a lot of potential employers?" but *"how* can I contact a lot of potential employers?" *The ability to resolve this question is at the very heart of your job search success.*

Enter Your Personal Computer!

Information on over 135,000 actual, professional employment opportunities (help wanted ads) in most career fields from employers coast-to-coast—updated weekly—resides in several computer databases just waiting for you to access.

Information on over 8,000,000 American employers who form the "hidden job market" is now available on CD-ROM—ready to help you prepare an endless number of potential employer mailing lists.

And the ability to distribute your resume to over 20,000,000 potential viewers—including millions of employers—now exists thanks to several computer database network services.

Which Strategy Should You Follow?

To maximize the number of employment opportunities that you can gain access to, to minimize the length of your job search, and to increase your chances of getting the job you want (rather than ending up taking only the job you can get), it is recommended that you use all three previous strategies. Responding to help wanted ads, working the "hidden job market," and distributing your resume to potential network contacts and employers can provide you with the greatest level of job hunting capability.

To connect to these databases and services, all you have to do is turn on your computer and (well, almost ... read on!).

Gain Access to Over 135,000 Help Wanted Ads Updated Weekly

The following two companies provide electronic access to over 135,000 new help wanted ads each and every week:

Help Wanted-USA

Description: Help Wanted-USA is a database of help wanted ads offered as a commercial service by Gonyea & Associates, Inc. Each week a team of employment consultants in over 50 cities across America collect information on employment opportunities to form the database. All positions are professional in nature and range from Accountant to Zoologist. The database is updated weekly and contains anywhere from 5000 to 10,000 ads. All ads contain information regarding the title of the job position, location and name of the company or recruiter offering the position, job description and qualifications, salary, and other important information. All ads are displayed for a two-week period. Job seekers are instructed to contact the company or recruiter listed in any ad matching their job search goals to apply for the position or to obtain more information about the position.

How to Use: The Help Wanted-USA database is accessible in the form of a searchable database to individuals who are members of America Online or to individuals who have access to the Internet. You may use the enclosed America Online software program to directly access the Help Wanted-USA database.

If for some reason you do not wish, or are unable, to directly access the database on any of the preceding network services, you may request (1) to have a search of the database conducted on your behalf on a weekly basis by an employment consultant and a list of help wanted ads found matching your career goals be provided to you, or (2) to obtain employment listings on diskette each week allowing you to search the full listings using your own personal computer.

Cost: There is no cost for individuals who wish to directly access the database on America Online, other than the regular monthly membership fee charged by the network service. For individuals who have access to the Internet,* there is no charge at all. For job seekers who wish to have a search done for them or to receive employment listings on diskette, a six-week subscription may be obtained for $39.95.

Note: To reach the Help Wanted-USA database through the Internet at Online Career Center, Gopher to *gopher.msen.com* or Telnet to *gopher.msu.edu*.

Advantages of Using This Service. You get to personally search the entire database and select only those jobs that you believe match your career goals and qualifications. You can conduct a local, state, regional, or nationwide search in only a matter of seconds. Because you are searching the database on-line, you get immediate results—full profile information on available positions that you may print out or download to your personal computer. You may use the service for as long as you wish at no cost if you are a member of America Online or the Internet.

How to Order. Use the enclosed America Online software program to access the Help Wanted-USA database. Otherwise, contact:

Gonyea & Associates, Inc.
3543 Enterprise Road East
Safety Harbor, Florida 34695
813-725-9600

While you're in the America Online Career Center checking out the Help Wanted-USA database, you might also check out the E-Span database of employment listings.

ClassiFACTS

Description. ClassiFACTS is an employment information service offered by North American ClassiFACTS® Inc. Under a cooperative arrangement with dozens of the largest newspapers across the United States, ClassiFACTS electronically compiles the help wanted ads from each newspaper into a single database. Job seekers may call a 1-800 number to have a search conducted of the database.

The ClassiFACTS database contains approximately 125,000 recruitment ads updated weekly. ClassiFACTS republishes these ads in the identical format as they appeared in the newspaper.

How to Use. Job seekers wishing to use the service should check the classified section of their local newspaper for a telephone number, or call 1-800-789-8974 to talk to a trained sales counselor. Job seekers will be asked to indicate (from a list of over 2000 titles) up to three job titles that represent the kind of position(s) they desire to find. Next, the job seeker identifies the cities, states, or regions where he or she would like to find employment. During the call a trained ClassiFACTS sales counselor will help the job seeker design the best database search to meet his or her particular needs. The job seeker is fully informed of how many ads are identified by the resulting search. ClassiFACTS will forward a personal publication (listing) of the matching recruitment ads each week for four weeks.

Cost. $29.95 for a four week subscription, and $4.95 for each additional week thereafter. Job seekers may call to change their search criteria at no additional charge, and may renew their subscription at any time. The subscription fee may be charged to Visa or MasterCard, or paid by personal check.

Search results may be obtained by first class mail, next day delivery, second day delivery, or same day fax. Some additional charges may apply depending on the preferred method of delivery.

Advantages of This Service. Job seekers can perform a local, regional, or nationwide job search accessing an extensive and up-to-date database of current employment ads, at a reasonable cost, without having to do anything more than place a toll free phone call!

How to Order. Check with your local newspaper to see if they are a ClassiFACTS affiliate or call 1-800-789-8974, or write to:

North American ClassiFACTSᵃ Inc.
2821 South Parker Road
Suite 305
Aurora, Colorado 80014

How to Gain Access to 8 Million "Hidden Job Markets" in the United States

Using a marvelous new CD-ROM program called Select Phone from ProCD, Inc., you may quickly and inexpensively obtain the name and mailing address on any one of over 8 million employers across the United States. The data contained on the *Select Phone* disc represents one of the largest, most accurate, and most up-to-date mailing list collections of employers available anywhere. Prior to the release of *Select Phone*, your only option for obtaining this amount and kind of information was to use expensive mailing list services. With *Select Phone* you can prepare an unlimited number of mailing lists of employers that you would like to contact to inquire about employment—for literally pennies a name.

By researching the companies you identify using *Select Phone*, and then by preparing and forwarding cover letters that outline how you may be of value to each employer, you can tap into the "hidden job market." See Chap. 4—Job Hunting the Electronic Way for more information about how to contact employers.

Select Phone

Description. Select Phone is a DOS-based system containing a series of 4 CD-ROM discs that collectively contain the following information on over 8 million U.S. businesses:

❏ Business name

❏ Street address

❏ City/state/zip

❏ Phone number with area code

❏ Business heading

❏ SIC Code (Standard Industry Classification)

In addition, Select Phone also contains telephone numbers for over 70 million residential listings in the United States.

With *Select Phone*, you can prepare an unlimited number of mailing lists of employers. For example, assume you wanted to apply to all banks and other financial institutions in New Jersey, New York, and Connecticut. To obtain this information would normally require days of research at your local library, or hundreds of dollars for mailing lists from commercial mailing list services.

Not anymore! With *Select Phone* you can prepare this list in only minutes.

Note: A Windows and Macintosh version interface are expected to be available in April and May of 1994.

How to Use. Simply select the type of business that you wish to contact using various menu options contained within the program, and then indicate the output format in which you wish to receive the data (such as text, mailing label, etc.). Within seconds, *Select Phone* will inform you as to how many employers it has found in its database and will then produce the output as instructed. Conduct some research of the companies on your list to determine which ones have a need for your expertise, and then you're ready to mail merge your list of employers with a cover letter. Finally, just enclose a copy of your resume and you've got the information necessary to reach the hidden job market!

Advantages of This Product. The beauty of *Select Phone* is that you can generate as many mailing lists as you wish without having to pay for each list—as is the case with traditional mailing list services, or other similar CD-ROM programs. For the cost of the program you can generate as many lists as you wish. In addition, because you can generate mailing lists in minutes, you also save the time and expense normally required to produce mailing lists the old fashioned way.

Cost. The suggested retail price of *Select Phone* is $299. The street price that is available from many software stores is around $150 to $200—shop around to find the best bargain. Do not be dismayed by the price. After you have finished using *Select Phone*, you may, like any other software program, resell the product to another job seeker. Let's say you buy it for $150, and then resell it for $100, your cost is only $50—far less than what you would pay for *one* mailing list from a commercial mailing list service! Many job seekers have found it easy to resell software by placing a classified ad in a local newspaper, or by contacting local user groups, or even software stores. You should have little trouble reselling *Select Phone*.

How to Order. Contact your local software stores, or mail-order software vendors, or call 1-800-99-CD-ROM, or write to:

Pro CD, Inc.
222 Rosewood Drive
Danvers, MA 01923

How to Place Your Resume in Front of Over 20 Million Potential Viewers

Worldwide Resume/Talent Bank Service

Description. The Worldwide Resume/Talent Bank Service is a resume posting service offered by Gonyea & Associates, Inc. Using this service, you may have your complete resume entered into an electronic database containing thousands of resumes of professionals in all career fields from across the nation and around the world.

The Worldwide Resume/Talent Bank service provides private individuals with an inexpensive means of advertising and marketing worldwide their career interests, expertise, and availability for employment, consulting, or other employment-related objectives.

You may elect to have your resume included in the worldwide database if you are interested in seeking full- or part-time employment, consulting opportunities, lecture engagements, or other forms of employment, or if you simply wish to advertise your professional interests, skills, and qualifications to other individuals as a means of networking around the world. Consider the Worldwide Resume/Talent Bank service to be the electronic equivalent of "who's who in American business."

The Worldwide Resume/Talent Bank database is accessible to over 20 million people worldwide. Anyone viewing your resume who is interested in talking to you can simply contact you per the directions you indicate in your resume. You may elect to be contacted by mail, phone, fax, or email.

New resumes are received daily into the database and are uploaded approximately every 10 days to the following computer network services:

Network services	Number of viewers
America Online	1,000,000
Internet (@ Online Career Center)	20,000,000
Total approximate viewing audience	21,000,000

Millions of employers, executives and professionals, and employment recruiters use the previous networks to find new employees, consultants, candidates, and individuals suitable for their employment needs. In addition, millions of private individuals use these services to network—to find people who have similar interests and skills.

Cost. $40.00 for a one-year subscription. Job seekers may renew their subscription as often as they wish.

How to Access. To have your resume entered into the Worldwide Resume/Talent Bank service, follow these directions depending on whether you wish to submit your resume electronically, on diskette, or printed:

Direction for submitting your resume *electronically:*

1. Using a word processing program, prepare a copy of your resume and save it as a "text" file. Consult your word processing user's manual for directions regarding how to save or convert a document as a text file.

Make sure nothing else resides in the file other than one copy of your resume.

Indicate at the bottom of your resume how you wish to be contacted, such as "Please contact me by mail or fax." Make sure you include the information that is necessary to contact you. Also, exclude any information, such as phone numbers, that you do not wish others to know.

2. Log onto America Online, access the email function menu area, and select the Compose New Mail item.

Enter the following information:

To: WWResume

Subject: Worldwide Resume/Talent Bank

In the message area, enter the following information:

- ❏ Your complete name
- ❏ Your residential address (street, city, state, zip)
- ❏ Your home phone number with area code
- ❏ Your Visa, MasterCard, or American Express number
- ❏ The expiration date of your credit card

3. Attach the file containing your resume. *Caution!* Double check this step—many people attach the wrong file by accident!

4. Select the "Send" button. Your message and resume will be emailed to WWResume (Gonyea & Associates).

Upon receipt of your message, your credit card will be charged $40.00 and your resume will be uploaded into the database, where it will remain for one full year. You will receive confirmation from Gonyea & Associates by email on America Online of the receipt of your order, as well as of the upload date your resume will be entered into the Worldwide Resume/Talent Bank. All resumes will be uploaded within 10 working days of receipt.

Direction for submitting your resume *on diskette:*

1. Using a word processing program, prepare a copy of your resume and save it as a "text" file.

Make sure nothing else resides in the file other than one copy of your resume. Indicate at the bottom of your resume how you wish to be contacted, such as "Please contact me via mail or fax." Make sure you include the information that is necessary to contact you. Also, exclude any information, such as phone number, that you do not wish others to know.

2. Save a copy of your resume on a 3.5" diskette (either PC or Macintosh format).

3. In a diskette mailer, mail your resume first class to:

Gonyea & Associates, Inc.
ATTN: Worldwide Resume/Talent Bank Service
3543 Enterprise Road East
Safety Harbor, Florida 34695

In an enclosed letter, provide the following information:

- ❏ Your complete name
- ❏ Your residential address (street, city, state, zip)

❑ Your home phone number with area code

❑ Your Visa, MasterCard, or American Express number and expiration date (or a check or money order made payable to Gonyea & Associates in the amount of $40.00)

❑ The format of your diskette (either PC or Macintosh)

Upon receipt of your order, and if appropriate, your credit card will be charged $40.00 and your resume will be uploaded to the database, where it will remain for one full year. You will receive confirmation from Gonyea & Associates by first class mail of the receipt of your order, as well as of the upload date on which your resume will be entered into the Worldwide Resume/Talent Bank. All resumes will be uploaded within 10 working days of receipt.

Directions for submitting your *printed* resume:

1. Mail a copy of your printed resume to:

Gonyea & Associates, Inc.
ATTN: Worldwide Resume/Talent Bank Service
3543 Enterprise Road East
Safety Harbor, Florida 34695

Make sure you indicate at the bottom of your resume how you wish to be contacted, such as "Please contact me via mail or fax." Make sure you include the information that is necessary to contact you. Also, exclude any information, such as phone number, that you do not wish others to know.

In an enclosed letter, provide the following information:

❑ Your complete name

❑ Your residential address (street, city, zip code)

❑ Your home phone number with area code

❑ Your Visa, MasterCard, or American Express number and expiration date (or a check or money order made payable to Gonyea & Associates in the amount of $45.00)

Upon receipt of your order, and if appropriate, your credit card will be charged $45.00 and your resume will be uploaded into the database, where it will remain for one full year. You will receive confirmation from Gonyea & Associates by first class mail of the receipt of your order, as well as of the upload date your resume will be entered into the Worldwide Resume/Talent Bank. All resumes will be uploaded within 10 working days of receipt.

Note:: An additional $5.00 data entry fee is required of all individuals who elect to mail in a printed resume.

9
Power Tools

This chapter contains profiles on over 160 electronic resources designed to be of value to career planners and job seekers. The resources found in this chapter are also useful to the following individuals and organizations who work with, or assist, career planners and job seekers:

❏ College career planning and placement services

❏ Company outplacement personnel

❏ High school and college guidance counselors

❏ Human Resource managers

❏ Information researchers and brokers,

❏ Libraries—public, private, corporate, and educational

❏ Military outplacement services

❏ Personnel directors

❏ Private career planning services

❏ Private employment agencies and services

❏ Rehabilitation therapists and counselors

❏ State employment agency counselors

❏ Vocational/career education teachers.

The profiles are arranged by title. For each resource listed, the following information is provided:

Name of the resource

Electronic Format—such as

❏ Audiocassette

❏ BBS (bulletin board service)

❏ CD-ROM

❏ Database

❏ Email

❏ Fax service

❏ Fax-back service

❏ Job hotline

❏ Magnetic tape

❏ On-line database

❏ On-line uploading service

❏ Phone service

❏ Radio broadcasting service

❏ Software

❏ Videotape

❏ Voice mail system

Reader Response Number. Each resource has its own unique number (e.g., P089). If you would like additional information about any resource listed in this chapter, note its reader response number and use the reader response card to obtain information by return mail.

Career Use. Each resource has been cross-referenced to the career development steps outlined in Chap. 2 (Career Planning the Electronic Way) and Chap. 4 (Job Hunting the Electronic Way). By noting the career use code(s) assigned to any resource, and by using the cross-reference table (see page 245), you can quickly determine how any resource may be of use to you. The codes include:

Codes	Corresponding Step
	Chapter 2—Career Planning the Electronic Way
PA	Personality Assessment
OE	Occupational Exploration
OP	Occupational Profiling
DM	Decision Making
PL	Planning
	Chapter 5—Job Hunting the Electronic Way
SEG	Setting Employment Goals
PST	Building a Professional Support Team
RT	Researching Targets—Identifying Your Employment Value
CV	Communicating Your Value—Shining Your Light
IT	Interviewing

Special. Certain resources coded as "special" are available at a cost beyond that which most individuals are willing to pay for career guidance, or are more appropriate for use by career and employment guidance professionals. Therefore, the items may be of more interest to companies and organizations that work with career planners and/or job seekers, and who have allocated budgets capable of purchasing such items.

Source. The name, address, phone number (and, if available and appropriate, the fax number and/or BBS number) of the company, organization, or individual offering the resource for sale.

Contact. The name of the person (or department) you should contact if you have questions about the resource. *Note:* If contacting the source for the purpose of ordering the resource, you should ask for Customer Service, *not* the contact name listed.

Description. Information regarding the use and value of the resource for career planners and job seekers.

Cost. The cost of the resource.

How to Obtain Resources

Many resources, especially software programs, CD-ROM discs, audiocassettes, and videotapes, can be obtained locally through various commerical retail stores. For other resources, contact the source listed in the profile.

Individual Purchase vs. Borrowing. Most of the resources found in this chapter are priced within the budget of most career planners and job seekers. However, some resources come with a high price tag. These expensive resources are not usually marketed to individual consumers, rather they are sold to schools, colleges, universities, libraries, companies, private employment services, and other similar corporate buyers. If you identify a resource that you would like to use, but determined that it is priced beyond your budget, it is suggested that you call various locations in your community to determine if the resource is available for your use at that facility. In the case of schools, colleges, universities, and libraries, you should be able to use the resource at no cost, or at a reasonable cost. In most cases, you will have to travel to the facility to use the resource, as the use of these resources is usually restricted to on-site use only.

Special Items. Some resources will have little or no direct value to individual career planners and job seekers. These resources are coded as "special." These resources are much more suited to the personnel management needs of companies and organizations. For example, a resume tracking program designed to enable companies to better manage the influx of resumes is of little value to the individual job seeker. However, it can be of great value to companies and organizations that wish to better manage the candidate application and screening process. Considering that this chapter will be used by individuals other than job seekers, it was determined to include these "special" listings.

Updating Service. Electronic resources for career planners and job seekers are being developed daily! Quarterly updates to this book are in development. If you would like to have your name added to the list of individuals who will be notified when each update is ready for distribution, please email your request to the author (James Gonyea) on America Online at screen name "CareerDoc." You will receive information by return email regarding when the next update will be available and how you may obtain a copy.

Recommended Resources. If you discover electronic resources that are not in this book, we would like to hear of them for possible inclusion in a future edition. Please send as much information as you can to the author, either by email or by regular mail.

!TRAK-IT AT;

Format: Software
Reader Response: P001
Career Use: Special
Source: !Trak-It Solutions
   485 Pala Avenue
   Sunnyvale, CA 94086
   Voice: 408-737-9454
   Fax: 408-737-9456

Contact: Carlene Enydey, Vice-President

Description: !Trak-It AT virtually automates all the time-consuming tasks associated with recruiting and screening new employees. The system tracks all pertinent applicant, recruiter, cost, and job requisition information, such as applicant skills, educational background, job titles, former employers, invitation schedules, resumes on hand, routing paths, employment letters, and status history, follow-up notes, and more.

AbraScan Resume Scanning System creates a direct connection between !Trak-It AT and the company's optical scanner to speed applicant data input as well as providing on-line resume review and searches.

Cost: A $25 Evaluation System for each product includes the user manual and actual running software with sample data.

"FIND-IT-511"

Format: Job Hotline
Reader Response: P002
Career Use: RT
Source: InfoVentures of Atlanta
   44 Broad St., NW
   Suite 710
   Atlanta, GA 30303-9718
   Voice: 404-222-2000

Contact: Jennifer Easterly

Description: "Find-It-511" is an interactive telephone service by Bell South/Cox Communications joint venture. "Find-It-511" provides a wide variety of information through the phone. Job seekers may call to obtain information regarding employment positions available from Georgia employers.

Cost: 50 cents per call.

//CAREER

Format: Database
Reader Response: P003
Career Use: OE, OP, SEG, RT, CV, IT
Source: Dow Jones News/Retrieval
   Dow Jones Business Information Services
   PO Box 300
   Princeton, NJ 08543
   Voice: 609-520-4638
   Fax: 609-520-4660

Contact: Customer Service
   Voice: 800-522-3567
   Fax: 609-520-4775

Description: //Career is a menu-driven database providing information from the National Business Employment Weekly (NBEW). Included in this database is NBEW Online, which contains timely articles on career management from the National Business Employment Weekly. //Career also offers regular reports on quarterly employment prospects as well as special reports on pertinent topics of interest to career planners and job seekers. Talent for Hire (situations-wanted ads from the NBEW) is also carried and updated monthly. Talent for Hire is a listing of professionals, managers, and executives nationwide who are in search of employment. Further, //Career offers articles

on how to tailor your resume to respond to an employer's specific needs; 10 rules for winning interviews; what to look for and what to avoid in advance-fee job-search services; hiring someone to write your resume; a guide to resume databases; and help writing a cover letter that will stand out. Job seekers may obtain software to access the service through a computer modem.
Cost: $19.95 annual fee plus $1.50/1000 characters of information.

1ST PLACE!

Format: Software
Reader Response: P004
Career Use: Special
Source: Academic Software
   PO Box 201958
   Austin, TX 78720-1958
   Voice: 512-918-8101
   Fax: 512-918-8118

Contact: Customer Service

Description: 1st Place! is an integrated software program designed for use by career placement services to increase the ability of the service to quickly and effectively match employers with job seekers. It allows instant matching between candidate profiles and various job criteria established by employers. A request for information from either an employer or job seeker can be filled instantly and with minimal staff participation. Students register using a disk-based procedure, which can store either a resume, an application, or a combination of both.
Cost: $1975.00

A PRACTICAL GUIDE TO FINDING A JOB IN TODAY'S FRENZIED MARKET

Format: Audiocassette
Reader Response: P005
Career Use: CV
Source: Maximum Potential
   PO Box 24618
   Tempe, AZ 85285-4618
   800-809-0165

Contact: Joanne Hawes

Description: This audiocassette is jam-packed with proven strategies for landing the ideal job. Covers everything from writing an effective resume to selecting your references, working with recruiters, and responding to advertisements. Includes sample resumes that get results. Ideal for listening while commuting to and from work.
Cost: $7.00

ABI

Format: Database
Reader Response: P006
Career Use: SEG, RT
Source: American Business Information
   5711 South 86th Circle
   PO Box 27347
   Omaha, NE 68127
   Voice: 402-593-4500
   Fax: 402-331-1505

Contact: Bill Kerrey, Vice-President

Description: ABI has compiled a database of approximatly 10 million U.S. businesses. Each profile includes the following information: Company name, address, contact person, number of employees, and the primary business activity. The ABI database can be used by job seekers to identify companies that match their employment goals, as well as to obtain basic information about a particular company to prepare for the job interview.
Cost: Furnished upon request.

ACADEMIC POSITION NETWORK

Format: On-line Database
Reader Response: P007
Career Use: RT
Source: William C. Norris Institute
      Suite 1548
      1 Appletree Square
      Bloomington, MN 55425
      Voice: 612-853-0225
      Fax: 612-853-0287
      Email: APN@EPX.CIS.UMN.EDU

Contact: E. Rex Krueger, Ph.D., Executive Director

Description: The Academic Position Network (APN) is an on-line database service accessible worldwide through Internet. It provides notice of academic position announcements, including faculty, staff, and administrative positions. Included are announcements for post-doctoral positions and graduate fellowships and assistantships. The announcement of a vacancy can be emailed or faxed to the APN where it will be uploaded within 24 hours. Job seekers have access to the information through Internet. A received announcement will be confirmed and will be provided with the written ad.

Cost: No cost to the job seeker. Service fees for placement of position announcements are as follows:
      One position $95
      Two positions $170
      Three positions $225
      Four or more positions $70 each when placed at the same time.
      Volume rates are available.

ACCESS ATLANTA

Format: On-line Database
Reader Response: P008
Career Use: SEG, RT
Source: Atlanta Journal-Constitution
      72 Marietta Street
      Atlanta, GA 30303
      Voice: 404-526-5151
      Voice: 404-526-5897
      Fax: 404-526-5258

Contact: David Scott, Publisher, Electronic Information Services

Description: The Atlanta Journal-Constitution provides an on-line database that allows job seekers an opportunity to access help wanted ads. This service is also accessible to Prodigy members.

Cost: $4.95 to $6.95/mo.

ACCESS ... FCO ON-LINE

Format: On-line Database
Reader Response: P009
Career Use: RT
Source: Federal Research Service, Inc.
      PO Box 1059
      Vienna, VA 22180-1059
      Voice: 800-822-JOBS
      Voice: 703-281-0200
      Fax: 703-281-7639

Contact: Nancy Cox, Vice-President/General Manager

Description: Access . . . FCO On-Line is a searchable database of thousands of federal job vacancies updated each weekday. Job seekers may search by GS Series, grade, location, eligibility, agency, or a combination of all. ACCESS is available 24 hours a day, 7 days a week through modem and an IBM compatible PC. ACCESS . . . FCO On-Line is used by individual job seekers and those organizations that aid job seekers in finding employment with the federal government. Hundreds of Federal Career Transition Centers subscribe to and use ACCESS to meet their outplacement needs.

Cost: Individual rates: $45/hr, $85/2 hrs, $120/3 hrs, $150/4 hrs. Unlimited monthly use—$50. New individual accounts pay a $25 set-up fee. Institutional rates available, call for details.

ACHIEVING YOUR CAREER

Format: Software
Reader Response: P010
Career Use: PST, RT, CV, IT
Source: Up Software, Inc.
      722 Lombard Street, #204
      San Francisco, CA 94133
      Voice: 800-959-8208
      Fax: 415-921-0939

Contact: Customer Service

Description: Achieving Your Career organizes the fundamentals of an effective job search to provide added inspiration for achieving one's career goals. The program contains 11 tools: resume templates; letter templates; database of 800 national companies; daily, weekly, and yearly calendars; contact and job lead tracking; progress summaries; research (on-line services, libraries, and magazines); interview questions; negotiation techniques, calling the right people and being remembered; and learning and evaluation. Career planners can furnish assignments and review printed reports, while job seekers can focus their energies for the best results.

Cost: $49.00

ADCo/ADVANCED CONCEPTS SERVICES

Format: On-line Database
       Software
Reader Response: P011
Career Use: RT
Source: ADCo/Advanced Concepts Services
      Dept. AC2
      PO Box 3281
      Lynnwood, WA 98046
      Voice: 206-546-8665
      Fax: 206-365-5055
      CompuServe 76020,3062

Contact: Nick Pearson

Description: ADCo/Advanced Concepts Services maintains a database of U.S. Government job openings provided by the Office of Personnel Management. The database, which is updated daily, is offered on PC diskettes (3.5" and 5.25" in both high density and double [low] density). Also offered is an electronic Career Guide which, in conjunction with the jobs database, provides job seekers with all the required information necessary to apply for a U.S. Government job.

Cost: $9.95

ADDRESS BOOK FOR WINDOWS

Format: Software
Reader Response: P012
Career Use: RT, CV
Source: Parsons Technology
      One Parsons Drive
      PO Box 100

Hiawatha, IA 52233-0100
Voice: 800-223-6925
Fax: 319-395-0102

Contact: Customer Service

Description: Address Book For Windows is an expandable database for storing names, addresses, and phone numbers of individuals and organizations. The program permits the organizing of names into categories, supplies a record finding feature and includes the capability to dial phone numbers automatically. Job seekers can build a database of contacts containing a virtual unlimited number of records. Address Book For Windows even includes a memo pad to make notes pertinent to individual records, such as best time of day to call.

This is an excellent program for keeping track of all the people one comes into contact with in the course of conducting career exploration and/or searching for employment.

Cost: $29.00

AIA ONLINE

Format: Software
On-line Database
Reader Response: P013
Career Use: SEG, CV
Source: American Institute of Architects
10550 Richmond Avenue, Suite 250
Houston, TX 77042
Voice: 800-864-7753
Voice: 202-626-7491
Fax: 202-626-7518

Description: AIA Online is an information and communication service accessible by modem-equipped computers. The service allows job seekers to search for available positions, employers to post help wanted ads, and individuals to obtain an electronic profile directory of architecture firms.

Cost: $25.00 per month plus 10 cents per minute for on-line use or 75 cents per minute flat rate.

AM/2000

Format: Software
Reader Response: P014
Career Use: Special
Source: SPECTRUM Human Resources Systems Corporation
1625 Broadway, Suite 2700
Denver, CO 80202
Voice: 800-477-3287
Fax: 303-592-3227

Contact: Suzanne Smith

Description: AM/2000 is a software program that allows employers to streamline their recruitment process by providing an Applicant Management System. AM/2000 allows a company to easily locate the status of any requisitions and current applicants based on various criteria, record and provide detailed information on education, work history, technical and professional skills, personal background, preferences, etc. Further, the system prepares and processes letters, labels, EEO/AAP information, and more. SPECTRUM also develops and markets other software systems relating to Human Resource management.

Cost: $6200.00

ANYTIME 2.0 FOR WINDOWS

Format: Software
Reader Response: P015
Career Use: RT
Source: Individual Software Incorporated
5870 Stoneridge Drive, #1

Pleasanton, CA 94588-9900
Voice: 800-822-3522

Contact: Customer Service

Description: AnyTime 2.0 for Windows is a personal organizer designed to make it easy for users to organize their schedules in the way that works best for them (7 view and enter options plus over 40 layout options). AnyTime has three main components: day planner, address book, and to-do list. The Quick Glance feature gives users a daily, weekly, monthly, or annual view of their schedule in either graph or calendar form and allows automatic revisions. Layouts can be designed from customized fonts, borders, colors. Schedules and calendars can be printed to fit popular paper-based organizers. Extra tools included with AnyTime are alarm reminder, warning of conflicting/overlapping appointments, search function, and automatic rollover of unfinished tasks.

Cost: $49.95

ATS-PRO

Format: Software
Reader Response: P016
Career Use: Special
Source: Human Resource MicroSystems
  160 Sansome Street, Suite 1450
  San Francisco, CA 94104
  Voice: 800-972-8470
  Voice: 415-362-8400
  Fax: 415-362-8595

Contact: Priscilla Eshelman, Marketing Manager

Description: Human Resources MicroSystems (HRMS) has developed ATS-Pro, a comprehensive applicant and requisition tracking system used by human resource and recruiting professionals. Developed in Microsoft FoxPro, ATS-Pro is available for Windows, DOS, and Macintosh users, either on a stand-alone PC or on a network. ATS-Pro matches applicants to openings by user-defined criteria and generates job postings, applicant correspondence, and interview schedules. ATS-Pro tracks the time and cost to fill job openings, analyzes recruiter effectiveness, documents all contact with applicants, and meets AA/EEO requirements.

Cost: Single user DOS and Macintosh ATS-Pro: $3500. Single user Windows ATS-Pro: $5000.

BASIC GUIDE TO RESUME WRITING AND JOB INTERVIEWS, THE

Format: Videotape
Reader Response: P017
Career Use: RT, CV, IT
Source: Vocational Biographies
  PO Box 31
  Sauk Centre, MN 56378-0031
  Voice: 800-255-0752
  Fax: 612-352-5546

Contact: Customer Service

Description: The Basic Guide to Resume Writing and Job Interviews is a 45-minute video teaching guide on how to find employment. It offers clear, practical tips and interesting examples. The video was written and produced by on-the-job employment professionals to ensure practical real-life advice.

Cost: $89.00

BEST DIRECTORY OF RECRUITERS, THE

Format: Software
Reader Response: P018
Career Use: PST
Source: Gove Publishing Co.
  The Original Resume Co.

1105 Lakeview Avenue
Gorman-Litchfield Plaza
Dracut, MA 01826
Voice: 508-957-6600
Fax: 508-957-6605

Contact: Tomas P. Gove
Steve Alborghetti

Description: The Best Directory of Recruiters, marketed by The Original Resume, provides over 2475 Executive Recruiter, Employment Agency and Management Consulting companies in over 8000 listings sorted with specifics, by specialty discipline, focused expertise, and state. Examples of listings are: hi-tech, medical, engineering, retail, energy, administration, general and international. The Best Directory provides the mailing address—most with key contact names in the organization—65 percent of the listings contain telephone and fax numbers. The company claims, "This is the most comprehensive publication known of this type available in computer disk available for computer merge flexibility ... the information provides the most cost effective impact for job seekers pursuing professional search organizations and companies looking for individuals with specific expertise and is a powerful outplacement publication."

Cost: Software—$99.99 plus shipping and handling. Discounts available for quantity.

BIO SCAN ON DISK AND BIO SCAN ONLINE

Format: Software
On-line computer database
Reader Response: P019
Career Use: SEG, RT
Source: Oryx Press
4041 N. Central Ave.
Suite 700
Phoenix, AZ 85012-3397
Voice: 800-279-6799
Fax: 800-279-4663

Contact: Karen Parry, Customer Service Director
Voice: 602-265-2651, ext. 621
Fax: 602-265-6250

Description: BioScan OnLine and BioScan on Disk are different versions of the same data. Both formats allow users to search (by an on-line database or as a downloaded file to a personal computer) an extensive database of company profiles and select companies according to various criteria, such as by business strategy, principal investors, agreements, products in development, R&D, investments, city, state, personnel, etc. Additional databases including business news are available. This service is primarily used by recruiters and agencies to gather background information useful in advising and preparing job seeking candidates for the interview process.

Cost: Approximately $1500.00

BROADCAST EMPLOYMENT WEEKLY

Format: BBS Job Hotline
Reader Response: P020
Career Use: RT
Source: Broadcast Employment Weekly
1125 W. Boone Ave.
Nampa, ID 83651-1812
Voice: 800-922-5627
Voice: 208-463-1951
Fax: 208-467-4097
BBS: 208-467-4110

Contact: Brian Denny, President

Description: Broadcast Employment Weekly is a Broadcast-Based job listing service. Listings from employers are entered into a database where they may be accessed by job seekers by BBS or Phone Hotline. Employment openings are available for radio stations (any position) and television stations (in Maintenance Engineering only) and cover positions from employers of the job listings available.

Cost: Subscription for the job seeker : $25 to $30 depending on the service.

BUILDING YOUR JOB SEARCH FOUNDATION

Format: Software
Reader Response: P021
Career Use: RT, CV
Source: Up Software, Inc.
       722 Lombard Street, #204
       San Francisco, CA 94133
       Voice: 800-959-8208
       Fax: 415-921-0939

Contact: Customer Service

Description: Building Your Job Search Foundation steps you through 192 key questions that strengthen the fundamentals of your job search. The program is divided into 16 sections (e.g., resume, letters, contacts, research, interview, negotiate, etc.), each developing skills and demanding time, thinking, and commitment. The objective of the program is to help job seekers more fully understand the fundamental concepts involved in an effective job search strategy. The program can be used by career planners for client assignments and print out results for progress review.

Cost: $29.95

BURWELL DIRECTORY OF INFORMATION BROKERS

Format: Software
       On-line Database
Reader Response: P022
Career Use: OP, SEG, RT
Source: Burwell Enterprises, Inc.
       3724 FM, 1960 West, Suite 214
       Houston, TX 77068
       Voice: 713-537-9051
       Fax: 713-537-8332

Contact: Joanne Pauline, Marketing Director

Description: The Burwell Directory on Disk is a full text searchable electronic version of Burwell's hard-bound annual directory. A PC diskette version is also available in 3.5″. The Directory provides contact information on more than 1500 information and research firms, as well as narrative descriptions of each firm's services and areas of expertise. The sophisticated job seeker or career planner can utilize Burwell's Directory to locate the precise firms which, in turn, can provide valuable research data on companies and potential employers. Burwell Enterprises is also a full-service information broker, providing on-line research for job seekers and career planners.

Cost: *The Burwell Directory of Information Brokers* (on disk) - $150. Book - $85. Book and Disk - $195. On-line searches —Call for estimate.

BUSINESS AMERICA ON CD-ROM

Format: CD-ROM
Reader Response: P023
Career Use: RT
Source: American Business Information
       5711 S. 86th Circle
       Omaha, NE 68127
       Voice: 402-593-4565
       Fax: 402-331-6681

Contact: Optical Products Division

Description: Business America on CD-ROM is a database of approximately 10 million U.S. businesses including company name, full address, contact name, title, phone, number of employees, sales volume, SIC code, and credit score. Searches can be made based on various criteria to provide targeted data for the job seeker or recruiter. A related component is American Yellow Pages on CD-ROM. American Yellow Pages includes the company name, address, phone, and SIC/Yellow Page heading. Information can be displayed or downloaded to a diskette or hard drive. The database is leased on a yearly basis. Semi-annual updates are provided.

Cost: $7500/year.

BUSINESS DATELINE

Format: On-line Database
CD-ROM Disk
Magnetic Tape
Reader Response: P024
Career Use: SEG, RT
Source: UMI
300 North Zeeb Road
Ann Arbor, MI 48106
Voice: 800-521-0600
Fax: 313-761-2920

Contact: Sales Department

Description: Business Dateline is an information database that provides access to complete articles drawn from over 450 regional business journals including business magazines, daily newspapers, and business wire services. Business Dateline can help research company executives, private industries/companies, or research a company's expansion plans or market share to assist the job seeker in his total interview preparation. This service, which is designed for use by both the job seeker and employer, can be accessed by purchasing a CD-ROM disk with monthly updates; or on-line through Dialog, Dow Jones News Retrieval, Nexis; or by purchasing a magnetic computer tape. Also available are several CD-ROM databases including ABI/INFORM, which provides access to over 1000 key domestic and international business markets.

Cost: CD-ROM disk with monthly updates: $3150/year. On-line: based on on-line charges. Magnetic computer tape: varies.

C-LECT JR.

Format: Software
Reader Response: P025
Career Use: DM
Source: Chronicle Guidance Publications, Inc.
66 Aurora Street
PO Box 1190
Moravia, NY 13118-1190
Voice: 800-622-7284
Fax: 315-497-3359

Contact: Kathy Lloyd, Customer Service Manager

Description: C-LECT jr. is a career guidance software program that helps middle school, high school, and college students identify career options (from a database of 700 occupations) that match their self-knowledge. Students first complete a workbook survey (10 to 15 minutes to complete), and then enter their answers regarding their preference for temperaments, interests, and educational choices into the software program. C-LECT jr. then selects appropriate occupations and prints the job titles for review and exploration. Students may check C-LECT jr.'s Career Profile Guide for details on any one of the 700 occupations contained in the database. The 700 jobs database represents approximately 90 percent of all occupations found in the American workplace.

Cost: $199.90 (includes software, 30 Student Workbooks, a Career Profile Guide, and an Instructor's Manual).

CAREER CAPABILITY SEARCH

Format: Software
Phone Service/On-line Database
Fax Service
Reader Response: P026

Career Use: OE, OP, DM, PL
Source: CapCo
      The Capability Corporation
      East 5805 Sharp
      Suite 103
      Spokane, WA 99212
      800/541-5006
Contact: Customer Service

Description: The Career Capability Search is a unique service that provides career planners with information about themselves, occupations, and the community(ies) where they wish to work to make sound career decisions. By supplying information about one's work history and preferred work locations, Career Capability Search can generate as much as a 40-page report that analyzes the client's work history, and then lists occupations that match the client's background with long-term labor market projections related to the client's skills and desired work locations. Labor market information is available for 3100 U.S. cities and 185 Canadian locations. Career Capability Search is designed to be used in conjunction with the EZ-DOT and Job Search Service programs (see profiles elsewhere in this chapter).

Cost: Phone-In Service: $75.00/report
Mail/Fax-In Service: $65.00/report
Modem Dial-Up Service: $25.00/report

CAREER DATABASE

Format: Database
Reader Response: 027
Career Use: SEG, CV
Source: Career Database
      PO Box 626
      Provincetown, MA 02657
      Voice: 508-487-2238
      Fax: 508-487-0371
Contact: Allan Wimer, Managing Director

Description: Career Database is a computer database containing several thousand resumes. The computer selects relevant data from the database and formats it into a career profile, which is then supplied to recruiters and prospective employers worldwide. The service is available to job seekers in all career fields. Career profiles are faxed to employers within hours of a request. Additional services include resume review, critique and writing, identification of potential employers, job hunting administrative support services, and technical analysis of a job seeker's strategy.

Cost: $50/yr.—individual price for inclusion in database.

CAREER DESIGN

Format: Software
Reader Response: P028
Career Use: DM, SEG, CV, IT
Source: Career Design Software
      PO Box 95624
      Atlanta, GA 30347
      Voice: 800-346-8007
      Fax: 404-321-6474
Contact: Customer Service

Description: Career Design is a complete career planning and job search guidance software program. This program is designed to help individuals clarify their career direction and land the job they want. Users are guided in uncovering their top skills and interests, in identifying their preferences for a work environment, in locating employers that may be interested in what they can offer, and in learning about how to interview and negotiate for the best employment agreement. Career Design includes a variety of tools for making the career or job transition, such as automated letter and resume preparation, interview training, and personal financial planning.

    The program is based on career planning methods originally developed by John C. Crystal, a founding leader in the field of job hunting techniques, and later popularized by Richard M. Bolles in his best selling book (*What Color Is Your Parachute?*). The techniques were also used by Crystal in his New York consulting firm to advise thousands of clients over the past 35 years.

Cost: $99.95

CAREER NAVIGATOR

Format: Software
Reader Response: P029
Career Use: CV
Source: Drake Beam Morin, Inc.
   PO Box 1400K
   Dayton, OH 45414
   800-345-JOBS

Contact: Customer Service

Description: Career Navigator is a software program that guides job seekers in conducting an effective job search. Using a built-in advice system, users are instructed in how to conduct a job search, how to write effective resumes and cover letters, how to handle an interview and negotiate a salary and benefits, and other related advice. Career Navigator includes a word processor with mail-merge capability, and a database for storing names and addresses of potential employers.

Cost: $49.95

CAREER OPTIONS

Format: Software
Reader Response: P030
Career Use: PA, OE, DM
Source: Peterson's
   202 Carnegie Center
   PO Box 2123
   Princeton, NJ 08543-2123
   Voice: 800-338-3282
   Fax: 609-243-2123

Contact: Customer Service

Description: Career Options guides users through the entire career selection process. The program helps to identify personal interests, skills, and preferences to find the best matching occupations. Career Options contains over 700 occupational descriptions including the education and training requirements necessary to pursue each career. The program is broad based, covering all training and educational levels.

Cost: $295.00

CAREER SEARCH

Format: On-line Database
Reader Response: P031
Career Use: SEG, RT
Source: Career Finders, Inc.
   21 Highland Circle
   Needham, MA 02194-3275
   Voice: 617-449-0312
   Fax: 617-449-4657

Contact: Theresa Gaudet/Sean Kavanagh

Description: Career Search provides an extensive database service whereby companies matching a job seeker's career objectives may be identified. This national employment search system provides an offline database search service with the option of downloading search results to a client's computer. Extremely rich in contact information, Career Search allows the job seeker, career planner, or recruitment agency to target potential employment opportunities using any number of criteria.

Cost: $4500/year and up.

CAREER SYSTEMS ONLINE

Format: BBS
Reader Response: P032
Career Use: RT
Source: Systems Personnel
PO Box 63
Chicopee, MA 01014
Voice: 413-592-4069
Fax: 413-592-9255
Modem: 413-592-9208

Contact: Donna Frappier

Description: Career Systems Online provides free access through modem to job listings for experienced professionals seeking jobs in the fields of MIS, Programming, Software Engineering, and Software Development. Jobs are located throughout the United States. Qualified job seekers call using their computer modem to view job listings in any geographic area. Employers call through voice to list jobs. This service is provided without cost to either the job seeker or employer.

Cost: Free.

CAREERTRACK

Format: Videotapes
Audiotapes
Reader Response: P033
Career Use: CV, IT
Source: CareerTrack, Inc.
Executive Department
3080 Center Green Drive
Boulder, CO 80301-5408
Voice: 303-447-2323, ext. 6006
Voice: 800-334-1018 (information and tape orders)
Fax: 303-443-6347

Contact: Jeff Hildebrant, Corporate Development Specialist

Description: CareerTrack, producers of the well known General Business Skills Seminars service, offers a series of video and audio tapes to aid individuals develop more effective management, communications, and sales and personal development skills. Employers can utilize these tapes to enhance the productivity of their existing work force. Job seekers can also utilize the tapes to strengthen their own skills to give themselves an advantage in the job search process.

Cost: $29.95 to $249.95.

CHEMJOBS

Format: Software
On-line computer database
Reader Response: P034
Career Use: SEG, RT, CV
Source: American Chemical Society
1155 16th Street NW
Washington, DC 20036
Voice: 202-872-6208
Voice: 202-872-6213
Fax: 202-872-4529

Contact: Louis Carrille
Program Assistant or
Amy Frankart/Cyndi Davis

Description: ChemJobs is an on-line database of members of the American Chemical Society. Members may enter their resumes and employers may list announcements regarding job openings both in industry and academia. The database may be searched on-line or data may be obtained on diskette.

Cost: $40 to $50 for 3 month's subscription.

CLASSIFACTS

Format: Phone Service/On-line Database
Reader Response: P035
Career Use: SEG, RT
Source: North American Classifacts, Inc.
      2821 South Parker Road
      Suite 305
      Aurora, CO 80014
      800/789-8974

Contact: Customer Service

Description: ClassiFACTS is an employment information service under cooperative arrangement with dozens of the largest newspapers across the United States ClassiFACTS electronically compiles the help wanted ads from each newspaper into a single database. Job seekers may call a 1-800 number to have a search conducted of the database. ClassiFACTS contains approximately 125,000 ads updated weekly. Search results may be obtained by first class mail, next day, or second day delivery, or same day fax.

    (See the Job Seeker's PowerPak chapter for more information.)

Cost: $29.95 for a four week subscription, $4.95 for each additional week thereafter.

COLLEGE COST EXPLORER—FUND FINDER

Format: Software
Reader Response: P036
Career Use: PL
Source: College Board Publications
      Department A 10
      Box 886
      New York, NY 10101-0886
      800/323-7155 (credit card orders accepted)

Contact: Customer Service

Description: Fund Finder, an extensive software program from one of America's premiere educational publishers, guides college-bound and college students in identifying sources of financial aid, including scholarships, internships, grants, and loans from a database of 3000 private and public sources and 2800 two- and four-year college sources. Ideally suited for professionals who advise students and parents about financial aid and planning.

Cost: $495.00

COLLEGE EXPLORER PLUS

Format: Software
Reader Response: P037
Career Use: PL
Source: College Board Publications
      Department A 10
      Box 886
      New York, NY 10101-0886
      800-323-7155 (credit card orders accepted)

Contact: Customer Service

Description: College Explorer Plus is an interactive search software program designed to help students identify undergraduate colleges and/or graduate schools that can match their educational plans, objectives, and needs. The database contains information on over 2800 undergraduate colleges and 1200 graduate schools. Various search criteria may be used, such as field of study, location, setting, tuition and fees, housing, and so on, to identify colleges and schools that can meet the user's needs. Developed by one of America's leading educational publishers. Ideally suited for professional guidance counselors.

Cost: $295.00

COMPANY BACKGROUNDERS

Format: On-line Database
Reader Response: P038
Career Use: OP, SEG, RT, IT
Source: Company Backgrounders
      1364 Kathy Lane
      Sebastopol, CA 95472
      Voice: 800-544-5924
      Voice: 707-829-9421
      Fax: 707-823-2713

Contact: Amelia Kassel, President, Marketing Base

Description: Company Backgrounders provides an indepth "company research service" targeted to the specifications provided by job seekers. Company Backgrounders conducts research designed to obtain the information as requested by job seekers, and then prepares reports providing the requested information to aid job seekers in conducting an effective job search, including preparing for the interview process.

Cost: $150 to $300.

COMPANY CONNECTIONS, THE COVER LETTER

Format: Software
Reader Response: P039
Career Use: CV
Source: Cambridge Educational
      90 MacCorkle Avenue SW
      So. Charleston, WV 25328
      Voice: 800-468-4227
      Fax: 304-744-9351

Contact: Customer Service

Description: Company Connections, The Cover Letter guides job seekers in writing and customizing cover letters. The software program also explains the objectives and functions of the cover letter, optimizing the use of the cover letter in the job search process.

Cost: Apple and IBM 5.25″ = $59.00 plus $10.00 shipping and handling. IBM 3.5″ = $64.00 plus $10.00 shipping and handling.

COMPU-JOB

Format: Software
Reader Response: P040
Career Use: RT, CV, IT
Source: Cambridge Educational
      90 MacCorkle Avenue SW
      So. Charleston, WV 25328
      Voice: 800-468-4227
      Fax: 304-744-9351

Contact: Customer Service

Description: Compu-Job provides users with a means of establishing life and employment goals, and a method of organizing the entire job search process. Components contained in the software program aid in finding job openings, following up on job leads, developing resumes, completing applications, interviewing, following up on interviews, and developing good work habits and relationships.

Cost: $129.00 plus shipping and handling.

CORPORATE FACT FINDERS, INC.

Format: On-line Database
      Fax-Back Service
      Software

Reader Response: P041
Career Use: SEG, RT
Source: Corporate Fact Finders, Inc.
        884 Westtown Road
        West Chester, PA 19382
        Voice: 800-220-3228
        Voice: 610-431-3708
        Fax: 610-431-0674

Contact: Sharon Dean, President
        Pam Baxter, Director of Finance and Marketing

Description: Corporate Fact Finders provides a custom research and analysis service for business: marketing and industry intelligence, including forecasts and statistics. Lists of targeted companies can also be obtained. The service can be utilized by job seekers, career planners, and employers as well. The information can be obtained on PC 3.5" HD disks; accessed from on-line database by Dialog, Dow Jones, Data Star, Data Times, Lexis/Nexis, and Newsnet; and by a Fax-Back service. Corporate Fact Finders can also be reached by CompuServe 75130,3644.

Cost: Minimum Fee—$500 prepaid for first project. Rush jobs add 25 percent of basic charges. For multiple projects the cost is negotiable.

CORPORATE JOBS OUTLOOK

Format: On-line Database
Reader Response: P042
Career Use: SEG, RT
Source: Corporate Jobs Outlook
        PO Drawer 100
        Boerne, TX 78006
        Voice: 210-755-8810
        Fax: 210-755-2410
        Voice: 800-638-8094 for HRIN

Contact: Jack W. Plunkett

Description: Corporate Jobs Outlook is a bi-monthly electronic on-line newsletter detailing hiring, training, advancement opportunities, salaries, benefits, and corporate culture at fast-growing American corporations. The service provides Human Resources contacts, corporate growth and hiring plans, description of business, including marketing, manufacturing, distribution, and data processing. The service further details the number of women and minorities in top posts; lists specific hiring and training methods and programs. Corporate Jobs Outlook is one of several database services offered by HRIN, the Human Resource Information Network, and is available on-line.

Cost: $169.99 yearly.

CORPTECH

Format: On-line Database
        Software
        CD-ROM
Reader Response: P043
Career Use: SEG, RT
Source: Corporation Technology Information Services, Inc.
        12 Alfred St., Suite 200
        Woburn, MA 01801-1915
        Order: 800-333-8036
        Voice: 617-932-3939
        Fax: 617-932-6335

Contact: Matt Blair, Account Executive

Description: CorpTech surveys 36,000 high-technology emerging companies each year with the objective of identifying the industry, products, size, and employment growth of each company. This information is available to job seekers, career planners, recruiters, and outplacement agencies on IBM PC (all diskette sizes), CD-ROM, On-line, and Internet (anticipated as of this writing).

Cost: Electronic CEO names from $195 to $6500 for all 36,000 companies electronically on a mobile hard disk. On-line access through DataStar is $3.00 per company profile.

CORS

Format: On-line Database
Reader Response: P044
Career Use: CV
Source: Cors
        Suite 300 East
        Itasca, IL 60143
        Voice: 708-250-8677
        Voice: 800-323-1352
        Fax: 708-250-7362

Contact: Customer Service

Description: Cors offers a full range of recruitment research services. For job seekers, a resume database contains over 15 million resumes which are sorted through a variety of means including government OCC and SIC codes, background skills, salary, and educational background. Cors also offers, for the employer, Recruitment Research Products, Multicultural Workforce Programs data, and Recruitment Intelligence Programs data in ASCII format if requested by the company/recruiter.

Cost: Resume database: $25. Research Intelligence: $500 to $6000. Updates: Free.

DATA SEARCH

Format: On-line Database
Reader Response: P045
Career Use: OP, SEG, RT
Source: Data Search
        170 Lexington Dr.
        Ithaca, NY 14850
        Voice: 607-257-0937
        Internet: Suef@tc.cornell.edu
        CompuServe: 70761,2055

Contact: Susan E. Feldman, Principal Associate

Description: Data Search researches various databases and provides information to job seekers, career planners, and employers. Data Search specializes in hard-to-find, unpublished information and serves as a total resource center. Job seekers who need background information on companies and other topics in order to appear knowledgeable for an interview or to make sound career choices may obtain data on diskette or on-line through the Internet.
Cost: $250 minimum.

DATABASE AMERICA

Format: Software
Reader Response: P046
Career Use: SEG
Source: Database America
        100 Paragon Drive
        Montvale, NJ 07645
        Voice: 800-223-7777 (in NJ, 201-476-2300)
        Fax: 201-476-2419

Contact: Steve Pullen, Sales Manager

Description: Database America offers a business database of over 10 million U.S. companies which may be selected by size of company, sales volume, geography (state, city, or zip code), and by business category. The information may be used for research, direct mail, or telemarketing campaigns. Customers may obtain data on diskette, CD-

ROM, 3x5 cards, or "peel-and-stick" labels.

Cost: Furnished upon request.

DIAL-A-JOB

Format: Job Hotline
Reader Response: P047
Career Use: SEG
Source: National Association of Interpretation
   PO Box 1892
   Fort Collins, CO 80522
   Voice: 303-491-6434
   Fax: 303-491-2255
   Hotline: 303-491-7410

Contact: Philip B. Tedesco, Office Manager

Description: Dial-A-Job is a service of the National Association of Interpretation whereby job seekers may access through recorded messages information about career, seasonal, and part-time positions submitted by various employers. Positions are from interpretation, environmaental education, and related fields. The listing is updated weekly.

Cost: All NAI members receive 10 weeks free per year. Otherwise, $10 per week. Positions may be listed at $10 per week, 2-week minimum.

DIAL-JAN

Format: BBS
Reader Response: P048
Career Use: Special
Source: Job Accommodation Network
   West Virginia University
   918 Chestnut Ridge Rd., Suite 1
   PO Box 6080
   Morgantown, WV 26506-6080
   Voice: 800-ADA-WORK
   Voice: 800-232-9675
   Voice or TDD: 800-526-7234 US
   Voice or TDD: 800-526-2262 Canada
   BBS: 800-DIAL-JAN
   Fax: 304-293-5407

Contact: Anne Hirsch, Barb Judy, or D. J. Hendricks
   Voice: 800-526-7234
   Fax: 304-293-5407

Description: Dial-Jan is a service sponsored by The President's Committee on Employment of People with Disabilities. Dial-Jan is a computer-based bulletin board offering information regarding possible accommodation technology and technique options for individuals with disabilities, as well as for individuals working and assisting individuals with disabilities.
Cost: Free.

DIALOG INFORMATION SERVICES

Format: On-line Databases
Reader Response: P049
Career Use: OE, OP, SEG, PST, RT
Source: Dialog Information Services, Inc.
   A Knight-Ridder Company
   Worldwide Headquarters
   3460 Hillview Avenue
   PO Box 10010

Palo Alto, CA 94303-0993
Voice: 800-3-DIALOG; 800-334-2564
Voice: 415-858-3785
Fax: 415-858-7069
DialSearch: 800-6-DIALOG; 800-634-2564
Contact: Sales Department

Description: DIALOG is a comprehensive on-line information source comprising 450 databases containing over 330 million articles, abstracts, and citations with particular emphasis on general news, business, science, and technology information. For career planners and job seekers, DIALOG can provide vast amounts of data on employers, industry trends, and other information to assist in targeting employment opportunities and preparing for interviews.

Cost: $295 start-up fee includes training, search documentation, and $100 of connect time credit. Renewal: $75/password.

DIRECT LINK

Format: Database
Job Hotline
Reader Response: P050
Career Use: OE, OP, PL, SEG, RT
Source: Direct Link for the Disabled, Inc.
PO Box 1036
Solvang, CA 93464
Voice: 805-688-1603
Fax: 805-686-5285
Contact: Linda Lee Harry, Executive Director

Description: Direct Link maintains an extensive database of information regarding disabilities. Employers can access Direct Link to obtain information on the American Disabilities Association. Job seekers and career planners can find resources for job training and placement, occupational skill training, and vocational rehabilitation.

Cost: No charge to the disabled or their family. Fees for professional use are furnished upon request.

DIRECTORY OF TOP COMPUTER EXECUTIVES

Format: Software
Reader Response: P051
Career Use: SEG, RT
Source: Applied Computer Research
11242 N. 19th Ave.
Phoenix, AZ 85029
Voice: 800-234-2227
Voice: 602-995-5929
Fax: 602-995-0905
Contact: Marketing Department

Description: The Directory of Top Computer Executives is a database available on diskette primarily for employers. Job seekers might also benefit from utilization of the data which provides contact names of MIS personnel in organizations across the country.

Cost: Diskettes from databases begin at $2000.

DUN'S MILLION DOLLAR DISK and MIDDLE MARKET DISK

Format: CD-ROM
Software
Reader Response: P052
Career Use: SEG, RT
Source: Dun & Bradstreet Information Services
Three Sylvan Way

Parsippany, NJ 07054-3896
Voice: 201-455-1881
Voice: 800-526-0651
Fax: 201-605-6911

Contact: Joseph Coveny
Account Executive-U.S. Sales
Voice: 800-624-5669, ext. 6411

Description: Dun's Million Dollar Disk contains a database of information comprised of 228,000 company profiles and 600,000 executive listings. The Middle Market Disk is a database of 150,000 company profiles and 400,000 executive listings. Both disks contain a custom report writer and free quarterly updates. Armed with the data contained on these disks, job seekers can target their executive job search in an informed manner to identify potential employers that match their career interests and needs.

Cost: Million Dollar Disk-$5295 (lease), Middle Market Disk-$3500 (lease).

E-SPAN

Format: On-line Database
Reader Response: P053
Career Use: SEG, RT
Source: E-SPAN
8440 Woodfield Crossing
Suite 170
Indianapolis, IN 46240
800-682-2901

Contact: Customer Service

Description: E-SPAN maintains a database of employment opportunities (help wanted ads) on America Online and CompuServe. Job seekers who are members of these network services may search the database for job announcements that match their career objectives. The database is updated weekly and contains approximately 1000 ads per week covering various professional occupations and employers nationwide.

Cost: Only the cost of the America Online and/or CompuServe membership.

EASY WORKING INSTANT RESUME

Format: Software
Reader Response: P054
Career Use: CV
Source: Spinnaker Software
465 Medford Street
Charlestown, MA 02129-9808

Contact: Customer Service

Description: Easy Working Instant Resume (for DOS and Windows) is an easy-to-use software program for creating professional looking resumes. The program contains ready-made templates to help users quickly create their own resumes. A spell checker and action words glossary are included to polish your resume. Change formats with a single click of your mouse. An on-line job hunting guide is also included offering advice regarding how to manage one's job search, succeed in the interview, and other important tasks.

Cost: $19.99

EDG/CITIZENS' SERVICES

Format: Software
Database
Reader Response: P055
Career Use: SEG, RT
Source: R. A. Publishing
1555 Delaney Dr., Suite 104
Tallahassee, FL 32308
Voice: 904-922-5161

Voice: 904-488-6354
Voice: 904-893-1639 (Evenings)
Fax: 904-487-4145
CompuServe: 74252,2320

Contact: Raja Adhikari

Description: Edg/Citizens' Services maintains a database of job openings (state jobs for Florida and private sector jobs nationwide). Job seekers indicate what type of positions they are interested in finding, and Edg/Citizens' does the searching of the database. Resulting information can be transmitted to the job seeker on diskette or through the CompuServe network service.

Cost: $15 for a 4-week listing.

ELECTRONIC TRIB

Format: BBS
Reader Response: P056
Career Use: OP, DM, PL, RT, IT
Source: The Albuquerque Tribune
P.O. Drawer T
Albuquerque, NM 87103
Voice: 505-823-3664
Fax: 505-823-3689
Modem: 505-823-7700 300, 1200, 2400 baud
Modem: 505-823-7701 9600, 14400 baud

Contact: Roy Buergi, Electronic Trib Editor

Description: The Electronic Trib is the on-line service of the Albuquerque Tribune. The Electronic Trib holds archives of the job advice columns of the Scripps Howard News Service. The latest installment of each column is offered each week. The archives go back to October 1993. Job seekers are able to access the BBS by modem to utilize the job advice information for their job search or career planning needs.

Cost: $20 for 3 months, $35 for 6 months, $50 for one year.

EMPLOYABILITY INVENTORY SOFTWARE PROGRAM, THE

Format: Software
Reader Response: P057
Career Use: RT, CV, IT
Source: Education Associates, Inc.
8 Crab Road
P.O. Box Y
Frankfort, KY 40602
Voice: 800-626-2950
Fax: 502-227-8608

Contact: Customer Service

Description: The Employability Inventory is an interactive computer software program designed to provide real-life situations that the job seeker would encounter during a typical job search. By requiring the user to decide which course of action he or she would take for each situation, the program helps the user become more familiar with effective job search strategies.

Cost: $79.99—Apple & IBM, $99.99—Windows.

ENCYCLOPEDIA OF ASSOCIATIONS

Format: On-line Database
Reader Response: P058
Career Use: SEG, RT
Source: Gale Research
835 Penobscot Building
Detroit, Michigan 48226-4094
Voice: 800-877-GALE
Fax: 313-961-6348

Contact: Customer Service

Description: With the Encyclopedia of Associations On-Line, you can access the most comprehensive compilation of nonprofit membership organizations and associations—over 88,000 in the United States and worldwide. Each entry provides complete information on their scope and activities, size, budget, publications, conventions and meetings, as well as contact details. Trade associations are the number one source of networking opportunities, specific training, and job banks. This on-line service is ideal for job seekers who wish to secure employment with professional associations, and may be accessed by modem through the Dialog Information Service. To learn how to connect with Dialog, call 1-800-334-2564.

Cost: $1.40/minute.

EURO PAGES ON CD-ROM

Format: CD-ROM
Reader Response: P059
Career Use: SEG, PST
Source: ProPhone, Inc.
       8 Doaks Lane
       Little Habor
       Marblehead, MA 01945-9866
       800/99-CD-ROM

Contact: Customer Support

Description: With Euro Pages, job seekers can easily and quickly identify the phone numbers, names, and addresses of 150,000 European companies. This database is ideal for job seekers interested in identifying companies overseas.

Euro Pages, like its companion program Select Phone, provides a variety of ways in which information may be searched and obtained, and does not contain a "metering" system. Data are available for the single, one-time cost of the program and comes with unlimited use.

Cost: Free when purchased with Select Phone. Call for cost if you wish to purchase separately.

EXEC-PC BBS

Format: BBS
       On-line Database
Reader Response: P060
Career Use: OE, OP, SEG, RT
Source: Exec-PC
       Elm Grove, WI 53122
       Voice: 414-789-4200
       Voice: 800-EXECPC-1
       Modem: 414-789-4360 14,400bps V.32bis
       Modem: 414-789-4210 2400bps
       Modem: 414-789-4500 28,800bps V.fast

Contact: Customer Service

Description: Exec-PC is the world's largest BBS with on-line offerings including searchable databases where companies post job openings and job seekers post resumes. In addition, the Want Ad Conference, Job Discussion forum is devoted to discussion of all job search concerns. Exec-PC also lists tens of thousands of clip-art images appropriate for use with cover letters and resumes. An interesting new addition to this resource is the concept of floppy disk-based resumes. This experimental area provides demos showing how a graphical, musical, entertaining multi-media style presentation on disk might look.

Cost: Three different plans ranging from $4/hour (local access from anywhere in the United States) to $75/year, $25 for 3 months (modem access).

EXECUTIVE DESK REGISTER OF
PUBLICLY HELD CORPORATIONS, THE

Format: Software
       On-line Database

Reader Response: P061
Career Use: SEG, RT
Source: Demand Research Corporation
     625 North Michigan Avenue
     Chicago, IL 60611
     312-664-6500
Contact: Roy W. Bernstein

Description: The Executive Desk Register contains information on approximately 5200 U.S. corporations and financial institutions currently trading on the New York Stock Exchange, the American Stock Exchange, and the NASDAQ National Market System. Each record contains the following information: company name and address, telephone number with fax, ticker symbol and exchange, full name of CEO and CFO, and primary industry classification. Ideal for job seekers who wish to create specialized mailing lists of potential employers. Updated daily and published monthly.

In addition to diskette, this database is also available on America Online (see Career Center).

Cost: One-month edition: $59.95. Quarterly subscription: $100. 12-month edition: $249.

EXECUTIVE SEARCH SYSTEM

Format: Software
     On-line Database
Reader Response: P062
Career Use: PST, RT
Source: Custom Databanks, Inc.
     13925 Esworthy Road
     Germantown, MD 20874-3313
     301-990-4010 (credit card orders accepted)
Contact: Jane Lockshin, President

Description: The Executive Search System is a software program containing information on nearly 4000 executive recruiters across the United States. The data are updated six times per year to ensure accuracy. Recruiters can be identified using a variety of search criteria, including location, industry and position specialties, and minimum salary. Resulting search data may then be merged with a personal letter to enable users to generate unlimited letters, envelopes, and mailing labels in much less time than by conventional means.

The Executive Search System may also be accessed in the Career Center on America Online.

Cost: $150.00

EXEC-U-TRAK

Format: Phone Service/Database
Reader Response: P063
Career Use: SEG, RT, CV
Source: Healthcare Financial Managers
     2 West Brook Corporate Center
     Suite 700
     West Chester, IL 60154
     Voice: 800-252-HFMA, ext. 308
     Fax: 708-531-0032
Contact: Brenda Harris, Associate at extension 301

Description: Exec-U-Trak provides a database of job seekers to potential employers. Specializing in health care financial managers, this service has, in addition to the placement service, a resume review service which includes personal coaching, critical commentary, and cover letter assistance. Also, a National Opportunities Bulletin containing positions for health care financial managers is available. Data are accessed by employers and job seekers by phone.

Cost: Exec-U-Trak is free to Healthcare Financial Managers Members, $2100 to employers; Resume review is $125 to members and $175 to nonmembers; National Opportunities Bulletin is $75 to members, $125 to nonmembers.

EZ-DOT

Format: Software
Reader Response: P064
Career Use: PA, OE, DM
Source: CapCo
       The Capability Corporation
       East 5805 Sharp
       Suite 103
       Spokane, WA 99212
       800-541-5006

Contact: Customer Service

Description: EZ-DOT is intended for use primarily by career and vocational guidance professionals who wish to assist clients with career selection, job restructuring, recruitment and placement, development of training programs, or performance evaluation. As a career planning tool, EZ-DOT allows users to input information about their interests and preference for involvement with data, people, and things. The program then compares the user's input to a database of over 12,000 occupations and generates a list of career options that match. The system is based upon the Dictionary of Occupational Titles with extensive reports available on each occupation. EZ-DOT is designed to be used in conjunction with the Career Capability Search and Job Search Service programs (see profiles elsewhere in this chapter).

Cost: $295.00

F1 SERVICES

Format: Database
       Software
Reader Response: P065
Career Use: RT
Source: F1 Services
       3141 Hood Street
       Suite 610
       Dallas, TX 75219-5021
       Voice: 214-528-9895
       Fax: 214-528-9819

Contact: Chris Dobson / Rob Peden

Description: F1 Services provides custom research services utilizing on-line databases, especially profiles of companies for candidates for executive level positions. The data also prepare candidates for interviews by informing them of prospect companies' mode of operation, prospects, and problems. F1 Services is used by outplacement firms. The data can be accessed by diskette.

Cost: Depends on particular search, ranging from $100 to $500 per company.

FED WORLD

Format: BBS
Reader Response: P066
Career Use: OP, SEG, RT
Source: National Technical Information Service
       Dept. of Commerce
       5285 Port Royal Road
       Springfield, VA 22161
       Voice: 703-487-4608
       Fax: 703-487-4009
       Modem: 703-321-8020
       Telnet from Internet: FedWorld.gov

Contact: Paul Melton

Description: Fed World is an on-line service of government information (including the Federal Jobs Listing service) offered by the National Technical Information Service. The Jobs Listing is a database of jobs available with the federal government, listed by regions and state and updated daily. Fed World also provides information concerning many government systems. This information may be valuable to job seekers who need more information as to how to go about beginning a career within the federal government.
Cost: Free.

FEDERAL OCCUPATIONAL AND CAREER INFORMATION SYSTEM

Format: Software
Reader Response: P067
Career Use: OE, OP, DM, SEG, RT
Source: NTIS Federal Computer Products Center
     United States Department of Commerce
     National Technical Information Service
     5285 Port Royal Road
     Springfield, VA 22161
     800-553-6847 (credit card orders accepted)
Contact: National Technical Information Service

Description: The Federal Occupational and Career Information System (FOCIS) is a software program designed to help career planners and job seekers explore career options with the federal government. The program contains three modules: career guidance, occupational information, and tips on how to get a job with the federal government. Users are asked to respond to questions, and the program then provides a list of career options. Information on over 360 white collar occupations and 450 agencies is provided.
Cost: $55.00

GENERAL BUSINESS FILE

Format: CD-ROM
Reader Resource: P068
Career Use: OP, SEG, RT
Source: Information Access Company
     362 Lakeside Drive
     Foster City, CA 94404
     Voice: 415-378-5200
     Voice: 800-227-8431
     Fax: 415-378-5369
Contact: Account Representative

Description: General Business File is a fully integrated database covering all aspects of business, management, company, and industry information. Career planners and job seekers can search specific company facts from investment reports, corporate profiles, and newspaper and journal articles within the database. Both groups will find basic and detailed information that will aid them in locating individual companies and industries that match their job seeking goals. Information contained in the database can aid job seekers in identifying potential employers, as well as in preparing for interviews with employers.
Cost: $10,500 and up for a one-year subscription.

GROWTH SEARCH SYSTEM

Format: Software
Reader Response: P069
Career Use: RT
Source: Custom Databanks, Inc.
     13925 Esworthy Road
     Germantown, MD 20874-3313
     301/990-4010 (credit card orders accepted)

Contact: Jane Lockshin, President

Description: The Growth Search System is a software program containing information on over 2100 of the fastest growing companies located throughout the United States. Using any number of search criteria, including: location, industry specialties, geographic preferences, and number of employees, job seekers can easily identify potential employers. Resulting search data may then be merge with a personal letter to enable users to generate unlimited letters, envelopes, and mailing labels in much less time than conventional means.

Cost: $250.00

HEADSUP

Format: Fax Service
　　　　E-mail
Reader Response:　　P070
Career Use: OP, SEG, RT
Source: INDIVIDUAL, Inc.
　　　　84 Sherman Street
　　　　Cambridge, MA 02140-9885
　　　　Voice: 800-414-1000
　　　　Fax: 800-417-1000

Contact: Jim Leightheiser, Product Manager

Description: HeadsUp is a personalized interactive daily news service.Each job seeker/subscriber builds his personal profile of interest topics. Each weekday morning, HeadsUp uses its computers to scan and filter more than 300 news sources around the world resulting in a selection of articles which match the personal profile. HeadsUp is then sent to the subscriber by fax or email before 8 a.m. Job seekers can build their profiles with topics covering their job interests, skills, or their preferred industry to find new companies that are growing and in need of new employees.

Cost: $695/year (includes 160 full text retrievals and $3.95 per article thereafter) or $29.95/month (includes 1 full text retrieval and $4.95 per article thereafter).

HUMAN RESOURCE INFORMATION NETWORK

Format: On-line Database
Reader Resource: P071
Career Use: OP, SEG, RT, CV + Special
Source: ETSI
　　　　1200 Quince Orchard Blvd.
　　　　Gaithersburg, MD 20878
　　　　Voice: 301-590-2300
　　　　Voice: 800-638-8094
　　　　Fax: 301-990-8378
　　　　Telex: 44-6194 NATSTAGAIT
　　　　EasyLink: 6228-6860

Contact: Jay McIver, Marketing Director
　　　　Billie LaPlaca, Manager Customer Service

Description: The Human Resource Information Network (HRIN) is an on-line database covering almost all aspects of human resources. One file lists job openings from 100 newspapers. Another file provides job outlooks of occupations. Also provided are files of job titles and job descriptions. HRIN is available primarily to Human Resource Managers, recruiters, and career planners. HRIN can be accessed by computer modem.

Cost: Three basic subscription plans—call for details.

IFMA JOB REFERRAL SERVICE

Format: Database
　　　　Software
Reader Response: P072
Career Use: CV
Source: International Facility Management Association
　　　　1 East Greenway Plaza, Suite 1100

Houston, TX 77046-0194
Voice: 713-623-4362
Voice: 800-359-4362
Fax: 713-623-6124

Contact: Research Specialist

Description: IFMA maintains a database of resumes of facility managers. The database may be searched according to criteria established by employers who wish to find appropriate candidates. Copies of matching resumes are then provided to the employer.

Cost: No cost to the job seeker. $295 per search requested by employers.

INDUSTRIAL DIRECTORIES ON DISKETTE AND CD-ROM

Format: Software
CD-ROM
Reader Response: P073
Career Use: SEG, RT
Source: Manufacturers' News, Inc.
1633 Central Street
Evanston, IL 60201
708-864-7000

Contact: Customer Service

Description: Manufacturers' News, Inc. offers extensive lists of U.S. industrial companies on diskette and CD-ROM. Industries are arranged by state, and users may purchase as many state collections as desired. Companies may be identified by manufacturing product, zip code, city, county, number of employees, SIC codes, sales volume, square footage, ownership type, area code, and executive title. Mailing labels and reports may then be generated.

Cost: Cost varies depending on which collection is desired. Call for quotes.

INFOWORKS

Format: On-line Database
Reader Response: P074
Career Use: OP, SEG, PST, RT, IT
Source: Infoworks
2033 Clement Avenue
Suite 222
Alameda, CA 94501-1317
Voice: 510-865-8087
Fax: 510-865-8089

Contact: Deborah H. Bryant

Description: InfoWorks is an information service bureau that searches on-line databases for data requested by job seeker clients. The information is then used to prepare a "Value Report" for the job seeker to assist him or her with career planning or searching for employment, and preparing for interviews. The Value Report may be forwarded by electronic mail, file transfer, or fax.

Cost: Cost varies—contact for specific quotes.

INSTANT JOB WINNING LETTERS

Format: Software
Reader Response: P075
Career Use: CV
Source: Career Labs
9085 East Mineral Circle, Suite 330
Englewood, CO 80112
Voice: 303-790-0505
Voice: 800-723-9675
Fax: 303-790-0606

Contact: Bill Frank

Description: Instant Job Winning Letters is an easy-to-use software program based on Bill Frank's book, *200 Letters for Job Hunters*. With this program, job hunters can easily and quickly write, edit, and print 200 different job hunting letters.

Cost: $39.95

INTELLIVIEW

Format: Phone Service
Reader Response: P076
Career Use: Special
Source: Pinkerton Services Group
      6100 Fairview Road, Suite 900
      Charlotte, NC 28210-3277
      Voice: 800-528-5745
      Voice: 704-552-1119
      Fax: 704-554-1806

Contact: Tracy Godfrey, Account Manager, IntelliView Service
James W. MacKenzie, Vice-President

Description: IntelliView is a structured interview training service system utilizing a computer and phone touch pad. Focused questions attempt to train individuals in how to identify and deal with the most relevant and candid responses that can produce a successful employment interview. The system provides feedback information regarding key areas that the individual should address and strengthen during the interview and any follow-up sessions that may take place between the employer and the job seeker.

Cost: Customized application: $35,000 plus $7 to $15 per administration.
Generic/shelf version: $5 to $15 based on volume of use.

INTERCRISTO

Format: Database
Reader Response: P077
Career Use: RT, CV
Source: Intercristo
      The Christian Career Specialist
      19303 Fremont Ave. N.
      Seattle, WA 98133-9906
      Voice: 206-546-7330
      Voice: 800-251-7740
      Voice: 800-426-1342

Contact: Jane Henry, Promotional Coordinator

Description: Intercristo is a Christian job referral service utilizing a computer database. Intercristo lists thousands of job openings worldwide, for Christian, nonprofit organizations. A job seeker's skills, interests, and background are matched to current openings with the listed organizations. Intercristo also produces a Career Kit, a self-study guide which helps evaluate a job seeker's strengths and weaknesses from a Christian perspective. The Career Kit utilizes, in part, audiotapes.

Cost: $45.00 for a 3 months' subscription to the job referral service.

J.O.B.

Format: BBS
      Audiocassettes
Reader Response: P078
Career Use: OE, PL, SEG, CV, IT
Source: National Federation of the Blind
      1800 Johnson Street

    Baltimore, MD 21230
    Voice: 410-659-9314
    Voice: 800-638-7518
    BBS: 410-752-5011

Contact: Lorraine Rovig, Director

Description: J.O.B. provides services to U.S. residents who are blind and looking for employment. J.O.B. provides training in how to conduct an effective job search. Training is provided by cassettes and through their national job magazine, which is also available on cassette. Many other job-related services for the blind are also offered on cassettes and through a national BBS service called the NFB Net. Services are designed to assist both job seekers and employers.

Cost: Free.

JOB AND CAREER BBS LIST

Format: BBS
Reader Response: P079
Career Use: RT, CV
Source: Online Opportunities
        PO Box 17
        Downingtown, PA 19335
        Voice: 610-873-2168
        BBS: 610-873-7170

Contact: Ward Christman, Executive Director

Description: Get on-line access to the latest verified searchable list of hundreds of job and career-oriented BBSs. Full contact information and detailed description of services offered. Use this list to locate BBSs in your field of interest. The most difficult part of a job or career change is finding out where to look for more information; this guide will help you locate what is available on-line.

   Free Philadelphia area resume database (employers subscribe to review resumes). Over 5000 current employment ads on-line. Career and job search information, corporate and recruiter databases, and career counseling available on-line.

Cost: $5.00.

JOBBANK HOTLINE, THE

Format: Job Hotline
Reader Response: P080
Career Use: SEG, RT
Source: The California Chicano News Media Association
        727 West 27th Street
        Los Angeles, CA 90007
        Voice: 213-743-7158
        Fax: 213-744-1809

Contact: Al Reyes, Executive Director
Cozette Munatones, Educational Programs Coordinator

Description: The JobBank Hotline offers the California Chicano News Media Association members a toll-free, 24-hour hotline where they can access information regarding media job openings. Over 50 jobs per week are in every media field from TV, radio, print, education, advertising, and public relations. The jobs are targeted for experienced job seekers as well as beginners.

Cost: Free to CCNMA members (membership fees are $35 for journalists and associate members, and $10 for students).

JOB BANK USA

Format: Phone Service/On-line Database
Reader Response: P081
Career Use: SEG, RT, CV

Source: Job Bank USA
  1420 Spring Hill Road
  Suite 480
  McLean, VA 22102
  800-296-1USA

Contact: Customer Service

Description: Job Bank USA is an employment matching service providing services for job seekers, as well as employers. The Career Advancement Service assists job seekers in identifying employment opportunities that match their career goals. The Recruiting and Outplacement Services are designed to help employers find qualified candidates. Job Bank USA provides an electronic network to unadvertised positions in all professions, crafts, and trades, at all management and skill levels, from employers throughout the United States and overseas. Job seekers can obtain information and assistance via the phone.

Cost: $75.00 per year for the Career Advancement Service. Call for volume discounts and other service prices.

JOB HUNT

Format: Software
Reader Response: P082
Career Use: SEG, RT, CV
Source: Scope International, Inc.
  PO Box 25252
  Charlotte, NC 28229-5252
  Voice: 704-535-0614
  Voice: 800-843-5627 Orders only
  Fax: 704-535-0617

Contact: Customer Service

Description: Job Hunt is a software program that contains profile information on over 6000 American companies. The full contact information on these companies includes company name, address, phone and fax, and a description of the company's line of business. Profiles can be searched by region or type of industry (S.I.C. Codes). Job seekers can quickly create and print personalized, mail-merged cover letters, follow-up letters, or other kinds of letters. Job Hunt can also print mailing labels, return address labels, and envelopes. The software includes a telephone dialer for making follow-up calls and a word processor. Included is a coupon for a mail-in free resume writing disk.

Cost: $49.95

JOB HUNTER

Format: Software
Reader Response: P083
Career Use: CV
Source: RESUMate, Inc.
  PO Box 7438
  Ann Arbor, MI 48107
  800-530-9310 (credit card orders accepted)

Contact: Chuck Schaldenbrand

Description: Job Hunter is a software program designed specifically for job seekers. With Job Hunter, you may store and organize information on all the people you come into contact with during the course of your job search. Records can be easily edited and printed out. Individuals stored in the database can be easily found using various search functions, including key words. Program includes a calendar/daily planner, form letters, and mailing labels.

Cost: $39.95

JOB LINK

Format: Job Hotline
Reader Response: P084
Career Use: SEG, RT
Source: The Employment Paper

209 Sixth Avenue North
Seattle, WA 98109
Voice: 206-441-4545
Fax: 206-441-4226
Hot Line: 206-517-JOBS (5627)

Contact: Customer Service

Description: Job Link is the telephone hotline component of The Employment Paper serving the Puget Sound and Seattle, Washington, areas. Job Link allows job seekers to call in and preview the week's employment ads, 24 hours a day, 7 days a week.

Cost: Free.

JOB NET

Format: Database
Reader Response: P085
Career Use: SEG, RT, CV
Source: Lutheran Social Ministries
919 North 1st Street
Phoenix, AZ 85004
Voice: 602-258-7201
Fax: 602-258-7275

Contact: Sue Neighbors, Director

Description: Job Net is a multidenominational project under the auspices of the Lutheran Social Ministries of the Southwest, which provides no-cost, and low-cost services for job seekers. The services include: a local database for both employers and job seekers, access to huge national databases of employer ads and educational resources, weekly networking meetings where job seekers can encourage each other, and referral to other counseling and electronic resources. Low-cost and no-cost job seminars are also available. For more information on assistance, or starting a Job Net support group in your church, contact Job Net, 1900 West Grant Road, Tucson, AZ 85745-1197, or the source reference above.

Cost: No cost or low cost to the job seeker.

JOB POWER SOURCE

Format: CD-ROM
Reader Response: P086
Career Use: OE, OP, PL, SEG, RT
Source: InfoBusiness, Inc.
887 South Orem Blvd.
Orem, UT 84058-5009
800-657-5300
801-221-1100

Contact: Customer Services

Description: This multimedia CD-ROM is a comprehensive source of information for career planners and job seekers. This program will guide you through the process of identifying your skills and matching them to a database of over 12,000 occupations as a means of selecting a career goal. Included are 200 in-depth occupational profiles, guides for writing resumes and cover letters, techniques of using networking, and how to interview and negotiate a salary. The program contains the text of many top-selling career and job hunting books and two hours of full color video.

Cost: $49.95

JOB SEARCH SERVICE

Format: Software
Phone Service/On-line Database
Fax Service
Reader Response: P087
Career Use: SEG, RT, CV

Source: CapCo
  The Capability Corporation
  East 5805 Sharp
  Suite 103
  Spokane, WA 99212
  800-541-5006

Contact: Customer Service

Description: To use the Job Search Service (JSS), job seekers first provide information about themselves, their desired work locations and occupational goals. JSS then produces extensive reports outlining specific resume writing tips for each kind of position for which the job seeker wishes to apply. JSS also provides detailed labor market data for each occupation, and an extensive list of employers (names and addresses drawn from a database containing 9 million business listings) allowing access to the "hidden job market" in any one of 3100 U.S. cities and 185 Canadian locations. JSS is designed to be used in conjunction with the EZ-DOT and Career Capability Search programs (see profiles elsewhere in this chapter).

Cost: Phone-In Service: $50.00/report
Mail/Fax-In Service: $40.00/report
Modem Dial-Up Service: $25.00/report

JOB SEARCH SYSTEM

Format: Software
Reader Response: P088
Career Use: OE, DM, SEG
Source: West Virginia Research and Training Center
  West Virginia University
  806 Allen Hall
  PO Box 6122
  Morgantown, WV 26506
  304-293-5313

Contact: Don McLaughlin

Description: The Job Search System (version 1.1) is a comprehensive software program that enables individuals and career guidance professionals to identify occupations (by Dictionary of Occupational Titles) that match an individual's preference for any one of several work traits, such as: interests; aptitudes; working conditions; preference for working with data, people, and things; preference for reasoning, math, and language requirements; environmental work conditions; physical demands; temperaments; and vocational preparation levels. The user's selections are compared against a database of over 13,000 occupations and a list of matching jobs can be generated. A description of each occupation is also available.

Cost: $200.00 plus shipping and handling.

JOBBS! BBS

Format: BBS
Reader Response: P089
Career Use: SEG, RT
Source: Alpha Systems, Inc.
  1510 Oakfield Lane
  Roswell, GA 30075-3013
  Voice: 404-992-8663
  Fax: 404-992-8663
  Modem: 404-992-8937

Contact: Bill Griffin, Sysop/President

Description: JOBBS! BBS is the oldest employment bulletin board service in Atlanta, Georgia. JOBBS! lists thousands of job openings from around the country, mostly high tech and engineering. The BBS also offers free job hunting advice and is free to job seekers.

Cost: Free to job seekers.

JOBLINE

Format: Job Hotline
Reader Response: P090
Career Use: SEG
Source: The Corporation for Public Broadcasting
901 E Street, NW
Washington, DC 20004-2037
Voice: 202-879-9600
Fax: 202-783-1019
JOBLINE: 202-393-1045

Contact: Follow voice instructions.

Description: JOBLINE is a hotline service provided to give job seekers an opportunity to access job announcements at public radio and television stations around the country with only one phone call. The listed jobs are updated weekly and available 24 hours a day. Using a touch-tone phone, job seekers can access new jobs only, or jobs available by category.

Cost: Only the cost of the phone call.

JOBSOURCE

Format: On-line Database
Reader Response: P091
Career Use: SEG, RT, CV
Source: The Hannah Group, Inc.
PO Box 1039
East Lansing, MI 48826-1039
Voice: 517-333-9093
Fax: 517-355-6479
BBS: call
Internet address: call

Contact: Bob LaPrad, Executive Director

Description: JOBSource is a new BBS database for job seekers and employers that is accessible worldwide through the Internet. It is utilized primarily by colleges and universities, corporations, government agencies, human resource consultants, job services, and professional societies and has a high concentration of agricultural and natural science employment listings. Employers may post help wanted ads, and job seekers may review ads and post resumes online.

Cost: Call.

JOBTRAK

Format: On-line Database
Voice mail system
Reader Response: P092
Career Use: SEG, RT
Source: JOBTRAK
1990 Westwood Blvd., Suite 260
Los Angeles, CA 90025
Voice: 310-474-3377
Voice: 800-999-8725
Fax: 310-475-7912

Contact: Ken Ramberg, Chief Financial Officer

Description: JOBTRAK provides an on-line computer database that is accessible by college career centers, students, and alumni on-line by computer, hard copy, as well as by voice mail. Employers can have their job listings transcribed into the on-line database and electronically transmitted to their choice of 200 college and university career centers. Over 90,000 employers have advertised their part-time, temporary, summer, and career opportunities through JOBTRAK.

Cost: No cost to colleges, students, and alumni. The cost to advertise an employment opportunity starts at $12.50.

JOURNAL FINDER

Format: Fax-Back Service
Reader Response: P093
Career Use: OP, PL, SEG, RT
Source: Dow Jones & Company, Inc.
Business Information Services
PO Box 300
Princeton, NJ 08543-0300
800-445-9454 (credit card orders accepted)

Contact: Customer Service

Description: Journal Finder allows customers to call an 800 number to request searches for articles from the following Dow Jones Publications: *The Wall Street Journal*, Barron's, the Dow Jones News Service, *The Asian Wall Street Journal* and *The Wall Street Journal Europe*. Callers may request either a search for a specific article or for any articles related to a topic. This service is ideally suited for career planners and job seekers looking for information on a particular industry, occupation, or economic trend, or on various employers in the news. Articles may be returned by fax or mail.

Cost: Mail: $10 for first article, $7 for each additional article. Fax: $12 for first article, $9 for each additional article.

LESKO'S COMPUTERIZED FEDERAL DATA BASE FINDER

Format: Software
Reader Response: P094
Career Use: OE, OP, PL, SEG, RT
Source: InfoBusiness, Inc.
887 South Orem Blvd.
Orem, UT 84058-5009
800-657-5300
801-221-1100

Contact: Customer Services

Description: One in a series of award winning software programs authored by Mathew Lesko, the Federal Data Base Finder provides quick and easy access to information about thousands of databases created by the federal government and available to the general public. The federal government spends taxpayer money to compile these databases, but nothing on advertising their availability to the general public. Info-Power is a must for anyone who wants immediate access to the vast numbers of databases available from the federal government. Most of the data are available free of charge, or for a small fee.

Cost: $99.95

LESKO'S INFO-POWER

Format: Software
Reader Response: P095
Career Use: OE, OP, PL, SEG, RT
Source: InfoBusiness, Inc.
887 South Orem Blvd.
Orem, UT 84058-5009
800-657-5300
801-221-1100

Contact: Customer Services

Description: One in a series of award winning software programs authored by Mathew Lesko, Info-Power provides access to more than $1 trillion worth of information developed by the U.S. government. Using the fast search program, users can quickly access information regarding government agencies, market studies, money lending programs, resources for investors, educational and grant programs, homeowners, entrepreneurs, career planners and job seekers, and much, much more. Info-Power is a must for anyone who wants immediate access to the vast library of information available from the federal government.

Cost: $59.95

LOTUS ORGANIZER

Format: Software
Reader Response: P096
Career Use: CV
Source: Lotus Development Corporation
55 Cambridge Parkway
Cambridge, MA 02142
617-577-8500

Contact: Customer Service

Description: One key to success in the job search is to keep detailed records of dates when certain tasks and meetings are to take place, names of people with whom you come into contact, and tasks that need to be completed. The Lotus Organizer has been rated as one of the best appointment and task scheduling software programs on the market today. Easy-to-use, flexible, and designed to operate intuitively, the use of an appointment/task scheduling software program, like Lotus Organizer, is highly recommended to all job seekers. Ideal for laptop users.

Cost: $89.95 (suggested retail).

MAINSTREAM

Format: Audiocassette
Videotape
Reader Response: P097
Career Use: CV
Source: Mainstream, Inc.
3 Bethesda Metro Center
Suite 830
Bethesda, MD 20814
Voice/TDD: 301-654-2400
Fax: 301-654-2403

Contact: Fritz Rumpel, Director of Information Services

Description: Mainstream provides a series of 14 audiocassettes including the following topics: "Finding Jobs Through Temporary Employment Agencies," and "Exploring Entrepreneurial Opportunities." The cassettes are specifically designed for job seekers with disabilities. The tapes provide practical advice from experts to assist individuals with disabilities in finding and securing employment. For employers, Mainstream provides two videocassettes on the topic of "Interviewing Applicants With Disabilities."

Cost: Audio—$9.95 Video—$59.95 each, or both for $89.95 plus $5 shipping and handling.

MARKETPLACE BUSINESS

Format: CD-ROM
Reader Response: P098
Career Use: SEG
Source: Marketplace Information Corporation
Three University Office Park
Waltham, MA 02154
800/999-9497

Contact: Customer Service

Description: Marketplace Business is a CD-ROM program (Windows or Macintosh formats) containing information on over 8 million U.S. businesses. Job seekers wishing to identify employers (especially for use in accessing the hidden job market) may do so using the program's powerful search function. Searches may be conducted by company name, address, phone number, business type (SIC codes), annual sales, number of employees, region, and other factors. The program contains a "metering" system whereby users purchase each mailing list that is created. Once the installed meter units are used, additional meter credits may be purchased.

Cost: $845.00

MARTIN GOFFMAN ASSOCIATES

Format: Database
        Software
Reader Response: P099
Career Use: SEG, RT, CV
Source: Martin Goffman Associates
        3 Dellview Drive
        Edison, NJ 08820-2545
        Voice: 908-549-5433
        Fax: 908-906-1687
Contact: Dr. Martin Goffman, Principal

Description: Martin Goffman Associates is a full service business and technical research organization. By searching databases on Dialog, Lexis/Nexis, BRS, Dow Jones, STN (Chemical Abstracts), NewsNet, Knowledge Express, and Data Star, plus many other databases, Martin Goffman Associates can locate positions and/or personnel for job seeking clients and/or employers. In addition to the targeted lists, MGA can provide background data on companies so that job seekers may target their career planning and job seeking efforts. The data from the search is supplied to job seekers through diskette or paper.

Cost: Furnished upon request.

MARTINDALE–HUBBELL LAW DIRECTORY

Format: On-line Database
        CD-ROM
Reader Response: P100
Career Use: SEG
Source: Mead Data Central
        PO Box 933
        Dayton, OH 45401
        Voice: 800-323-3288 Subscription information
        Fax: 908-665-2898
        (CD-ROM Version)

        Martindale-Hubbell—A Reed Reference Publishing Co.

        121 Chanlon Road
        New Providence, NJ 07974
        Voice: 800-526-4902
        Fax: 908-464-3553
Contact: Customer Service

Description: The Martindale-Hubbell Law Directory is available on CD-ROM and on-line through the Lexis/Nexis services. The Directory lists more than 800,000 lawyers and law firms with profiles and contact information. Job seekers (law school graduates and lawyers) use the Directory to target law firms for positions. Using CD-ROM or on-line technology job seekers can search the Directory by multiple criteria. Also, Lexis/Nexis (A Mead Data Central component) offers the Martindale-Hubbell and Lexis Student Directory, an on-line resume service for graduating law students.

Cost: CD-ROM $995/year.

MEDIALINE

Format: Phone Service (Voice Mail Box System)
Reader Response: P101
Career Use: SEG, RT, CV
Source: MediaLine
        PO Box 51909
        Pacific Grove, CA 93950-6909
        Voice: 408-648-5200
        Fax: 408-648-5204

Contact: Mark Shilstone, Manager

Description: MediaLine is a jobs phone hot line for the television industry. Jobs that are listed daily are divided into 5 categories and made available to job seekers by voice mail. Employers may enter jobs by phone or fax. Also available from MediaLine is a Resume Tape Critique service. MediaLine in not a 900 service.

Cost: $40 to $46 for a 6-week subscription.

MEXICAN BUSINESS REVIEW

Format: On-line Database
Reader Response: P102
Career Use: SEG, RT
Source: Mexico Information Services, Inc.
     PO Box 11770
     Ft. Worth, TX 76110
     Voice: 800-446-0746
     Voice: 817-924-0746
     Fax: 817-924-9687

Contact: Lee Thurburn

Description: The Mexican Business Review is the largest electronic database of information about Mexico available in the United States. It can be accessed by a BBS and data can be retrieved by diskette. The database contains data on laws, codes, Constitution, regulations, the Diario Official, books, magazines, articles by experts and research reports, financial reports on Mexican companies, the NAFTA, the NAFTA Side Agreements, statistics and international email. Over 20,000 Mexican companies are listed in the searchable database. Job seekers and career planners can utilize this resource to develop long- and short-range career plans. Further, the available data can be useful in targeting appropriate businesses for employment searches.

Cost: One time set-up fee of $60. Minimum annual fee of $120.

MLA JOBLINE

Format: Phone Hotline
Reader Response: P103
Career Use: RT
Source: Medical Library Association
     Suite 300
     6 N. Michigan Ave.
     Chicago, IL 60602-4805
     Voice: 312-419-9094
     Fax: 312-419-8950
     Jobline: 312-553-INFO (4636)

Contact: Kate E. Corcoran, Director of Membership Development

Description: MLA Jobline allows job seekers with a touch-tone phone to access information on available jobs within the medical library field. Each job is categorized by various factors allowing the job seeker to quickly identify occupations matching certain preferences. The listings of medical library positions is both national and international in scope.

Cost: No charge to users. For listing, contact directly.

MODULAR C-LECT

Format: Software
     CD-ROM
Reader Response: P104
Career Use: OE, DM
Source: Chronicle Guidance Publications, Inc.
     66 Aurora Street
     PO Box 1190

    Moravia, NY 13118-1190
    Voice: 800-622-7284
    Voice: 315-497-0330
    Fax: 315-497-3359

Contact: Kathy Lloyd, Customer Service Manager

Description: Modular C-Lect is an on-line career development software. Users can explore career decision making and planning options through five different modules. It helps users access which careers would fit their temperaments and interests. Designed to be used by job seekers, Modular C-Lect can be found in many academic or counseling settings, such as schools, colleges, libraries, and private employment placement services, and is best used prior to, or at the time of, entering the active job seeking market.

Cost: $900.00

MOODY'S COMPANY DATA

Format: CD-ROM
Reader Response: P105
Career Use: SEG, RT
Source: Moody's Investors Services
    99 Church Street
    New York, NY 10007
    Voice: 212-553-4351
    Fax: 212-553-4700
    Orders: 800-342-5647

Contact: Jeff Cohen, Assistant Vice-President, Sales Planning and Development

Description: Moody's Company Data is in-depth business and financial information on more than 10,000 publicly held U.S. corporations. Moody's provides very comprehensive company business descriptions and histories, coupled with full listings of officers, directors, and other contact persons. The data can be searched on CD-ROM to identify potential employers, utilizing over 160 textual/financial and geographic criteria.

Cost: $3000 to $6000.

MOODY'S INTERNATIONAL COMPANY DATA

Format: CD-ROM
Reader Response: P106
Career Use: SEG, RT
Source: Moody's Investors Services
    99 Church Street
    New York, NY 10007
    Voice: 212-553-4351
    Fax: 212-553-4700
    Orders: 800-342-5647 sales dept.

Contact: Jeff Cohen, Assistant Vice-President, Sales Planning and Development

Description: Moody's International Company Data is in-depth business and financial information on more than 8000 companies in over 90 countries. Moody's provides very comprehensive company business descriptions and histories, coupled with full listings of officers, directors and other contact persons. The data can be searched on CD-ROM to identify potential employers, utilizing over 160 textual/finacal and geographic criteria.

Cost: $3500 to $7000.

NANDO.NET

Format: BBS
Reader Response: P107
Career Use: SEG, RT
Source: The News & Observer
    215 South McDowell Street
    PO Box 191

Raleigh, NC 27602
Voice: 919-836-2808
Fax: 919-836-2814
Modem: 919-829-3560
Modem: 919-558-0500
Telnet: Merlin.NandO.net (login as guest)

Contact: Denise J. Jones

Description: NandO.net is the BBS of the *News & Observer Newspaper*, of Raleigh, NC. The BBS provides employment classified ads daily (after 6 p.m. on the day prior when they normally appear in the newspaper).

Cost: $15 to $30/month.

NATIONAL AD-FAX

Format: Fax-back Service
Reader Response: P108
Career Use: SEG, RT
Source: National Ad Search
PO Box 2083
Milwaukee, WI 53201
Voice: 800-992-2832
Fax: 414-351-0836

Contact: Scott D. Morey

Description: National Ad-Fax collects help wanted ads from 75 Sunday newspapers each week and combines them into 55 job categories. This fax back service compiles over 2200 help wanted ads each week geared toward the managerial, executive, professional, and technical segments of the workforce. Ads are faxed Wednesday from the previous Sunday.

Cost: One-week trial subscription = $15.00 per category, 4 weeks = $50.00, 8 weeks = $80.00.

NATIONAL CAREER APTITUDE SYSTEM

Format: Software
Reader Response: P109
Career Use: DM
Source: Chronicle Guidance Publications, Inc.
66 Aurora Street
PO Box 1190
Moravia, NY 13118-1190
Voice: 800-622-7284
Fax: 315-497-3359

Contact: Kathy Lloyd, Customer Service Manager

Description: The National Career Aptitude System is a career guidance software program designed to measure a student's ability—or aptitude—in a variety of occupational skill areas including: understanding business situations, clerical speed/accuracy, logical reasoning, mechanical reasoning, numerical concepts, and understanding personal/social situations. After entering information and responding to on-line questions, the user may receive directions regarding how to conduct additional occupational exploration, how to choose an appropriate educational direction, and which occupations (from a database of over 1000 jobs) match his or her strengths and weaknesses.

The program is appropriate for students and young adults in grades 10 or higher.

Cost: $295.00 (software plus instructor's manual).

NATIONAL RESUME BANK

Format: On-line Database
Reader Resource: P110
Career Use: CV
Source: National Resume Bank
3637 Fourth Street North

Suite 330
St. Petersburg, FL 33704
Voice: 813-896-3694
Modem: 813-822-7082

Contact: NRB Headquarters

Description: The National Resume Bank is an on-line job database developed to allow job seekers an opportunity to enter their resumes for review by employers. Employers can search the database by their personal computer. The National Resume Bank began three years ago as a member service to the Professional Association of Resume Writers.

Cost: $40 to list a resume. No cost to employers to search the database.

NATIONAL TRADE DATA BANK EXPORT COLLECTION/CD-ROM

Format: CD-ROM
Reader Response: P111
Career Use: OE, OP, PL, SEG
Source: U.S. Department of Commerce
National Trade Data Bank
Economics and Statistics Administration
Office of Business Analysis
Room 4885, HCHB
Washington, DC 20230
202-482-1986 (credit card orders accepted)

Contact: Office of Business Analysis

Description: This two CD-ROM system contains the full text of many books, directories, and publications developed by the U.S. Department of Commerce. One publication, called the *U.S. Industrial Outlook*, contains in-depth projection reports outlining the future for 50 major industries, including such areas as: construction, chemicals, telecommunications, environment, health care, entertainment, finances, and many more. If you're interested in where your industry is going in the next few years, this is the source of information you'll need.

This information may also be accessed from the Career Center area on America Online.

Cost: $37.00

NEOBOOK PROFESSIONAL

Format: Software
Reader Response: P112
Career Use: CV
Source: NeoSoft Corporation
354 NE Greenwood
Suite 108
Bend, OR 97701
800-545-1392
503-383-7195 - BBS

Contact: Customer Service

Description: For job seekers who wish to create electronic resumes for distribution through on-line services and diskette, Neobook Professional is an ideal choice. With Neobook Professional, anyone—programmers and nonprogrammers—can easily and quickly create interactive, multimedia software programs (e.g., resumes, catalogs, books, sales literature, presentations) that run on any DOS computer. Neobook Professional combines text, graphic images, audio, and control buttons all into one package and includes powerful illustration and animated presentation modules. Neobook Professional also produces .EXE programs which may be distributed royalty-free.

Cost: $89.95 (Download free demo from BBS).

NETWORKING CAREERS ONLINE

Format: On-line Database
Reader Response: P113
Career Use: SEG, RT, CV
Source: Network World, Inc.
   161 Worcester Rd.
   Framingham, MA 01701
   Voice: 508-875-6400
   Fax: 508-820-1283
   Modem: 508-620-1160 (up to 9600 baud)
Contact: William Reinstein

Description: Networking Careers Online is an on-line database system providing listings of current job opportunities appropriate for computer network specialists. Networking Careers Online is utilized by job seekers and employers alike to identify job openings and obtain company background information.
Cost: Free.

NORTH COAST MERIDIAN

Format: On-line Database
Reader Response: P114
Career Use: RT, CV
Source: North Coast Meridian
   Executive Search Consultants
   Route 52 and Maple Avenue
   Pine Bush, NY 12566
   Voice: 914-744-3061
   Fax: 914-744-3961
Contact: Charles F. Thomaschek

Description: North Coast Meridian is a recruiter of manufacturing professionals of varying disciplines. North Coast Meridian maintains a large database that contains specific information and resumes on candidates. The company conducts a search of its own database as well as of a few national databases in order to match candidates and jobs. North Coast Meridian's open listings can be accessed on National Recruiting Databases and College Alumni Databases (through BBS).
Cost: Free to job seekers and career planners.

NORTHWEST HIGH TECH

Format: Software
Reader Response: P115
Career Use: SEG
Source: Resolution Business Press, Inc.
   11101 NE 8th Street, Suite 208
   Bellevue, WA 98004
   Voice: 206-455-4611
   Fax: 206-455-9143
   Internet: rbpress.aol.com
Contact: Karen Strudwick

Description: Northwest High Tech provides profiles of 1800 to 1900 computer companies for job seekers who wish to secure employment with firms in the computer industry. The data are provided on diskette from the main database.
Cost: $150.00 (includes easy-to-use database program).

NOTES UNLIMITED

Format: On-line Database
Reader Response: P116
Career Use: SEG, RT
Source: Notes Unlimited
      14301 Swan Lane
      Gulfport, MS 39503-8752
      Voice: 800-729-4491
      Fax: 800-729-4491
      Internet: 76256.2135@compuserve.com
      Compuserve: 76256,2135
Contact: Cliff Williams

Description: Notes Unlimited scans various on-line databases to provide general, business, and company information. A response with information, or a plan detailing how the information will be obtained, will be provided to customers within 24 hours of a request. The company provides business information and positions by city which can be combined to give job seekers background information about various companies that they are considering for employment. Notes Unlimited's on-line searches include the following sources: Dialog, Lexis/Nexis, Dow Jones, Data-Star, Easynet, over 1000 databases, thousands of library card catalogs, and over 15,000 journals. The job seeker calls in, Notes Unlimited provides the on-line search and then provides the results to the job seeker.

Cost: Call for free estimate not to exceed budget prior to search.

OBSERVER ONLINE BBS

Format: BBS
Reader Response: P117
Career Use: OE, OP, SEG, RT, CV
Source: Charlotte Observer
      PO Box 30308
      Charlotte, NC 28232-0308
      Voice: 704-358-5249
      Fax: 704-358-5258
      Modem: 704-358-5072

Description: Observer Online is a BBS provided by the Charlotte, NC Observer newspaper for the benefit of its readers. As with many BBS systems, its content is controlled by its users, therefore a wide variety of information and activities are available. As a true community BBS, job seekers may use it to network and search for job possibilities (full-time, part-time, work at home, etc.), and employers may use it to advertise for new employees.
Cost: Free.

OCCUPATIONAL OUTLOOK HANDBOOK—1994/95 ON CD-ROM

Format: CD-ROM
Reader Response: P118
Career Use: OE, OP
Source: U.S. Government Printing Office
      Superintendent of Documents
      PO Box 37194
      Pittsburgh, PA 15250-7954
      202/783-3238 (credit card orders accepted)
Contact: Customer Service

Description: The Occupational Outlook Handbook - 1994/95 on CD-ROM contains the entire text of the printed version of the latest Occupational Outlook Handbook (OOH). The OOH contains detailed profiles on the vast majority (over 90%) of occupations found in the American workforce. The OOH is published every two years, and represents one of the most comprehensive, single sources of occupational information available anywhere. The OOH is developed by the Bureau of Labor Statistics. Such information as duties, salary, future employment need, training and qualifications, related occupations, and sources of additional information are available for each occupation profiled. A must for every career planner and job seeker seeking information about various occupations.
Cost: $35.00

ONLINE INTERNATIONAL

Format: On-line Database
　　　BBS
Reader Response: P119
Career Use: SEG, RT, CV
Source: Online International
　　　PO Box 27245
　　　Corpus Christi, TX
　　　Voice: 512-850-8905
　　　Fax: 512-850-8905
　　　BBS: 512-850-8255

Contact: John Spofford, CEO

Description: Online International maintains a BBS containing an on-line database of job openings (federal, state, and general), candidate resumes, and other general information for job seekers.

Cost: No cost to access employment information. $20 per year to post resume.

ONLINE SOLUTIONS

Format: On-line Uploading Service
Reader Response: P120
Career Use: CV
Source: OnLine Solutions
　　　1584 Rt. 22B
　　　Morrisonville, NY 12962
　　　Voice: 518-643-2873
　　　Fax: 518-643-0321
　　　Modem: 518-643-0134
　　　America Online: CareerPro1
　　　CompuServe: 73512,3174
　　　Prodigy: RSNA65A

Contact: Wayne M. Gonyea, President

Description: OnLine Solutions provides leading-edge full text resume upload service to Help Wanted-USA's Worldwide Resume/Talent Bank located on various computer network services, including America Online, National Videotex, and the Online Career Center on Internet. Job seekers and career planners can place their resume, through this service, on the information superhighway, where it may be seen by 20 million on-line members. With full text upload capabilities, OnLine Solutions can fully profile each job seeker's qualifications. Resumes may be accessed by employers, employment recruiters, and Help Wanted-USA's nationwide team of employment consultants. Job seekers may submit their resumes to OnLine Solutions by mail, fax, disk, or email through on-line computer services.
Cost: $40 per resume.

ORIGINAL RESUME CO., THE

Format: On-line Database
Reader Response: P121
Career Use: CV
Source: The Original Resume Co.
　　　A Sales and Marketing Associates Company
　　　1105 Lakeview Avenue
　　　Gorman-Litchfield Plaza
　　　Dracut, MA 01826
　　　Voice: 508-957-6600
　　　Fax: 508-957-6605

Contact: Tomas P. Gove
　　　Steve Alborghetti

Description: The Original Resume Company is a Sales and Marketing Associates Company providing resume preparation and resume marketing services for job seekers in the United States. Once the job seeker has registered with Original Resume and a resume is in the computer database, all changes and work may be ordered by telephone. The Original Resume prepares and laser prints a personalized and signed cover letter, resume, addressed and stamped envelope usually within 24 hours of the phone call. The Original Resume also accesses employment databases and responds for the job seeker.

Cost: $98.00 registered resume listing with PIN# - Average $7.00 per letter response.

PERFECT RESUME, THE

Format: Software
Reader Response: P122
Career Use: CV
Source: Permax, Inc.
      PO Box 826
      Woodstock, NY 12498
      800-233-6460

Contact: Customer Support

Description: The Perfect Resume software program (designed by Tom Jackson, one of America's leading career development experts), allows job seekers to quickly and easily produce professional resumes and employment letters. Using his vast experience with thousands of job seekers, Jackson guides you through every step of the resume construction process creating a resume that will showcase your talents and qualifications. Advice is also available to help you master the interview. Change formats instantly to suit your needs. Spell checker and mail merge functions included. A must for all serious job seekers and resume writing professionals!

Cost: $59.95 (DOS and Windows).

PINKERTON INFORMATION CENTER

Format: Database
Reader Response: P123
Career Use: Special
Source: Pinkerton Services Group
      6100 Fairview Road, Suite 900
      Charlotte, NC 28210-3277
      Voice: 800-528-5745
      Voice: 704-552-1119
      Fax: 704-554-1806

Contact: Fred Giles, Vice-President Information Sales
      James W. MacKenzie, Vice-President

Description: Pinkerton Information Center is a background database service bureau. The Center provides electronic reporting and verification of academic credentials, work experience, driving records, credit reports, social security numbers, civil and criminal court records, and hundreds of other facts. Employers can access the database to provide information to assist in the selection of potential employees.

Cost: Furnished upon request.

POWERMATCH

Format: Database
Reader Response: P124
Career Use: Special
Source: PowerMatch
      625 Ellis St., Suite 303
      Mt. View, CA 94043
      Voice: 415-962-1425
      Fax: 415-962-2686

Contact: Deborah Mussomeli, Marketing Coordinator

Description: PowerMatch is a fully integrated employment management system which includes resume scanning, management reporting, ad hoc report writing, full text searching, and other applicant tracking features. PowerMatch is used by employers as a database of prospective employees. The system captures all key information gathered through the interview cycle of all prospective candidates as well as the information captured on the resume.

Cost: Site license: Software for one file server with five workstations is $24,500.

PRO/FILE RESEARCH

Format: Software
Reader Response: P125
Career Use: SEG, RT
Source: Pro/File Research
PO Box 602
Flourtown, PA 19031-0602
Voice: 800-776-0927
Voice: 215-643-3411
Fax: 215-643-3626

Contact: Bob Bronstein, President

Description: Pro/File Research uses a variety of electronic databases (subscription and on-line) to provide electronic search services for people in career transition. The service also functions as the research department for career consulting professionals who choose not to have their own research equipment and staff. In addition to targeting jobs, the service also offers the National Job Scan, a search of help wanted display ads in major newspapers across the country as well as a journal search of trade periodicals. The results of the searches can be delivered on disks for PCs and Macs for an additional charge. The service takes the results of many searches and will produce cover letters, envelopes, and mailing labels.

Cost: Varies depending on the nature of the project. Recruiter searches start at $75. Company searches start at $120. The National JobScan starts at $50.

QUICK & EASY

Format: Software
Reader Response: P126
Career Use: RT
Source: DataTech
6360 Flank Drive #300
Harrisburg, PA 17112
Voice: 717-652-4344
Fax: 717-652-3222

Contact: Customer Service

Description: Quick & Easy is a software program designed to aid job seekers in filling out and managing the SF-171 (Federal Application for Employment) form. The program prints forms and data on blank paper using any Windows printer or any one of 50 supported printers under DOS. The program features: unlimited work experience data printed one or two per page; automatic calculation, formatting, and printing of continuation sheets; save to disk and update; ASCII import; word processor and spell checker. For job seekers interested in federal employment, this program is a real time saver. Quick & Easy is available for DOS or Windows.

Cost: $49.95

QUICKEN

Format: Software
Reader Response: P127
Career Use: Special
Source: Intuit
155 Linfield Drive
Menlo Park, CA 94026
415-322-3689

Contact: Customer Service

Description: Quicken (for DOS, Windows, and Macintosh) is an easy but powerful software program for managing personal and business finances. Since job seeking expenses are tax deductible, job seekers should consider using Quicken to handle their checking, savings, cash transactions, investments, loans, credit cards, assets and liabilities during their job search process. Quicken can print checks, budget finances, balance your checkbook and many other financial tasks. Easy graphical interface.

Cost: $69.95

RACHAEL P. R. SERVICES

Format: Fax-Back Service
Reader Response: P128
Career Use: SEG
Source: Rachael P. R. Services
     513 Wilshire Blvd, #238
     Santa Monica, CA 90401
     Voice: 310-326-2661
     Fax: 310-326-2825

Contact: Janis Brett-Elspas, President

Description: Rachael P. R. Services publishes a job newsletter for full-time and free-lance writers, PR, advertising and marketing, and journalism professionals. The job newsletter is available by fax-back service.

Cost: $39 per two-months' subscription.

READY TO GO RESUMES

Format: Software
Reader Response: P129
Career Use: CV
Source: Ten Speed Press
     Box 7123
     Berkeley, CA 94707
     Voice: 800-841-BOOK

Contact: Customer Service

Description: Ready To Go Resumes provides self-teaching resume templates in a variety of styles and formats. With step-by-step resume writing guidelines built into the templates, job seekers can create powerful, state-of-the-art resumes in about an hour. The program requires a word processor, Word Perfect, MS Word/DOS, MS Word/Windows, or MS Word/Macintosh. Ready To Go Resumes is widely used in state employment offices nation-wide.

Cost: $39.95 plus $2.50 shipping.

RELIABLE SOURCE, THE

Format: On-line Database
     BBS
Reader Response: P130
Career Use: OP, SEG, RT, CV
Source: The American Occupational Therapy Association, Inc.
     PO BOX 1725
     Rockville, MD 20840-1725
     Voice: 301-948-9626
     Fax: 301-948-5512
     Fax: 301-948-5529
     Voice Mail: 301-948-9633
     TDD: Only 800-377-8555

Contact: Scott Ferguson, Program Manager

Description: The Reliable Source is an on-line information system for Occupational Therapists. The system offers a variety of information. One area of information is dedicated to on-line databases, including a job bank listing hundreds of occupational therapy-related jobs available across the country. Also included in the database area are references to many topics of interest to Occupational Therapists, and therefore of value to job seekers looking for additional information about the field.

Cost: $75 to $300/year.

RESTRAC

Format: Database
Reader Response: P131
Career Use: Special
Source: MicroTrac Systems
       1 Dedham Place
       Dedham, MA 02026
       Voice: 617-320-5600
       Fax: 617-320-5630

Contact: Christie Curreri   Voice: 617-320-5322
       Gregory Morse   Voice: 617-320-5351

Description: RESTRAC Enterprise is a fully integrated Windows client/server-based staffing system for organizations of 1000 or more employees. The system allows HR departments to scan up to 2000 resumes per day, turning resume volume into a rich candidate source. Recruiters can then perform searches on the full text of resumes, and route the top ones to hiring managers by fax or email. Because the system is based on industry standards in corporate computing, it can be implemented in a single department, or deployed across the entire organization linking many recruiting sites together to share resumes and applicant data. Benefits to employers include reduced costs, speed and effectiveness of identifying qualified candidates, and instant reporting for EEO compliance and management. RESTRAC helps corporate HR departments provide a more courteous and timely response to applicants (acknowledgment letters, etc.). If a company has a central employment response center, the system makes it feasible to provide just one location for applying to any job at any location in the company.

Cost: Furnished upon request.

RESUMATE

Format: Software
           Database
Reader Response: P132
Career Use: Special
Source: RESUMate, Inc.
       PO Box 7438
       Ann Arbor, MI 48107
       Voice: 800-530-9310
       Voice: 313-429-8510
       Fax: 313-429-4228

Contact: Chuck Schaldenbrand, CEO

Description: RESUMate is a search and match software program for both permanent and temporary agencies. The software can access candidates, clients, job orders, and may offer mail merge, data entry through scanning, and an integrated calendar system. A companion product, RESUMate REMote allows a single RESUMate database to be shared by several nonnetworked PC's. This product package is primarily targeted toward employers, recruiters, and agencies.

Cost: $784 to $2284.

RESUME FILE, THE

Format: On-line Database
           BBS
Reader Response: P133
Career Use: SEG, RT, CV
Source: The Resume File
       2470 Stearns Street, #309

Simi Valley, CA 93063
Voice: 805-581-4940
Modem: 805-581-6210

Contact: Steve S. Hawley

Description: The Resume File (currently containing over 900 resumes) provides services to help employers and job seekers find each other. It provides a fresh resource for companies looking for prospective employees to fill positions for themselves or their clients. The File also contains employment ads placed in its classified section by employers. The job seeker can access the employment ads by modem.

Cost: Varies: no cost for any company wishing only to list help wanted ads.
$144/year for a full access subscription.

RESUMÉ-LINK

Format: Software
Reader Response: P134
Career Use: Special
Source: Resumé-Link
PO Box 218
Hillard, OH 43026
Voice: 614-777-4000
Fax: 614-771-5708

Contact: Greg Ruf, President

Description: Resumé-Link is a service provided primarily to college and university Career Planning and Placement Services, MBA Career Placement offices, professional associations, outplacement firms, and job fair companies for producing customized Resume Referral Systems. The software program enables clients to produce their own customized resume database, which they may then resell to their clients.

Cost: By quote per specific request.

RESUME ON A DISK

Format: Software
Reader Response: P135
Career Use: CV
Source: Personal Data Concepts
PO Box 987
Byron, IL 61010
Voice: 800-MED-DISK

Contact: Gary Krautwurst, President

Description: RESUME ON A DISK is a software product that allows job seekers to prepare an electronic resume on disk (including a photo) that can then be transmitted to employers and recruiters on-line or by a computer diskette. Personal Data Concepts will also transmit a job seeker's electronic resume electronically to employers. The resume text and photo may be easily upgraded as needed.

Cost: $35.95

RESUME PROCESSOR AND LETTERWRITER

Format: Software
Reader Response: P136
Career Use: CV
Source: Vocational Biographies
PO Box 31
Sauk Centre, MN 56378-0031
Voice: 800-255-0752
Fax: 612-352-5546

Contact: Customer Service

Description: This "create your own" word processing software program formats custom resumes, cover letters, and job interview follow-up letters. The program overcomes writer's block by giving structure to the creation of resumes and job search letters. Readily useable by "hunt and peck" typists, there is no need for word processing skills or knowledge of DOS commands. Its flexibility allows the user to experiment with format without having to retype data.

Cost: $199.00

RESUME PROFESSIONAL

Format: Software
Reader Response: P137
Career Use: CV
Source: Richard C. Leinecker
PO Box 2567
Reidsville, NC 27323-2567

Description: Resume Professional is a resume writing software program that can facilitate many of the time consuming tasks associated with preparing a resume. Resume Professional may be obtained directly from the developer by mail, or downloaded from America Online (see computer forum area). Version 2.0 includes Contact Tracker, a program that enables you to easily track correspondence and phone calls; and The Electronic Resume Maker, a program that creates disk-based resume presentations.

Cost: Shareware—$20 registration fee.

RESUMEMAKER

Format: Software
Reader Response: P138
Career Use: PST, RT, CV, IT
Source: Individual Software Incorporated
5870 Stoneridge Drive, #1
Pleasanton, CA 94588-9900
Voice: 800-822-3522

Contact: Customer Service

Description: ResumeMaker includes tools for creating resumes and cover letters. The software program is structured for users to enter personal data into one of three resume types (chronological, functional, or performance) that reflect the particular demands or requirements of your job target. Also included is a library of broadcast, cover, and thank you letters; a built-in word processor for custom letters and correspondence; spell checking and mail merge capabilities. Special features of ResumeMaker are a target company's manager, job activity tracker, scheduler and address book. A copy of *What Color Is Your Parachute?* is also included in the Windows version.

Cost: $49.95 (DOS, Macintosh, or Windows available).

RESUMIX

Format: Software
Database
Reader Response: P139
Career Use: Special
Source: Resumix
2953 Bunker Hill Lane
Santa Clara, CA 95054
Voice: 408-764-9215
Fax: 408-727-9893

Contact: Joseph Huilo

Description: Resumix is a software application that automates the hiring process by combining advanced technologies to scan resumes into a computer-based system, automatically extract key candidate information, and create a database of resumes which can then be matched against open position requisitions. Job seekers will benefit by having their resumes and the information contained therein turned into an electronic data resource, available to all recruiters within various organizations. Also offered is Resumix Service Bureau for smaller organizations.

Cost: $25,000 and up.

SEARCH BULLETIN

Format: Software
Reader Response: P140
Career Use: SEG
Source: The Beacon Group
   Village Centre,
   PO Box 641
   Great Falls, VA 22066
   Voice: 703-759-4900
   Fax: 703-759-4901
   Orders: 800-486-9220

Contact: Nancy Schretter, Publisher
   Cathy Smith, Administrator

Description: The Search Bulletin provides access to 400 to 500 unadvertised job leads per month in the $65K to $350K range in the areas of general management, marketing and sales, finance and accounting, consulting/corporate planning, operations management, information services, and human resources. The job leads are sourced through a nationwide network of over 1000 companies, search firms, investor groups, search researches, and members.

Cost: $97 for quarterly membership. No other cost to either job seeker or employer.

SELECT PHONE

Format: CD-ROM
Reader Response: P141
Career Use: SEG, PST
Source: ProPhone, Inc.
   8 Doaks Lane
   Little Harbor
   Marblehead, MA 01945-9866
   800-99-CD-ROM

Contact: Customer Support

Description: With Select Phone, job seekers can obtain every white page telephone directory number in the United States, with the name and address of the owner of each number! Select Phone contains over 72 million residential and 8 million business listings. The program has a powerful search program built in allowing users to identify phone numbers by one or any combination of factors, such as: street address, telephone number, city, state, zip, area code, business heading, and SIC (Standard Industry Classification) codes. Select Phone is an excellent resource for identifying the "hidden job markets"—employers who exist, but have not advertised employment openings. With Select Phone, you can easily and quickly prepare mailing lists of employers in any industry, anywhere in the United States.

  Select Phone does not contain a "metering" system whereby users pay for each mailing list produced. The program allows for unlimited use of the listings for the single cost of the program.

  See the Job Seeker's PowerPak, Chap. 8, for additional information.

Cost: $299.00—includes free copy of Euro Pages (see profile for more information).

SKILLSEARCH

Format: Phone Service/On-line Database
Reader Response: P142
Career Use: RT, CV
Source: SkillSearch Corporation
   3354 Perimeter Hill Drive
   Suite 235
   Nashville, TN 37211
   Voice: 800-252-5665
   Fax: 615-834-9453

Contact: Customer Service

Description: SkillSearch is a custom employment search service provided on a confidential basis to white collar and technical professionls interested in finding new career opportunities. Job seekers complete a questionnaire form outlining their background which SkillSearch uses to create a profile on each candidate and to match employers to prospective employees. SkillSearch monitors the job search process, sends the appropriate contact letters, and notifies the job seeker regarding further action. Employers may access the data by calling SkillSearch.

Cost: $65 to enroll and $15 each year thereafter.

SMARTSEARCH2

Format: On-line Database
Reader Response: P143
Career Use: Special
Source: Advanced Personnel Systems, Inc.
     4167 Avenida de la Plata #126
     Oceanside, CA 92056
     Voice: 619-941-2800
     Fax: 619-941-3287

Contact: Doug Coull

Description: Advanced Personnel Systems, Inc. offers a scanning-based resume retrieval and applicant tracking software package called SmartSearch2 to corporate departments and personnel agencies. SmartSearch2 enables employers to search thousands of resumes to locate the appropriate candidate. Software is supplied to the employer to facilitate the on-line database search capability.

Cost: $10,000 to $100,000.

SPRINTFAX®

Format: Fax Service
Reader Response: P144
Career Use: Special
Source: Sprint TeleMedia
     6666 West 110th Street
     Overland Park, KS 66211
     Voice: 913-661-8372
     Voice: 800-366-3297
     Fax: 913-661-8326

Contact: Sharon L. Lundeen, Marketing Communications Specialist

Description: HR Departments can utilize Sprintfax® Broadcast Distribution to send position vacancy information to recruiters. Sprint Document on Demand allows employers and recruiters to respond immediately to requests for information by fax. Sprintfax® claims superior fax resolution because of their all fiber-optic network.

Cost: Call for quote.

STANDARD AND POOR'S

Format: On-line Database
Reader Response: P145
Career Use: SEG, RT
Source: Standard and Poor's Corporation
     25 Broadway
     New York, NY 10004
     Voice: 212-208-8300
     Fax: 212-412-0498

Contact: Phil Ellenberg, Product Manager
     Voice: 212-208-8283
     Fax: 212-412-0305

Description: Standard and Poor's extensive on-line databases permit comprehensive searching of over 70,000 executives, 45,000 privately held companies, and 10,000 publicly traded companies. In addition to being a high-powered recruitment tool for employers and executive recruitment agencies, this service can also benefit job seekers and career planners who wish to obtain critical information regarding potential employers. Standard and Poor's data also are available on CD-ROM and through the DIALOG and Mead Data Central network services.

Cost: Prices vary depending on formats and data distributions source used. For example DIALOG is $84/hour, $2 download per full printed record.

STARTEXT

Format: On-line Database
Reader Response: P146
Career Use: SEG, RT
Source: StarText
       Fort Worth Star Telegram
       400 West Seventh Street
       PO Box 1870
       Fort Worth, TX 76101
       Voice: 817-390-7400
       Voice: 817-390-7905 Orders Only
       Fax: 817-390-7797

Contact: Marla Hammond, StarText Office Manager

Description: StarText is the electronic information service of the *Fort Worth Star/Telegram*. StarText includes classified ads from the *Star/Telegram*. Job seekers may access help wanted ads 24 hours a day, and actual ads can be previewed from 6 p.m. of the prior day to the actual newspaper release. The StarText Business Edition has one column on new jobs and several columns on careers.

Cost: $9.95 to $14.95/month.

STONICK RECRUITMENT

Format: Radio Broadcasting Service
Reader Response: P147
Career Use: Special
Source: Stonick Recruitment
       10160 Grove Lane
       Cooper City, FL 33328
       Voice: 305-680-6322
       Fax: 305-680-6327

Contact: Chris Stonick, President

Description: Stonick Recruitment is a Radio Recruitment Consulting Service. This service provides services to companies that wish to recruit qualified employees through radio advertising. Stonick Recruitment works with radio stations and companies all over the United States to develop radio recruitment campaigns. The actual format, a 60 -second advertisement run 24 hours a day on Sunday, Monday, and Tuesday, develops responses from currently employed candidates.

Cost: Market pricing—call for quotes.

TECHMATCH REGISTRY

Format: Software
       On-line Database
Reader Response: P148
Career Use: Special
Source: TechMatch Registry
       1117 S. Milwaukee Ave.
       Forum Square, Bldg. D-1
       Libertyville, IL 60048

Voice: 708-549-9557
Fax: 708-549-7429

Contact: Douglas J. Baniqued, President

Description: TechMate Registry is a service using an on-line computer database that provides validated research information to clients who are looking to staff information technology positions. Techmate Registry also provides a service to individuals within the information technology field who wish to have their names included in the research database. Also offered is a turnkey software package and executive search and consulting services.

Cost: $2000 to $3000.

TECHNOLOGY REGISTRY™

Format: On-line Database
Software
Reader Response: P149
Career Use: CV
Source: QuestLink Systems, Inc.
616 Carolina Street
San Francisco, CA 94107
Voice: 415-641-3838
Fax: 415-821-7953

Contact: William M. Hassebrock, President

Description: For employers, the Technology Registry™ provides real-time access to a database of more than 200,000 executives in over 35,000 corporations through an on-line Windows-based database search software system. Copies of all data obtained from a search can be faxed or downloaded to the subscriber's local computer. In addition, by mid-1994, the Technology Registry™ will be made available to job seekers who wish to make their resumes available to employers. Job seekers will submit their career data on the Floppy Resume, a unique diskette using software designed as a career management tool. Once the job seeker's Floppy Resume data are in the database, it is immediately available to employers and recruiters. Techology Registry™ is designed as a career management service in addition to being a job search tool.

Cost: Furnished upon request.

ULTIMATE JOB FINDER

Format: Software
Reader Response: P150
Career Use: PA, OE, OP, DM, PL, SEG, PST, RT, DV, IT
Source: Planning/Communications
7215 Oak Avenue
River Forest, IL 60305
Voice: 708-366-5200
Voice: 800-829-5220
Fax: 708-366-5280

Contact: Dan Lauber

Description: Dan Lauber's The Ultimate Job Finder is a computer software resource that contains all the resources included in Lauber's three job hunting books; *Professional's Private Sector Job Finder*, *Government Job Finder*, and *Non-Profits' Job Finder*. The Ultimate Job Finder, containing over 5000 listings in a searchable database format, directs you to Electronic Job Hotlines, Electronic Job-Matching Services, Computerized Job and Resume Databases, Online Computer Job Services, and many more electronic resources of value to the job seeker, career planner, employer or professional involved in electronic job and employer matching. Use of appropriate search words will present those resources, which are electronic in nature or use. The resulting information is comprehensive and easy to access. Available in Windows and DOS versions, The Ultimate Job Finder is an indispensable tool in the job seeker's electronic search repertoire. The Ultimate Job Finder also provides specialty and trade periodicals, job ads, and directories that list information not on software.

Cost: Regular edition: $49.95. Professional edition: $79.95 (includes one free update and discounts on licenses for use on a network).

UNIVERSITY PRONET

Format: On-line Database
Reader Response: P151
Career Use: CV
Source: University ProNet
    3803 East Bayshore Road, Suite 150
    Palo Alto, CA 94303
    Voice: 800-726-0280 (corporate)
    Fax: 415-691-1619

Contact: Director, University ProNet

Description: University ProNet is a private database of alumni resumes. It's owned by 16 universities including Stanford, MIT, University of Michigan, Carnegie Mellon University, UCLA, University of Texas at Austin, Ohio State, University of California at Berkeley, Caltech, Yale, Columbia, Cornell, University of Chicago, University of Illinois, University of Pennsylvania-Wharton, and the University of Wisconsin-Madison. Alumni submit their resumes by computer diskettes and update them annually. The company provides executive searches for employers, but limits the searches to individuals participating in the program.

Cost: Alumni: $35 for lifetime membership. Employers: Varies depending on the size of the subscription purchased, ranging from $2500 to $35,000/year. Contact your individual Alumni Association for details.

US DEPARTMENT OF COMMERCE, BUREAU OF CENSUS

Format: On-line Database
    BBS
Reader Response: P152
Career Use: SEG, RT
Source: U.S. Department of Commerce
    Bureau of Census
    Personnel Division
    Room 3124, FB 3
    Washington, DC 20233
    Voice: 301-763-5780
    Voice: 800-638-6719
    TTY: 301-763-4944
    Modem: 800-451-6128

Contact: Sandra Loew
Voice: 301-763-5780

Description: Job seekers who have access to a personal computer with a modem can access information on current vacancies available from the Bureau of Census for the Washington, DC area.

Cost: Free.

VENTURE SEARCH SYSTEM

Format: Software
Reader Response: P153
Career Use: RT
Source: Custom Databanks, Inc.
    13925 Esworthy Road
    Germantown, MD 20874-3313
    301-990-4010 (credit card orders accepted)

Contact: Jane Lockshin, President

Description: The Venture Search System is a software program containing information on over 1300 top venture firms located throughout the United States. Using any number of search criteria, including: location, industry specialties, and geographic preferences, job seekers interested in seeking employment with venture firms (or the client companies they represent) can easily identify potential employers. Resulting search data may then be merged with a personal letter to enable users to generate unlimited letters, envelopes, and mailing labels in much less time than conventional means.

Cost: $250.00

VERMONT DEPARTMENT OF EMPLOYMENT AND TRAINING

Format: Software
       On-line Database
       BBS
Reader Resource: P154
Career Use: OE, OP, PL, SEG, RT, IT
Source: Vermont Department of Employment and Training
       Office of Policy and Information
       PO Box 488
       Montpelier, VT 05601
       Voice: 802-828-4321
       Voice: 800-924-4443 *Within Vermont*
       Voice: 802-828-4108 *Outside Vermont*
       Voice: 802-828-4322 *Outside Vermont*
       Fax: 802-828-4022

Contact: Michael Griffin
       Voice: 802-828-4153

Description: The Vermont Department of Employment and Training has various electronic resources available to job seekers. They include:

VTOIS Vermont Career Information System. This is a computer software program designed for counselors, career planners, and job seekers. With this system, the user may obtain data for all occupations and training programs available in the state of Vermont, and cross-reference occupations to a database of career resource materials.

DET Bulletin Board. This is an electronic bulletin board that is accessible using a personal computer and modem. It provides up-to-date Vermont Labor Market information and job openings.

Economic Development and Employer Planning System. This resource includes a computerized database of national, state, and area information that allows the user to prepare reports that will assist in job interviewing and decision making.

Transition Opportunities System. A computerized system specifically designed for military personnel facing relocation by the military or to assist military personnel in securing employment upon leaving military service.

Cost: No cost to job seekers.

VOCATIONAL BIOGRAPHIES CAREER FINDER

Format: Software
Reader Response: P155
Career Use: OE, DM
Source: Vocational Biographies
       PO Box 31
       Sauk Centre, MN 56378-0031
       Voice: 800-255-0752
       Fax: 612-352-5546

Contact: Customer Service

Description: This career interest survey software program generates a list of 20 career options that most closely match the interests of the user, based on 18 simple questions. The program also provides direction for career exploration by pinpointing several specific careers an individual might find most interesting. It allows the user to compare interests with those of people in specific occupations, and offers basic information about 452 job titles, plus references for additional information.

Cost: $298.00

WEST VIRGINIA EMPLOYMENT SERVICE

Format: Hot line
        Database
        Fax service
Reader Response: P156
Career Use: SEG
Source: West Virginia Bureau of Employment Programs
        112 California Ave.
        Charleston, WV 25305
        Voice: 304-558-0219
        Fax: 304-558-3449
        Hot Line: 800-252-JOBS

Contact: Allen Wright, Assistant Director of Programs

Description: The West Virginia Employment Service provides a database of information on high-tech and computer-related job openings. Employment information may be obtained by a telephone hotline. Employers are invited to fax their job orders to any Job Service office.
Cost: No cost to West Virginia residents.

WILSON BUSINESS ABSTRACTS

Format: On-line Database
        CD-ROM
         Computer Magnetic Tape
Reader Response: P157
Career Use: SEG, RT
Source: The H. W. Wilson Company
        Indexing Services
        950 University Avenue
        Bronx, NY 10452
        Voice: 800-367-6770
        Voice: 718-588-8400
        Fax: 718-590-1617

Contact: Customer Service

Description: The H. W. Wilson Company Indexing Services continually searches 345 of today's leading business magazines. The resulting information is used to produce the Wilson Business Abstracts, which provides references for corporations and trends in business opportunities for career planners and job seekers. The data can be accessed through on-line database and can be obtained on CD-ROM and computer magnetic tape.
Cost: CD-ROM: $2495.00. Computer magnetic tape: variable. On-line database: variable.

WRITER'S RESEARCH REPORT

Format: BBS
Reader Response: P158
Career Use: SEG, RT
Source: National Writers Association
        1450 S. Havana, Suite 424
        Aurora, CO 80012
        Voice: 303-751-7844
        Fax: 303-751-8593

Contact: Sandy Whelchel, Executive Director

Description: Writer's Research Report is a Bulletin Board Service (BBS) maintained by the National Writers Association for use by its members to assist them in finding publishers, agents, and freelancing opportunities. A second service, called the BBS's Jobnet service assists members with matching their skills with possible employers. The service benefits both job seekers and employers.
Cost: $50 to $60 membership.

YOU'RE HIRED!

Format: Software
Reader Response: P159
Career Use: RT, CV, IT
Source: DataTech
 6360 Flank Drive #300
 Harrisburg, PA 17112
 Voice: 800-556-7526
 Fax: 717-652-3222
Contact: Customer Service

Description: You're Hired! is an automated job search and resume software program for Windows. The program helps create resumes and cover letters and even automates much of the resume building process. By selecting different options, you are prompted with questions to help you best describe your skills and experience, or you can use pre-written descriptions that are included with the program. Other program features include: contact and job lead manager; interview assistant; cover letter writer; and SF-171 data conversion for federal and civilian job applications.

Cost: $29.95 plus $5.00 shipping.

YOU'RE HIRED!

Format: Software
Reader Response: P160
Career Use: IT
Source: DataWell
 13852 Echo Park Court
 Burnsville, MN 55337-4776
 Voice: 612-432-5109
 Fax: 612-891-5727
 CompuServe: 71355,470
 Internet: 71355.470@compuserve.com
Contact: Stu Tanquist, President
Orders: PsL
 PO Box 35705
 Houston, TX 77235-5705
 Voice: 800-242-4775
 Voice: 713-524-6394
 Fax: 713-524-6398

Description: You're Hired! is a computer-based job interview simulator that offers job seekers practical training in how to answer difficult interview questions. The interactive process asks common challenging interview questions in a lifelike simulation and records elapsed times as the response is given. If advice and coaching are required or desired, users can call up the on-line Help program to receive professional advice as well as the individual's own reminder notes.

Cost: $26.95

10

The America Online Career Center

This chapter will guide you in using the Career Center—America's premiere electronic career and employment guidance service offered exclusively on the America Online computer network service. Now, for the first time, professional career development information and guidance are available to you through your personal computer.

Welcome to the America Online Career Center!

As founder and director of the Career Center, I would like to welcome you to the first and only service of its kind. Created in 1989, the Career Center has been used by tens of thousands of on-line members to satisfy their career development needs. In only a few minutes, you'll be connected to America Online and will be able to use any of the online career guidance services.

Enclosed with this book you will find a free copy of the America Online (AOL) software program. If for some reason, your copy is missing, please call America Online at 1-800-827-6364 to obtain a replacement copy free of charge. Also, the enclosed copy is for PC DOS machines. If you wish to obtain a free copy of the America Online software program for Windows or Macintosh, please call America Online for a free copy, or you may purchase a copy of either version at most computer software stores.

Before you begin, make sure you have the following materials:

❑ A copy of the America Online software program

❑ Your registration number and password (enclosed with your diskette)

❑ A working, standard phone line

❑ A Hayes® or Hayes-compatible modem (at least 2400 baud)

❑ Your Visa, MasterCard, Discover Card, or American Express card, or your checking account and transit number

While not required, a mouse is highly recommended for maximum ease of use of the AOL program.

The America Online program does not come with, nor does it require the use of a user's manual. The program is relatively easy to use and plenty of help is available online. However, to best understand and utilize the many features, functions, and services that are available with this service, it is recommended that you obtain a copy of *The Official America Online Tour Guide*, written by Tom Lichty. This excellent book is available from most bookstores and computer software stores and can also be ordered online (use keywords *tour guide* to get to the AOL Products Center area).

How to Install the Program

Follow the directions supplied with your copy of the America Online software program to install a copy onto your computer system.

How to Get to the Career Center

If necessary, turn on your computer and start the America Online program to display the sign on screen.

1. Sign on to America Online.

2. You can get to the Career Center several ways:

Option 1—Using Your Mouse. Click on the *Browse the Service* (or Departments) button, and then click on the Learning & Reference area button, and then *double* click on the Career Center item found in the large scrolling list box.

Option 2—Using Your Keyboard. Press the tab key until the *Browse the Service* (or Departments) button is highlighted, then press the enter key. Press the tab key again until the Learning & Reference area button is highlighted, then press the enter key. Using the down arrow key, highlight the Career Center item found in the large scrolling list box, then press the space bar.

Later, once you become more familiar with using America Online, you might want to consider using the keyword function or editing the Go To menu to enable you to quickly access the Career Center. See the on-line Help area for more information.

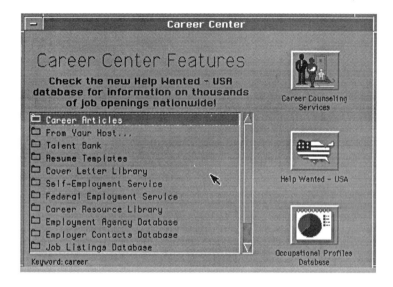

Well, you've finally made it to the Career Center.

The Career Center contains many services that can help you with your career planning and job hunting needs. Please note that new services are added on a regular basis, and old services are edited or deleted when necessary. Therefore, the list that follows may not match exactly the list of services you actually find once you get on-line.

The main Career Center screen is divided into four areas:

1. *Scrolling List Box*: In the large box or window area, you will find a list of most of the services available from the Career Center.

   Mouse users—double click on any item to access the area.

   Keyboard users—using the down arrow key, select the item you wish to access and press the space bar.

2. *Career Counseling Services Icon*. This icon will lead you to another area in the center where you can obtain information regarding online career counseling services, the bulletin board area where you may leave questions for response by the counseling staff, and/or access the Counseling Chat Room.

   Mouse users—double click on the icon to access the area.

   Keyboard users—press the tab key until this icon is highlighted, then press the enter key to access the area.

3. *Help Wanted-USA Icon*. This icon will take you to the Help Wanted-USA search screen where you can immediately access thousands of help wanted ads.

Mouse users—double click on the icon to access the area.

Keyboard users—press the tab key until this icon is highlighted, then press the enter key to access the area.

4. *Occupational Profiles Icon.* This icon will take you to the occupational literature area where you can gain access to information on hundreds of different occupations.

Mouse users—double click on the icon to access the area.

Keyboard users—press the tab key until this icon is highlighted, then press the Enter key to access the area.

Following is an alphabetical list of all the Career Center services available at the time of the writing of this book.

Note: As you roam through the Career Center, it is strongly suggested that you first review those areas that are labeled "About ...". For example, *About the Career Center.* Any item containing the word "About ..." provides you with basic information and instructions for using the service affiliated with the "About ..." label. It is recommended that you read these files before attempting to use any service or database.

About the Career Center. Use this area to learn more about the purpose of the Career Center service, including a description of all available services and information. You should check this area frequently as this is where information regarding new services and databases is posted.

Article Archives. Use this area to view or download any of the many articles that have been written and saved for your use. Articles are written by professional career counselors and other professionals and cover topics of interest to career planners and job seekers.

Article of the Month. Use this area to view or download the article featured for the current month. These articles change approximately every month depending on the general interest in the article.

Ask the Counselor. Use this area to leave a message or question for one of the professional on-line career counselors to respond to. Use this bulletin board if you have a career development question or concern that does not require an immediate response. You can expect a response usually within 48 to 72 hours.

Career Counseling Services. Use this area to schedule a private counseling session with a professional counselor—a time when you can meet on-line privately to discuss your career planning and/or job hunting problems and needs. All counselors are professionally trained, hold appropriate educational degrees and certifications, and have extensive employment experience. Each counselor has been carefully selected to bring certain skills and knowledge to the center. A complete profile on each counselor is available online to aid you in selecting the counselor who can best meet your needs.

Due to the popularity of this service, it is suggested that you check the Appointment Book in the Career Center early in the week to reserve a time for your use.

Career Guidance Services. Use this area to gain access to various career guidance materials and services that can help you discover which occupations may be best for you as career goals. You can download various workbook and inventory materials, as well as gain access to an extensive career analysis service designed to help you discover occupations suitable as career goals.

Career Resources Library. Use this area to obtain information on hundreds of career planning and job hunting resources (books, software programs, CD-ROM disks, online databases, audio and video cassettes, fax services, etc). If you are in need of career development resources, you're likely to find them here!

Counseling Room. Use this area to meet with the career counselor at the time you have scheduled to discuss your career needs. The "chat" capability of America Online allows you to communicate in real-time, instantly keyboard-to-keyboard—all from the comfort of your easy chair and computer. You may also use this area (when it's unoccupied) to meet and chat with other America Online members.

Cover Letter Library. Use this area to view and/or download sample employment cover letters that you may edit and use in your own job search. These letters can save you time, as well as help you prepare professional looking letters.

Employer Contacts Database. Use this area to obtain information on thousands of employers nationwide—information that can help you better understand the business objectives and activities of those employers that you are interested in contacting regarding employment. If you're looking for "hidden job market" employers, this area can help.

Executive Search Firms. Use this area to access information on hundreds of executive recruiting firms nationwide—including specific recruiters who may be able to help you secure employment.

Federal Employment Service. Use this area to gain access to information regarding federal employment opportunities, including profiles of hundreds of federal departments and agencies, and instructions regarding how to find, apply for, and secure employment with the federal government.

Financial Aid Service. Use this area to gain access to information about financial aid resources that may help you secure financial assistance to underwrite the cost of your education.

Job Listing Database. Use this area to gain access to thousands of employment opportunities (help wanted ads) from employers coast-to-coast. These ads cover hundreds of professional positions from Accountant to Zoologist, and are updated weekly. Growing daily, this area often contains more than 5000 weekly help wanted ads. This is one of the most popular services in the Career Center.

Occupational Profiles. Use this area to access detailed information about any one of hundreds of different occupations, such information as duties, salaries, entrance qualifications, future employment outlook, etc. Information on thousands of occupations is available.

Resume Templates. Use this area to view and download sample resumes that you can use as guides when creating your own resume, to upload a copy of your completed resume for viewing by other America Online members, or to download resumes of other members for your own review.

Self-Employment Service. Use this area to view and/or download profiles of individuals who have started successful home-based businesses, and/or to purchase one of the home-based, computer-assisted business opportunities offered by the Career Center.

Talent Bank. Use this area to enter your mini-resume into the Career Center Talent Bank, and/or to search the Talent Bank for resumes of other America Online members. The Talent Bank is an excellent means of letting the hundreds of thousands of America Online members—many of whom are employers—know you are available for employment!

The Talent Bank is part of the Worldwide Resume/Talent Bank service offered by Gonyea & Associates. See Chap. 8 for more information about this service.

US Industry Projections. Use this area to access information regarding the future of over 50 major U.S. industries over the next ten-year period.

How to Contact the Author. If you wish to contact the author regarding your career needs, you may either send me an email message or sign up for a private counseling session.

To sign up for a private counseling session, see the Appointment Book item in the Career Counseling Services area in the Career Center.

To send email, use the Compose Mail option on the Mail menu.

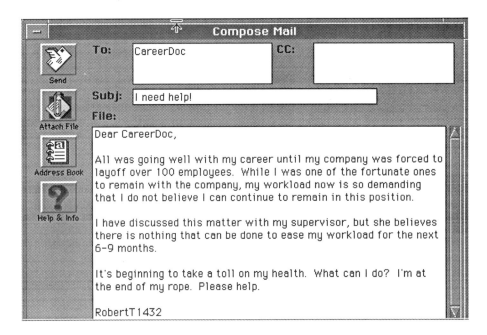

Address your email to James Gonyea, using the screen name *CareerDoc*. Depending upon the volume of mail received, you can expect a response to your email within 48 to 72 hours.

Additional AOL Services of Interest

An easy way to discover many of AOL's services and features is to select the Discover AOL button on the Welcome screen that first appears when you connect on-line.

Spending a little time offline reading Tom Lichty's book, *The Official America Online Tour Guide,* can also help you get the maximum use from your membership.

Cross-Reference Table

Profiles to Career Development Steps

To identify electronic resources that can help you accomplish various career development steps outlined in this book, follow these directions:

1. Determine which career development task(s) you wish to complete. Your choices are listed in the following—note the code for each task selected.

2. Move down the column labeled with the code(s) you have selected to identify all related electronic resources.

3. Move to the appropriate page(s) in Power Tools, Chap. 9, for a description of each resource you have selected.

Additional resources are available in the Career Center on America Online, as well as in the chapters dealing with the Internet, Commercial Computer Network Services, Bulletin Board Services, and the Job Seeker's PowerPak.

Career Planning Tasks (Chap. 2)

Code	Task
PA	Personal Assessment—resources that can help you learn more about your interests, skills/aptitudes, values/needs, and behavioral traits.
OE	Occupational Exploration—resources that can help you identify occupations that exist in the American workplace.
OP	Occupational Profiling—resources that can help you understand the nature of various occupations you may be considering, with such information as duties, qualifications, and the like.
DM	Decision Making—resources that can help you decide which career direction is best for you to pursue.
PL	Planning—resources that can help you determine which steps you should take to reach your new career goals.

Job Hunting Tasks (Chap. 4)

Code	Task
SEG	Setting Employment Goals—resources that can help you identify and prepare of list of employers that may be able to offer you employment.
PST	Building a Professional Support Team—resources that can help you identify professional employment recruiting services.
RT	Researching Targets—Identifying Your Employment Value—resources that can help you determine how you may be of value to those employers on your target list.

CV Communicating Your Value—Shining Your Light—resources that can help you prepare effective resumes, letters of employment, and other written materials necessary for securing employment.

IT Interviewing—resources that can help you master the art of interviewing.

Special Additional resources of value to job seekers, employers, and professionals who work with career planners and job seekers.

Cross-Reference Table
Profiles to Career Development Steps

Profiles	PA	OE	OP	DM	PL	SEG	PST	RT	CV	IT	Special
P001											X
P002								X			
P003		X	X			X		X	X	X	
P004											X
P005									X		
P006						X		X			
P007								X			
P008						X		X			
P009								X			
P010							X	X	X	X	
P011								X			
P012								X	X		
P013						X			X		
P014											X
P015								X			
P016											X
P017								X	X	X	
P018							X				
P019						X		X			
P020								X			
P021								X	X		
P022			X			X		X			
P023								X			
P024						X		X			
P025				X							
P026		X	X	X	X						
P027						X			X		
P028				X		X			X	X	
P029									X		
P030	X	X		X							
P031						X			X		
P032									X		
P033									X	X	
P034						X		X	X		
P035						X		X			
P036					X						
P037					X						
P038			X			X		X		X	
P039									X		

Cross-Reference Table											
(Continued)											
Profiles	PA	OE	OP	DM	PL	SEG	PST	RT	CV	IT	Special
P040								X	X	X	
P041						X		X			
P042						X		X			
P043						X		X			
P044									X		
P045		X				X		X			
P046						X					
P047						X					
P048											X
P049		X	X			X	X	X			
P050		X	X		X	X		X			
P051						X		X			
P052						X		X			
P053						X		X			
P054									X		
P055						X		X			
P056			X	X	X			X		X	
P057								X	X	X	
P058						X		X			
P059						X	X				
P060		X	X			X		X			
P061						X		X			
P062							X	X			
P063						X		X	X		
P064	X	X		X							
P065								X			
P066			X			X		X			
P067		X	X	X		X		X			
P068			X			X		X			
P069								X			
P070			X			X		X			
P071			X			X		X	X		X
P072									X		
P073						X		X			
P074			X			X	X	X		X	
P075									X		
P076											X
P077								X	X		
P078		X			X	X			X	X	
P079								X	X		

Cross-Reference Table
(Continued)

Profiles	PA	OE	OP	DM	PL	SEG	PST	RT	CV	IT	Special
P080						X		X			
P081						X		X	X		
P082						X		X	X		
P083									X		
P084						X		X			
P085						X		X	X		
P086		X	X		X	X		X			
P087						X		X	X		
P088		X		X		X					
P089						X		X			
P090						X					
P091						X		X	X		
P092						X		X			
P093			X		X	X		X			
P094		X	X		X	X		X			
P095		X	X		X	X		X			
P096									X		
P097									X		
P098						X					
P099						X		X	X		
P100						X					
P101						X		X	X		
P102						X		X			
P103								X			
P104		X		X							
P105						X		X			
P106						X		X			
P107						X		X			
P108						X		X			
P109				X							
P110									X		
P111		X	X		X	X					
P112									X		
P113						X		X	X		
P114								X	X		
P115						X					
P116						X		X			
P117		X	X			X		X	X		
P118		X	X								
P119						X		X	X		

Cross-Reference Table
(Continued)

Profiles	PA	OE	OP	DM	PL	SEG	PST	RT	CV	IT	Special
P120									X		
P121									X		
P122									X		
P123											X
p124											X
P125						X		X			
P126								X			
P127											X
P128						X					
P129									X		
P130			X			X		X	X		
P131											X
P132											X
P133						X		X	X		
P134											X
P135									X		
P136									X		
P137									X		
P138							X	X	X	X	
P139											X
P140						X					
P141						X	X				
P142								X	X		
P143											X
P144											X
P145						X		X			
P146						X		X			
P147											X
P148											X
P149									X		
P150	X	X	X	X	X	X	X	X	X	X	
P151									X		
P152						X		X			
P153								X			
P154		X	X		X	X		X		X	
P155		X		X							
P156						X					
P157						X		X			
P158						X		X			
P159								X	X	X	
P160										X	

Topic Index

Resource Index

About the Author

James C. Gonyea, President of Gonyea and Associates, Inc. is widely recognized as an expert in the field of career and employment guidance, especially in the use of electronic resources for career planning and job placement. For over 22 years, Mr. Gonyea has personally counseled thousands of clients in how to realize a more enjoyable and prosperous career. Thousands of additional adults and students have benefited from his innovative career guidance techniques through the use of many of his career guidance software programs and books, including *Career Options, Career Quest, The Perfect Career, Working for America*, and *Career Selector 2001*.

In 1989, Mr. Gonyea created the nation's first electronic career and employment guidance service, called the Career Center, available on the America Online computer network service. Anyone with a personal computer and a telephone modem may access the Career Center by subscribing to America Online (now with over 1,000,000 members nationwide) and use any of the Career Center services, including private on-line counseling from professional guidance experts.

Most recently, Mr. Gonyea created Help Wanted-USA and the Worldwide/Resume Talent Bank, two of the nation's premiere employment listing services. Help Wanted-USA electronically publishes 5000 to 10,000 employment help wanted ads weekly via America Online, National Videotex, and the Internet to a viewing audience in excess of 30 million people. The Worldwide Resume/Talent Bank contains resumes of job seekers accessible to millions of employers worldwide.

Mr. Gonyea and his wife, Pamela, operate Gonyea and Associates, Inc. and, together with their daughter, reside in New Port Richey, Florida.

America Online's Top Ten List
What can <u>YOU</u> do with America Online?

1. Access the resources of the "information superhighway" through America Online's INTERNET CENTER!

2. Send electronic mail to thousands of other subscribers on many different networks.

3. Read the latest issue of TIME *before* it hits the newstand.

4. Easily download files from a library of thousands.

5. Tap into computing support from industry experts at online conferences and easy-to-use message boards.

6. Have "real-time" conversations with other members, join clubs, and read your favorite specialty magazines.

7. Monitor your stock and mutual fund investments in your own personal portfolio.

8. Make airline and hotel reservations, and even do some shopping.

9. Search the encyclopedia or get help with homework.

10. Find out the latest information about the world of entertainment through Hollywood Online and Rocklink.

AND BEST OF ALL, YOU CAN TRY AMERICA ONLINE FREE!

If you've never experienced America Online — now is the time. There's a world of services available for you to discover, and they're all at your fingertips! We've included the Windows™ version of the America Online software at the back of this book, along with TEN FREE trial hours online.

America Online is also available in Macintosh® and DOS platforms. **If you need a different disk type or have questions about connecting, call us at:**

1-800-827-6364

Reader Response Card

Directions:

Circle the numbers of the electronic resources for which you would like to receive additional free information. In addition to free information, you will receive a free registered copy of **You're Hired** ($27.00 value— an IBM compatible computer software program that simulates the job interview process to provide you with the practical training needed to beat out the competition and land the job you want.

You will also receive an electronic catalog (in ASCII text formatted on an IBM compatible 3.5" diskette) of other resources, both electronic and non-electronic, that are useful to career planners and job seekers. Please specify below if you prefer to receive the catalog on a Macintosh diskette.

Complete the Return Information section below. Enclose $5.00 for shipping and handling payable to Diverse Data, Inc., and this card in an envelope and mail to:

Diverse Data, Inc.
PO Box 1548
Tucson, AZ 85702-1548

P001	P002	P003	P004	P005	P006	P007	P008	P009	P010
P011	P012	P013	P014	P015	P016	P017	P018	P019	P020
P021	P022	P023	P024	P025	P026	P027	P028	P029	P030
P031	P032	P033	P034	P035	P036	P037	P038	P039	P040
P041	P042	P043	P044	P045	P046	P047	P048	P049	P050
P051	P052	P053	P054	P055	P056	P057	P058	P059	P060
P061	P062	P063	P064	P065	P066	P067	P068	P069	P070
P071	P072	P073	P074	P075	P076	P077	P078	P079	P080
P081	P082	P083	P084	P085	P086	P087	P088	P089	P090
P091	P092	P093	P094	P095	P096	P097	P098	P099	P100
P101	P102	P103	P104	P105	P106	P107	P108	P109	P110
P111	P112	P113	P114	P115	P116	P117	P118	P119	P120
P121	P122	P123	P124	P125	P126	P127	P128	P129	P130
P131	P132	P133	P134	P135	P136	P137	P138	P139	P140
P141	P142	P143	P144	P145	P146	P147	P148	P149	P150
P151	P152	P153	P154	P155	P156	P157	P158	P159	P160
P161	P162	P163	P164	P165	P166	P167	P168	P169	P170

Return Information:

Name: _____

Street Address: _____

City/State/Zip _____

[ ] Check here if you prefer the catalog on a Macintosh diskette.